Someone To Talk To

SOMEONE TO TALK TO

Mario Luis Small

OXFORD
UNIVERSITY PRESS

OXFORD
UNIVERSITY PRESS

Oxford University Press is a department of the University of Oxford. It furthers
the University's objective of excellence in research, scholarship, and education
by publishing worldwide. Oxford is a registered trade mark of Oxford University
Press in the UK and certain other countries.

Published in the United States of America by Oxford University Press
198 Madison Avenue, New York, NY 10016, United States of America.

Library of Congress Cataloging-in-Publication Data
Names: Small, Mario Luis, author.
Title: Someone to talk to / Mario Luis Small.
Description: New York, NY : Oxford University Press, [2017] |
Includes bibliographical references.
Identifiers: LCCN 2017009352| ISBN 9780190661427 (hardcover) |
ISBN 9780190661434 (updf) | ISBN 9780190661441 (epub)
Subjects: LCSH: Social networks—Case studies. | Graduate students—
Social networks—United States—Case studies. | Confidential communications—
United States—Case studies. | Interpersonal communication—
United States—Case studies.
Classification: LCC HM741 .S5853 2017 | DDC 302.3—dc23
LC record available at https://lccn.loc.gov/2017009352

For Tara

CONTENTS

PREFACE

When I try to explain to my friends what I have been studying for this book, I ask them a kind of question used in sociological surveys to elicit respondents' networks: "There are people with whom we talk about matters that are personally important. Who are those people for you?"

If I were asked that question at the time I drafted this preface, I would answer by naming my fiancée, a former college classmate to whom I am still close, and a dear childhood friend with whom I never lost touch. When my friends are asked the question, they typically answer in a similar way: they name a spouse, one or two friends or family members, and one or two close colleagues or professionals. These three or four people are known to sociologists as the network of "strong ties," the close friends and family members who provide support when people need a confidant.

But then I ask my friends a different pair of questions that would seem to capture the same issue. First, "What are the most personally important matters that currently concern you?" In my case, at the time I wrote this paragraph, the answer would be clear: my upcoming nuptials, the declining health of one family member, and, frankly, all of the anxieties concerning this book. Each of these matters has been stressful, and at times overwhelmingly so, over several months. Each has also been quite personal, and if I am honest with myself I would probably not confess publicly that I was even stressed about them were I not doing so for the purpose of this preface. My friends, when asked, offer their own version of a similar answer; they list worries that typically involve their work, their finances, their own or a loved one's health, and their family or relationships.

The second question, though, matters more, because it asks people what they have actually done: "Now, consider the topics you listed, say, the last one. Think of the last time you talked to anyone about that topic. Who was it?"

The last person I spoke to is a sociologist at a different university. Before I first drafted this paragraph, we were on the phone to discuss a future academic conference. To make conversation, she asked how I was doing, and since I had been working on this book, I blurted out that I was stressed about it, concerned about the difficulty of producing a manuscript that treats complex topics with the care that they deserve but avoids unnecessary jargon. Striking that balance had been harder than expected. We talked about it—I vented, in fact—for 15 or so minutes.

This colleague was not a close friend. In fact, I had ever only seen her, in person, twice, including the time we first met. If you had asked me whether I would ever confide something as personal as my anxieties about a book to someone I had only seen twice, the answer would obviously be negative. And if you had asked me to name my close friends, I would never have thought to include her in the list. In fact, there is practically no way to have worded the abstract question at the start of this preface—whom do you typically talk to?—that would cause me to list her as one of the people I would be willing to confide personal matters to.

Every time I have repeated this exercise—asking the first question and then the second two—I have consistently found that, for at least one and usually more of the matters that people found personally important, the last person they had actually talked to was someone they had not first named as a confidant, and was neither a family member nor a close friend. Sometimes, they had confided in someone entirely surprising, like a hairdresser or a long-lost acquaintance they had randomly run into. In fact, judging from their actual experience, my friends seem willing to confide personal matters to a vast network of people, including some who are so distally related they might as well be strangers.

This book is the product of my attempt over several years to understand whom we turn to when we need someone to talk to, and why. Confiding in others is an elementary way of seeking social support. It is an essential component of our mental health and well-being. It is a primary means to avoid a sense of isolation. It is a need that cuts across class, race, gender, and other differences and advantages. And it is a fundamental part of how we relate to our social networks. Understanding how we confide in others would mean grasping something at the root of the social nature of the self.

Soon after I started the project, I realized that the standard tools of network analysis could only take me so far. A good network analyst would first specify the network and then try to determine how people use it. That is, I would first identify the most important people in the lives of those I studied and then examine how they chose whom to talk to among these. But that approach would have missed the colleague to whom I had vented unexpectedly about my book. In fact, I soon began to wonder if the power and rapid growth of network analysis as a field had produced what Daniel Kahneman has called a "theory-induced blindness" that undermined how we answered simple but fundamental questions.

How people decide whom to confide in—the question is not complicated. Yet the standard tools were pushing me to answers I found untenable, since they required assumptions—about how people make decisions and how they relate to different kinds of ties—that clashed repeatedly with what I observed in the field. Even elegant rules of thumb about the difference between strong and weak ties seemed far too often inconsistent with lived experience. To understand what people actually did, I had to change perspectives. As a result, my inquiry became not only sociological but also epistemological, and the book eventually probed not only how people use their networks but also how we should study such questions.

When it comes to whom they turn to for support, people do not quite do what they say they are inclined to do. As evidenced by their actions, they are willing to cast a wider net than might seem rational; they are more sensitive to expectations and responsive to opportunities than either they themselves or network theorists seem to believe. People will go far to avoid this core form of isolation, the feeling that the difficulties of poverty, illness, loss, or failure must be confronted alone.

Yet understanding why requires unshackling one's thinking from the powerful chains of network science. The principles of the latter work better as tools than as articles of faith. Understanding how people mobilize their networks requires beginning not with structure but with *practice*, not with the composition of a network but with the motives behind a decision.

I arrived at this problem not through the deductive methods standard in the field but very much inductively, as I found myself frustrated by the inability of several elegant theories to account for what I was observing. Along the way, as I asked question after question to many of my colleagues, I accumulated a number of debts, both personal and professional. Some of the most important were to journal reviewers. As I began to think about these questions I produced three papers—one sole authored, one coauthored with Christopher Sukhu, and one coauthored with Vontrese Deeds Pamphile and Peter McMahan—that were published in the journal *Social Networks*. Several tables are reproduced here with permission. The editors and anonymous reviewers improved my thinking on these questions immeasurably. Chris, Voni, and Peter were astute, hard-working graduate students who quickly made the shift from research assistants to collaborators. A version of Chapter 6 was presented at the "Pragmatism and Sociology" conference in 2015 at the University of Chicago. Early ideas were also presented to the Social Interactions, Identity and Wellbeing group of the Canadian Institute for Advanced Research; at the 2013, 2014, and 2015 Sunbelt Meetings of the International Network for Social Network Analysis; and at a 2016 Radcliffe Institute conference on Ego Networks in the Era of Network Science. A large number of people provided ideas, critiques, complaints, or questions that forced me to think more deeply, more precisely, or more imaginatively about what I was uncovering: George Akerlof, Peter Bearman, Roland Benabou, Irene Bloemraad, Alison Wood Brooks, Elizabeth Bruch, Ronald Burt, Kathleen Cagney, Damon Centola, Mina Cikara, Anna Counts, Matt Desmond, Steven Durlauf, Claude Fischer, Henk Flap, Filiz Garip, Rachel Kranton, Clemens Kroneberg, Michèle Lamont, Edward Laumann, Jennifer Lee, Miranda Lubbers, Peter Marsden, John Levi Martin, Tey Meadow, Michael Norton, Devah Pager, Betsy Paluck, Paolo Parigi, Brea Perry, Bernice Pescosolido, Todd Rogers, Robert Sampson, Kristen Schilt, Ned Smith, Kate Stovel, and Jocelyn Viterna. Some of them read passages, entire chapters, or one of the early papers; others read nothing but asked questions that troubled me for weeks or months; all of them helped immensely. Ron, Claude, and Peter Marsden, pioneers in the study of personal networks, helped me correct some errors in my account of their own roles in an exciting time in the history of survey methods for network research. Laura Adler, Kelley Fong, Robert Manduca, and Bernice Pescosolido read the manuscript from cover to cover and provided invaluable feedback; Tara García Mathewson did the same, for multiple drafts. The four thoughtful reviewers for Oxford University Press were helpful in various ways. Although I benefited greatly from the kindness of all of these people, I stress that my acknowledgment of their help should not be read as their endorsement of my book.

James Cook at Oxford was a supportive, enthusiastic editor when this manuscript was little more than an idea. As I was developing the book, collaborating to organize sessions and conferences proved invaluable. Sessions organized with Bernice Pescosolido and Brea Perry, and with Ned Smith and Tanya Menon, at the International Network for Social Network Analysis were a great source of ideas. Organizing a conference on ego network analysis with Bernice, Brea, and Ned—with the generous support of the Radcliffe Institute at Harvard University and the Indiana University Network Science Institute—proved an exceptional opportunity to think and refine my ideas about what has been missing from network analysis. Readers will also detect the strong intellectual influence of the works of John Dewey, Claude Fischer, Mark Granovetter, Daniel Kahneman, Clyde Mitchell, Bernice Pescosolido, Alfred Schutz, Georg Simmel, and Herbert Simon.

I also thank my undergraduate and graduate students at the University of Chicago and Harvard University, who in many seminars over several years unwittingly helped me think through these ideas. I especially thank the reading group on qualitative network analysis at Harvard, a group that provided invaluable feedback on a near-final version of the manuscript. For their institutional and financial support, without whom this project would be impossible, I especially thank the Canadian Institute for Advanced Research, the University of Chicago, and Harvard University. Finally, and most important, I thank the graduate students at Hillmount University, women and men whose generous time and willingness to share their experiences with my team and me were indispensable. A few of them were kind enough to read draft chapters, those in which their lives were extensively profiled, to help me assess whether I got their story right. I am grateful beyond words. To them and all the interviewees: I hope that expressing your difficulties so generously will help other people overcome theirs.

Someone To Talk To

PART I

The Question

Introduction

 M uch of our everyday life consists of managing the difficulties that befall us. Many such difficulties, on top of their particular annoyances, pains, or complications, are also emotionally fraught. The prospects of divorce, the stress of a recent job loss, the fear of an imminent eviction, the news of a cancerous growth—these and other stressors drain one's emotional reserves, and often stimulate the need to talk. So do those difficulties that require a course of action, such as whether to end a pregnancy, to publicly come out of the closet, to come clean about a dishonest act, or to finally make the move to a retirement home.[1] Whether venting or brainstorming, talking can make a difference. To live is to experience emotional difficulties—but when the strain is sustained, the prolonged worry and stress can harm mental and physical well-being. And while talking is no panacea, people have found repeatedly that confiding in others improves their mental state.[2]

Philosophers have made the point for centuries. As Adam Smith wrote, "How are the unfortunate relieved when they have found . . . a person to whom they can communicate the cause of their sorrow? Upon his sympathy they seem to disburthen themselves of a part of their distress."[3] Immanuel Kant proposed that "[w]e all have a strong impulse to disclose ourselves," and he called "such self-revelation" a "human necessity."[4]

Scientists have now made the point as well, with abundant evidence to support it. Research in medicine, psychology, and sociology has increasingly found that when people confide in others their mental and physical health improves; when they do not, it suffers. As early as 1985, a major review of the existing studies concluded that having confidants seemed to buffer against the effects of stressful events (such as losing one's job) and ongoing difficulties (such as feeling economic strain); it was accompanied by lower anxiety, less clinical depression, and fewer symptoms of physiological stress.[5] Many studies have since affirmed these findings. A study of the spouses of suicide and accidental-death victims found that those who confided in others after the death of the loved one ruminated less and reported lesser illness.[6] A dramatic study of breast cancer patients found that those randomly assigned to confide their problems in others and to perform mental exercises lived almost twice as long after the intervention as the control group, about 37 versus 19 months.[7] In fact, the mere act of expressing one's difficulties appears to improve health. For example, a study of patients with asthma found that those randomly assigned to write about stressful life events had significantly improved lung function four months later.[8] A critical review of the literature concluded that, across 13 randomized control studies, written expression had improved "physical health, psychological well-being, physiological functioning, and general functioning."[9]

Studies showing help

These findings are not surprising; they are consistent with the enormous body of work documenting the measurable effects of social support.[10] Support promotes health through several different mechanisms, and the ability to confide in others may be one of the most important. Though researchers have yet to unravel precisely how and why, the conclusion seems clear: when people are facing difficulties, talking to others makes a difference.[11]

Nevertheless, confiding one's problems is risky. Since sharing one's difficulties requires exposure, trusting the wrong person can hurt rather than help. How much it hurts will depend on how private, important, morally charged, or otherwise sensitive the difficulty is. The consequences can be emotional. Consider the exposure involved in confessing that one has failed an important test, has cheated on a spouse, has decided to apply for food stamps, has entertained suicide, or has become regrettably pregnant. Confiding in the wrong person may lead to embarrassment, frustration, despair, depression, or worse. The consequences can also be social. Consider the potential loss of privacy. Some years ago a White House intern unwittingly found her problems shared with the entire world by confiding her affair with her boss to the wrong person. While few of our personal difficulties would make international news, many of our private worries would damage our social relations if they suddenly became public knowledge. Ponder the news of the unexpected pregnancy or the act of marital disloyalty. Confiding in a person who violates that trust may mean turning a private matter into a public crisis. The consequences can also

Potential consequences

be professional. Consider that most employers place a premium on confidence and competence, and exposing oneself in a work-related context may hurt one's reputation, shaping how others treat and evaluate one in the long run. Seeming weak, immoral, or troubled can seriously and even permanently undermine one's professional prospects. In short, to confide in another person is to become temporarily vulnerable in potentially serious ways. Everyone understands this fact: though talking to others is essential, it is also fraught with risk.

For this reason, to whom people confide their difficulties is an unusually clear window into whom, in practice, they trust. And how they make the decision reveals a lot about how they think about those they are connected to, how they manage their problems, and what they judge or value when using their networks for support. That is, as one of the most elementary forms of support, confiding in others provides an especially unencumbered view of what researchers have variously called "help-seeking behavior," the "activation of social ties," or the "mobilization of social networks."[12] To understand this decision is to grasp fundamentally one core aspect of people's relations to their networks.

Thus, this book is driven by a simple but consequential question: when people need a confidant, when they need someone to talk to about a personal difficulty, how do they decide whom to talk to? *question of the book*

There is a common-sense answer to this question: since confiding in others requires personal exposure, people will tend to approach only those to whom they are close. It is the answer, for example, that both Kant and Smith proposed. Kant seemed to believe that the kind of trust required for true disclosure "can exist only between two or three friends."[13] Smith found it self-evident that since we can "expect less sympathy from a common acquaintance than from a friend[,] we cannot open to the former all those little circumstances which we can unfold to the latter."[14] In fact, that seems to be the answer most Americans would provide. A recent survey asked representative adult Americans who they would first talk to if they felt "just a bit down or depressed," and 91% reported they would turn to either a family member or a "close friend."[15] Certainly, particular circumstances will call for a given close friend or family member, rather than others. Yet being vulnerable ultimately requires trust, and it makes sense that the kind of trust needed for personal matters of emotional import is reserved for one's inner circle.

The common-sense answer is consistent with current social theory. Sociologists of networks have proposed that most people have a "core discussion network," a set of close friends and family they turn to regularly when they have important matters to talk about. It is the network *current theory → close ppl.*

of individuals to whom people are strongly tied. Because this network comprises strong, not weak ties, several expectations follow. Since strong ties tend to be in-bred, the people in this network are likely to be close to one another. Because of its density, this network is likely to be steady and stable—it will change and evolve, as all of them must, but only slowly and deliberately, over the life course. And just as people will first turn to the inner circle, they will also avoid those outside it, lest exposing private feelings proves a costly error. As a set of distinguished sociologists has recently written, "There are some things that we discuss only with people who are very close to us. These important topics may vary with the situation or the person—we may ask for help, probe for information, or just use the person as a sounding board for important decisions—but these are the people who make up our core network of confidants."[16]

These ideas are sensible. But they are so consistent with common sense that they have rarely been tested. They are so foundational to how we understand ourselves—after all, who would trust personal matters to people they are not close to?—that they are taken for granted, more assumed as a matter of course than subject to empirical scrutiny.

Someone To Talk To examines these ideas directly, probing how people actually make this decision over the course of their everyday lives and unraveling the implications of the process. The book argues that most of these ideas are either only partly true or else largely inconsistent with the facts. People are far more willing to confide personal matters to those they are not close to than they are inclined to believe about themselves, than network theory would propose, and than social science is likely to uncover without expanding the way it studies networks.

This book shows that people are not always close to those they call their confidants. Furthermore, these confidants do not always know one another, because they are colleagues, therapists, priests, or random friends with no reason to interact with one another. Yet named confidants are still whom people say they confide in, not necessarily those they have actually confided in—they represent belief, not behavior. When we uncover whom people have actually talked to, the picture differs even more. Certainly, people often confide in their spouses and others they are close to. Yet rather than consistently turning to their spouses, friends, or family, people will often studiously avoid their inner circle for many of the issues they most care about, precisely because the expectations involving many of these relationships make them too close for comfort. At times the best confidant is one with some distance.[17] And though people might believe otherwise about themselves, they will repeatedly, willingly, and even without much reflection confide deeply personal matters to individuals they are not close

[handwritten margin note: arguing main narrative]

to, even to those they barely know. In fact, approaching individuals they are not especially close to appears to be what adult Americans do more than half the time they confide in others. Their decisions, in the end, are motivated less by affection than by pragmatism, and more by their institutional and organizational contexts than research has hitherto acknowledged.

In sum, this book proposes that people are far more willing to confide in individuals they are not close to than common sense suggests, because *reasons for confiding to a distant* they are less deliberative, more sensitive to expectations, less attached to the past, and more responsive to context than normally believed. Networks of emotional support are thus at once smaller and larger than typically proposed. They are smaller because strong ties are too complicated in concrete ways to be consistently reliable sources; they are larger because, when deciding whom to talk to, people seem to seek empathy, respond to opportunity, and pursue pragmatic options far more than they consider how close they are to potential confidants.

Some decades ago, the people who called themselves network researchers, in anthropology, psychology, and sociology, spent much of their energy analyzing and thinking deeply about questions of this kind. They pondered what motivated people to approach others, how psychology, emotion, expectations, and context joined to shape behavior. Today, that moniker often refers to those who analyze increasingly large datasets using ever more powerful computers to map the underlying structure of networks and their consequences. Network research has exploded, spreading from sociology, psychology, and anthropology to economics, physics, neuroscience, chemistry, and many other fields. This revolution has led to an effort to uncover common structures across networks of great diversity—of people, firms, nations, airports, computers on the web, neurons in the brain, and many others.[18] Some of these studies now involve millions of connections among hundreds of thousands of nodes. The signal image for the field today is the sociogram, the usually dense web of nodes and ties that graces the covers of dozens of popular science books and that represents with clarity the ultimate object of attention: the network structure.

But social networks are no ordinary networks, for people, and only people, have interests, preferences, insecurities, emotional needs, gut feelings, a belief in good and bad, a sense of obligation, and the capacity to trust. People can and do maintain complex relations that confound the easy heuristics—strong versus weak or positive versus negative—often used to capture network ties. People can at once love yet hate another, feel joy yet envy for a friend's success, and disdain a competitor while seeking their approval. They can love a relative yet feel queasy when discussing certain topics. They can trust a total stranger in the aisle seat on a plane. The complicated nature of social relationships, and the contexts where those relationships take place, inevitably shapes decisions about whom to turn to when seeking a confidant.

This book, therefore, begins where structural network research ends. It homes in on not the macro but the micro, not the functioning of large structures but the actions of the individual. It does not reject the well-established notion that people's decisions are shaped by network structure—in fact, it takes as given that structure matters and makes frequent use of the insights of that field. Yet the book shifts the focus of attention from the network to the decision to ask for help. The concern is not structure but practice. There are neither sociograms nor taken-for-granted assumptions about people's motivation. Rather than focusing on what people say they typically do, the book pays careful attention to what they have actually done, seeking to reconstruct the varied and complex factors that affect the decision to confide in another person.

The book does so by digging deep into a case study, following a set of people small enough that their motivation, thinking, and decisions about whom to trust with what can be examined with some care. It follows people as they enter a new context with new challenges and stresses, a context where forming a new set of confidants is an option, yet retaining the lifelong inner circle of support that many are presumed to have remains appealing.

Someone To Talk To begins by following the experiences of a set of graduate students in three academic departments over the course of their first year in their programs. First years often exhibit a boot-camp quality that heightens stress, undermines mental health, and repeatedly creates the need to talk—not merely about work but also about life goals, marriage, health, finances, and more. The book probes the students' worries, concerns, and struggles, asking whom they turned to when they needed a confidant and why. It finds reason to reject a number of beliefs about how people confide in others while developing an alternative view of social support, one in which actors are neither mostly affective nor mostly instrumental but, instead, mostly pragmatic in their decisions about expressing vulnerability, and one in which contexts—the institutional spaces where people spend their daily lives—are at least as important as network structure in shaping their decisions.

Nevertheless, most people are not in graduate school, and even graduate students only experience their first year for a short 12 months. Having probed deeply the views, actions, and decisions of a small set of people in a unique and analytically strategic context, the book then examines nationally representative populations. It separates the elements that [handwritten: compares study to greater nation] should be unique to this case from the patterns of decision making that should, in theory, be common across adult Americans. It then tests these major propositions against several national datasets either newly released or else original to this project. The large-sample analyses with representative data make clear that while the experience of graduate school is unique, the students' reactions to it are not, with respect to whom to confide in and how. Most people, in their own contexts, confide in others in similar ways and probably for similar reasons.

The following chapter briefly reviews what researchers have found about [handwritten: Ch. 1] these questions and points to reasons for considering an alternative. The subsequent five chapters, all focused on the graduate students, are five separate but highly connected studies that constitute the heart of the book. Chapter 2, "Weak-Tie Confidants," begins by following tradition. It examines the students' "core discussion networks" and finds that, contrary to [handwritten: Ch. 2] traditional expectations, many of the ties appear to be weak, not strong. Chapter 3, "Beyond Named Confidants," shows that shifting from belief to action—from the perceived network to the decision to ask for help— [handwritten: Ch.3] confirms the finding, and also shows that students even talked to many people they did not name as discussion partners. These two chapters jointly make clear that students had no problem turning to weak ties to confide serious matters; the subsequent three chapters examine why.

Chapter 4, "Incompatible Expectations," shows that part of the reason is their avoidance of strong ties. Students avoided strong ties for particular difficulties when they feared that what they would expect of the potential [handwritten: Ch.4] confidant might not be compatible with what the confidant would expect about him- or herself, as a result of the formal and informal norms and rules surrounding the relationship. Institutional expectations of this kind affect many kinds of relationships, and often matter more to people's reluctance to confide in others than the strength of the tie.

Chapter 5, "Relevance and Empathy," shows that students did not just approach weak ties when avoiding strong ones, but also at times pursued them deliberately. They did so when they had reason to believe the poten- [handwritten: Ch. 5] tial confidant was likely to be fully or partly empathic—to understand their concerns from their own perspective—with respect to a given difficulty. They often found that empathy in one of several different forms of similarity, suggesting a mechanism through which homophily, people's tendency to associate with those who resemble them, operates. Ultimately, students valued empathy more than they feared being hurt.

Chapter 6, "Because They Were There," takes these questions even further, probing how much the students' decisions about whom to talk to were [handwritten: Ch. 6]

ch. 6

deliberative as opposed to spontaneous—whether they assessed pros and cons before deciding whom to ask or, instead, as one might to the person on the plane, spontaneously spilled their emotions on the spot. The chapter shows that spontaneous decisions of this kind are far more common than presumed, consistent with both classic propositions in pragmatist philosophy and recent experiments in behavioral economics. It suggests that several conditions regarding the space of interaction and institutional expectations may make such decisions more likely.

The final chapters look beyond the graduate experience. Graduate school, after all, is a unique institution, and the generalizability of the findings beyond the case must be addressed. Chapter 7, "Empirical Generalizability," presents each of the book's core propositions about what people do, and assesses it against nationally representative data on adults in the US. Relying on original surveys and newly released findings from other national studies, it confirms that though the students' experiences are unique, their responses to the latter are not. Graduate students largely behave the way everyone else does.

Chapter 8, "Theoretical Generalizability," considers the extent to which the concepts developed to explain the students' behavior are portable to other situations. After summarizing the perspective developed in the book, it shows that the perspective, which shifts focus from structure and its consequences to practice and its contexts, can help us think differently about matters as varied as when people will keep depression secret from their close ones, why people may avoid reporting sexual assault, how people may decide whom to come out to, and why even competitors can be among a person's best confidants.

CHAPTER 1

Confidants

Whom do people turn to when they need a confidant? It is no surprise that survey respondents would answer by invoking close friends and family. No rational person would be expected to do otherwise, given the exposure involved and the high costs of confiding in the wrong person.

That answer would further be confirmed by network social theory. Network theorists believe that most people have a core network with whom they discuss important matters.[1] Thought to represent people's close, intimate, trustworthy, and socially supportive partners, the "core discussion network," sometimes called the personal discussion network or the core social network, may be one of the most important concepts in the analysis of the networks of individuals over the past 30 years. To understand why, some history is instructive.

popular social network theory

BRIEF HISTORY OF AN ANSWER

Network-related thinking is as old as thinking itself. Aristotle proposed that the strength of ties among friends derives from their similarity and repeated interaction.[2] Hume argued that people will tend to associate with those with similar characteristics.[3] And Adam Smith proposed that friends made better confidants than acquaintances.[4] But the thinking that directly informed contemporary network analysis began to crystalize across the social sciences in the late 19th century. Perhaps no early thinker had a greater impact than Georg Simmel, who viewed individuals as involved in multiple intersecting "webs" of affiliations, and derived the implications for individual and group behavior. Simmel laid the foundation for many topics now standard in network analysis, such as the study of brokerage.[5] Early anthropologists also theorized using network-related ideas, particularly through the study of long and complicated kinship ties, which they often represented using sociograms. Psychiatrist and theorist J. L. Moreno, working in the 1930s, produced one of the first analyses of group and individual behavior that was based primarily on sociograms.[6] Over the course of the 20th century, researchers in several institutions, including anthropologists at the University of Manchester, psychologists at MIT, sociologists at Columbia University and the University of Chicago, and organizational scholars and later sociologists at Harvard University, developed various aspects of network analysis, along the way convincing scientists of all stripes that sociograms could effectively represent the structure of a group, that network patterns might recur across different kinds of contexts, and that graph theory could be a powerful tool to analyze networks quantitatively.[7] This fascinating history is richer than could possibly be described here given our purposes. Linton Freeman's *The Development of Social Network Analysis* provides an exceptionally well-informed account.[8]

Among this large and diverse collection of 20th-century researchers, one set of sociologists became interested in the networks of large populations, differing in this respect from anthropologists, psychologists, and sociologists of group behavior. Though anthropologists and psychologists usually asked different kinds of questions, they shared a tendency to study small groups, such as tribal clans in central Africa, elementary school children on the East Coast, or college students in a single campus.[9] Studying small groups simplified the task of mapping all interpersonal connections within a set of people, creating the foundation of "sociocentric" analysis, the study of a group's network structure. But by the 1960s, survey-based researchers had become dissatisfied with the limits of small-group research. Sociologists such as Edward Laumann, Barry Wellman, and Claude Fischer hoped to understand the personal networks of individuals in society as a whole. They were inspired in part by researchers such as Paul Lazarsfeld, who with colleagues in the 1940s had run representative surveys in small cities where people were asked to name who influenced their decisions.[10] The new survey researchers yearned to capture how North Americans understood their class position, formed bonds with others, maintained friendship relations, or found social support.[11] This kind of research required both large-scale representative surveys and an "ego-centric" perspective, where respondents would be asked about the composition of their personal networks.[12] One of the first to conduct such surveys was Laumann, who was interested in how religion and class shaped people's friendship choices, and thus, the structure of associations in society as a whole. Using the 1965–66 panel of the Detroit Area Study, he asked a representative sample of white males in the city to name the "three men who are your closest friends and whom you see most often."[13] The survey then asked respondents about the characteristics of these friends, including their religion, class background, and—importantly—relations to one another. This study and others by Laumann, Wellman, Fischer, and others began to map the personal networks of large populations.[14]

Nevertheless, no existing survey collected network data on a national sample. No social scientist could describe with confidence the personal network of the average American. In the late 1970s, Ronald Burt, a young scholar trained at the University of Chicago, began an assistant professorship at the University of California, Berkeley, sitting in an office on the same floor as Fischer. Fischer had recently interviewed more than a thousand Northern Californians about many aspects of their personal networks, in one of the most extensive surveys of its kind. Fischer had asked more questions about the personal support networks of a large population than any in recent memory—the questions included the names of whom respondents turned to when discussing personal matters, whom they consulted for important decisions, whom they talked to about hobbies, whom they approached when borrowing money, and so on. Intrigued by Fischer's data and convinced of the importance of large-sample network research, Burt believed it should be possible to collect network data from a national population of Americans.

Burt approached the organizers of the General Social Survey (GSS), which had been interviewing nationally representative samples of Americans yearly since 1972.[15] The idea would be to ask all GSS respondents a question that, as Laumann's and Fischer's had, would elicit a set of names—a name generator question. These names and the relations between them would constitute the respondent's personal network.

But there was a problem. When taking a survey, responding to name generator questions takes longer than answering typical demographic or attitude questions, because name generators are almost always followed by "name interpreters," additional questions about the characteristics of the people named and—even more time consuming—additional questions about the particular ties between each pair of named persons. Even a single name generator, with the follow-up questions, could take as many as 11 more minutes, already a costly proposition.[16] Surveys were and still are expensive—every minute counts.

Burt examined the 11 name generators that Fischer had asked his Northern California respondents several years earlier and became convinced that, if only one could be asked, it should probably be the question

Fischer asked about whom people turned to when they had "personal matters" to discuss. Fischer himself was skeptical of the use of a single question, since he had learned that any one question often misses important people in respondents' networks.[17] Yet Burt doubted the possibility of convincing the GSS board to agree to any more than one question, and figured one was better than none. Burt presented a proposal, and after some negotiation, the board agreed to add a question to the 1985 survey, settling on a modification in the final wording: "From time to time, most people discuss important matters with other people. Looking back over the last six months, who are the people with whom you discussed matters important to you?"[18] Respondents were asked to produce actual names, nicknames, or pseudonyms of the confidants, about whom further questions were then asked. Two years later, Marsden published one of the first papers on the social networks of a nationally representative sample of Americans. The average American, it turned out, reported about three confidants.[19]

The significance of this simple question to the study of personal support networks is difficult to overstate. This was the first survey to collect national network data, and researchers everywhere seeking to apply the science of networks to other representative populations emulated the authoritative GSS and its single, cost-effective question. The question has motivated scores of surveys—it has been asked of national populations as varied as the United States, the Netherlands, and China, and of local populations as diverse as the towns of Santa Ana and Irvine, the cities of Atlanta and Macau, and the state of North Carolina.[20] It has been used to study the networks of adults 18 and older, of mothers in Head Start programs, of managers in large and small companies, of poor people in cities, and of women and men facing retirement.[21] It has been used to understand questions as diverse as how people attain happiness, how they react to natural disasters, how they form their political opinions, how they invest in social capital, how they make use of social media, how they respond to neighborhood poverty, and how well they maintain their health.[22] The results of studies based on this question have been published in hundreds and possibly thousands of articles in countless news outlets, including the *New York Times*, the *Wall Street Journal*, the *Los Angeles Times*, and the *Washington Post*. While social scientists have created many name generators to study networks, no single name generator has been asked more often or of larger populations or across more countries or in more important studies than this one.

Though the question was initially motivated by practical and empirical concerns, it was also built on a theoretical foundation. As Burt explained in 1984, "Intimacy stated in terms of discussing personal matters is the proposed criterion. The respondent is asked to focus on emotionally close ties in which specific matters of a personal nature have been discussed."[23] Burt was not actually interested in whom people confided in; he was interested in capturing the intimate ties of a sample of Americans, and this approach provided a vehicle. But the question, he reasoned, would encourage respondents to think of close relationships. Marsden agreed: "The theoretical case favoring 'discussing important matters' as a name generator was the view that influence processes and normative pressures operate through intimate, comparatively strong ties."[24] This interpretation of what respondents might think about—intimate relations, rather than just acquaintances—seemed sensible. It was unlikely that this or any other single national measure of Americans' ties would capture the full range of people's acquaintances, including people they were only loosely connected to.

But over time, as the question was replicated across surveys, these early theoretical notions were solidified into a much firmer set of assumptions. First, the name generator responses became increasingly interpreted as measures of people's closest friends and family. As early as 1990, Gwen Moore wrote an important paper comparing the networks of women and men in the United States, using the 1985 GSS name generator. She was unambiguous about what she thought the data represented: "Because persons named were likely to be those to whom respondents felt close, these network data are best seen as measures of strong ties. For most respondents these were subsets of a more extensive network of strong ties."[25] By the 2000s, as interest in isolation and social support continued to rise, the idea of a "core discussion network"—the people we turn to when discussing important matters—was an agreed-upon element of the intellectual discourse, with the GSS name generator the key tool to produce that measure. Soon enough, the twin ideas emerged: the tool produced respondents' close friends and family, and people turn to close friends and family when discussing important matters. An idea about what the question elicited became a theory about how people confide in others.

solidifying "strong ties" theory

The notion was widespread. For example, an influential team of sociologists in the Netherlands used a variation of the question in a survey of more than 1,000 Dutch respondents, hoping to understand the core networks of the Dutch. The authors provided a careful rationale for their chosen measure: "While people can have many network members and even many friends, they do not tend to discuss important personal matters with every one of them, but only with those they really trust. We therefore use the word 'confidant' to indicate these core discussion network members."[26] But perhaps the most careful account was produced in a highly cited study by Miller McPherson, Lynn Smith-Lovin, and Matthew Brashears on the core discussion network, a study that suggested, using the name generator asked by the GSS in 1985 and 2004, that Americans had become more isolated over the past few decades. That finding has been highly controversial.[27] However, their understanding of what they were measuring has not. Indeed, in their careful discussion of the rationale behind employing the GSS question, the authors seemed to capture not only the prevailing scholarly understanding but also common sense: "There are some things that we discuss only with people who are very close to us. These important topics may vary with the situation or the person—we may ask for help, probe for information, or just use the person as a sounding board for important decisions—but these are the people who make up our core network of confidants."[28] When people have important matters to discuss, they will turn to the people they are close to.[29] For some researchers, it is "only" to the people they are close to.

DEEPER FOUNDATIONS

But this view did not just depend on a survey question.[30] It found further support in ideas widely accepted among network scholars about the differences between strong and weak ties. The origin of those ideas lay in a highly influential 1973 paper by Mark Granovetter. Granovetter defined strong ties as those characterized, among other things, by the intimacy or "mutual confiding" of the two parties, the extent to which each served as confidant for the other.[31] He argued that strong ties tend to be in-bred, in the sense that a person's close friends are likely to be connected among themselves. This characteristic made strong ties resilient, highly supportive, and reliable. But if strong ties tend to be connected among themselves, he argued, then only weak ties are likely to be bridges between networks of strongly tied groups. This insight, the core contribution of the paper, convinced social scientists that weak ties had their own important kind of strength.[32]

Most of the work inspired by Granovetter's paper focused on the newfound importance of weak ties across many kinds of settings. But the basic insights about strong ties encouraged the work of experts on social support who were beginning to explore what a network-based perspective could offer to their field. For years, scholars of social support had paid little attention to the incipient network science. In the 1980s, they began to take note—network science could improve what science understood about how people get help from others. Prominent among them was Wellman. In 1981, he chided students of support for ignoring that one of the most important differences between relationships is their strength: "Ties vary not only in their content but also in the intensity with which they manifest that content; one tie may provide much more emotional support or financial aid than another." He continued: "Yet many network and support system analyses have treated all ties as equal in strength, that is, as having the same amount of resources flowing through them."[33]

In fact, Wellman began to argue that a comprehensive understanding of social support required distinguishing strong from weak ties: "While there is some evidence that stronger ties (however measured) provide more support, weaker ties often provide more diverse support because they access a greater number and variety of social circles."[34] In a later study with Scot Wortley based on a survey of residents of a Toronto suburb, Wellman refined the idea that different kinds of ties provided different kinds of support, clarifying precisely what strong ties could offer and testing the idea against empirical data. The authors distinguished emotional support— the kind we have discussed as what a person gets from a confidant—from other kinds, such as the provision of small services, financial assistance, and so on. One of their core findings was consistent with what researchers had come to expect: people reported receiving emotional support from their strong ties.[35]

These and other studies reinforced the idea that different ties provide different things, with strong ties providing emotional support. In a review of the research inspired by his seminal paper, Granovetter would 10 years later describe in a pithy statement what by then had become a rule of thumb: "Weak ties provide people with access to information and resources beyond those available in their own social circle; but strong ties have greater motivation to be of assistance and are typically more easily available. I believe that these two facts do much to explain when strong ties play their unique role."[36] If people's ties could be divided into weak and strong, then weak ties provide information; strong ties provide the kind of support one expects of a confidant. Network principles thus came to buffer an even deeper reading of the meaning of that powerful survey question.

Weak vs. Strong ties

THREE REASONS TO BE SKEPTICAL

In spite of this work, the simple idea that when people need a confidant they will actually choose someone close—rather than merely saying they will—has rarely been tested.[37] It is so consistent with common sense, so cemented in the collective consciousness, and so implied by elementary principles in network analysis that it has hardly seemed worth examining.

skepticism

But I see at least three reasons to be skeptical that people will turn to strong ties when seeking a confidant as consistently as they say they do.

The first is the difference between belief and reality. Though people may believe they only trust those they are close to, they may be wrong about what they do in practice.[38] While the notion that people may be wrong about how they use their own networks may be far-fetched, it has been supported strongly in many studies. In fact, it is the primary conclusion of the research over many years by anthropologist H. Russell Bernard, oceanographer-turned-network-analyst Peter Killworth, and their colleagues. In various settings and with different types of populations, the authors have tracked people's interactions with their network members and then, separately, asked them about their interactions. For example, a group of deaf individuals who knew one another was asked to rank each of the others by how much contact over teletype (TTY) communications they had. Their actual communications were then logged over three weeks. Only about half the time was participants' ranking of their top communicant the actual top, second, third, or even fourth person they most talked to.[39] In a separate study, a team observed every interaction among a group of 30 faculty, graduate students, and staff in one program in one university for a week. They then asked each person in the program to rank others by the amount of interaction over the previous week. Even in tasks as simple as correctly categorizing others under the most contacted versus least contacted halves of the distribution, participants were only right about half the time.[40] The authors have conducted many such studies, most of them finding, as the authors have written, that "[p]eople do not know, with any accuracy, those with whom they communicate."[41] In fact, a recent study suggests that people tend to be wrong about a large number of everyday aspects of their own behavior.[42] Over the course of their everyday activities, people may actually confide in people different from those they think they typically do.[43]

The second reason to be skeptical is that people may, in fact, have reason to avoid their close friends and family. Strong ties are more complicated than other relationships, and they may dissuade someone seeking a close friend or family member as a confidant, for many reasons. Network analysis itself would propose that a person's strong ties are likely strongly connected among themselves. If so, then any information acquired by one member of the group has the potential to be quickly acquired by all others, such that any private issue shared with a strongly tied person would not remain private for long. Confessing something embarrassing to one's mother might mean the whole family will soon know. That threat might make family or close friends at times the people to avoid, rather than

① belief vs. reality

② complicated

approach. Simmel suspected something similar, that the complications of strong ties may encourage people to avoid them in favor of strangers, who might be able to provide some objectivity.[44]

The third reason to be skeptical is that people may not be as distrustful as assumed when deciding whether to confide in people they are not close to. Confiding in others, in the end, is a decision, and at least two aspects of how people make decisions may matter. One is that people do not always think carefully before acting. Since confiding personal matters makes people vulnerable, a rational actor would pause to think before confiding to ensure that the potential confidant is trustworthy. But a growing body of research in the psychology of decision making and behavioral economics has shown that people are often not rational precisely in the sense of not pausing to think before they act.[45] The idea is not that people are stupid; it is, as psychologist Daniel Kahneman has put it, that they sometimes deliberate extensively before acting and sometimes act intuitively, spontaneously, and without much reflection on the consequences. The fact that people often act intuitively may be the reason they find themselves confiding in a total stranger on a two-hour flight—the flight mate just seemed trustworthy.

ppl may think/pause before talking to someone they know

The other important aspect of decision making is that the context of interaction may make potential confidants seem more trustworthy. Whether deliberatively or instinctively, people do not decide to confide in others in the abstract. They do so while lying in bed next to their spouses, sitting at work next to their colleagues, kneeling at pews next to their churchmates, or jogging at treadmills in the midst of other runners. People spend their lives at work, church, fitness centers, schools, bars, neighborhood restaurants, sports leagues, social groups, union halls, country clubs, and countless other organizational contexts surrounded by others with common interests and needs. The sociologist Scott Feld has called these "foci" of social activity; elsewhere I have referred to this as the "organizational embeddedness" of social networks.[46] These contexts may affect how willing people are to confide in someone who might otherwise be an acquaintance or a stranger. For example, in one study I found that mothers in New York City were surprisingly willing to confide personal matters to parents they did not know well but saw often through their children's daycare center.[47]

willingness

The analyst may find it mathematically convenient and theoretically elegant to assume that people have one set and stable network of confidants; that they always have these individuals in mind; and that, when needing to talk, they simply choose the most appropriate from within this group of three or four. But when people are going about their business, in the contexts where they do, they might just do whatever they can given their circumstances, not think too much about consequences, or otherwise make decisions that undermine common-sense notions about how they should behave.

TOWARD AN ANSWER

While these three notions provide reason to doubt the status quo, whether any of them reflects reality can only be answered empirically. Such a project requires three things. First, it requires probing what people do, rather than think they do. Rather than asking people whom they feel comfortable confiding in or otherwise attempting to reconstruct their network, it requires examining whom they have actually turned to when needing someone to talk to. One way of doing so might be conducting an ethnography, following a group or community and capturing the experience as it takes place. However, an ethnographer cannot, by definition, observe the private conversation between two people.[48] An alternative is to interview.[49] In that context, rather than asking people what they might do or even what they typically do, it requires uncovering what they have actually done, based on a reconstruction of their actual experiences.

Second, it requires probing why people decided to do what they have done. That probe involves at a minimum asking people to account for their decisions. While that question might be posed in a survey, a questionnaire with fixed items and little rapport between researcher and respondent gives the latter little reason to provide anything but short, incomplete, or unreflective answers. Even the open-ended questions often used in surveys would likely produce thin answers to what theory already would suggest is a complex set of questions.[50] Furthermore, some people may explain their actions in ways that reflect not their true motivations but their need to represent themselves well.[51] And others may be unable to explain their actions at all. In such situations, social scientists typically deploy experiments, which may be designed to capture implicit biases and uncover underlying motivations. However, such experiments rarely capture people as they make decisions outside the laboratory in the course of their everyday experiences. Moreover, an experiment cannot be used to test explanations for decisions people have already made—and, as we have discussed, to answer our questions we must probe not what people think but what they have actually done in practice. Thus, understanding motivation requires asking people to account for both the confidants they approached and those they did not through qualitative, guided, but open, free-flowing interviews. The process requires not only an empathetic ear but also a skeptical eye and an inquisitive disposition; it requires developing a relationship over time, knowing people far better than a single interview makes possible, allowing them to talk in depth, and then pursuing answers where they lead, probing contradictions in their statements, and asking both factual and hypothetical questions to get deep into respondents' naturally occurring decision-making process.

Third, because the decision to approach a confidant may be shaped by the context of social interaction, answering our question requires understanding context—specifically, the organizational spaces in which people decide to confide in others and the institutional norms, rules, and expectations that govern interaction in those spaces. The challenge, however, is the ubiquity of context. Every interaction happens in some context: there is no such thing as a context-free setting we might use as a counterfactual for comparison, to understand how context shapes social interaction.[52] Even online interactions, wherein people might confide in someone through a web application or platform, occur within an institutional context—the norms of online discourse, the rules instituted by the service, and the constraints imposed by the platform.

(margin annotation: ③ understanding context)

Given such conditions, the greatest leverage for the social analyst to understand context is change. When people experience major shifts in the life course, such as starting school, changing jobs, marrying, having children, divorcing, or retiring, the contexts of their regular activities often change.[53] This change is analytically useful for at least two reasons. First, it provides an opportunity to examine the evolution of the core discussion network. People may retain their old ties, add new ones, or some of both, and they may do so quickly or slowly. The responsiveness of the network to circumstances can be explored. Second, and more important, it provides an exceptional opportunity to examine what people actually do. Since major life changes, even positive ones such as having children, tend to produce emotional stresses, they drive people to turn to confidants often, creating multiple events—instances during which a person confided in someone—to examine who was approached, how, and why. As people enter a new context, manage the stresses of that change, and slowly find their way to new routines, the role of the context in the process can be examined as it is taking place.

For the study, I decided on graduate students beginning their programs because they faced such circumstances. My research assistants and I followed a cohort of first-year PhD students in three academic departments—a laboratory science, a social science, and a humanities department—in a large institution I call Hillmount University. (The model followed the tradition of early network classics such as Theodore Newcomb's 1961 *The*

Acquaintance Process, a study of 17 college freshmen over their first year.) All of them adults with an existing core discussion network, these three dozen or so graduate students entered a new institutional context, where the stresses of change could be expected, and where they could either rely on their existing ties, form new ones, or do some of both.

The serious stresses that first-year graduate students face have been well documented. They are entering a challenging new environment with high performance expectations and scores of unfamiliar people to manage and negotiate. They also often experience a range of concerns not unique to their conditions, including performance anxiety, racial discrimination, and poverty. Not surprisingly, deep anxiety, debilitating stress, and depression are common. In fact, their experiences have been used as a prime case to test the life-change hypothesis, the idea that "significant life events strain the adaptive capacities of the individual even when successful, causing 'cumulative wear and tear' on the body and, thus, greater vulnerability to disease."[54] To whom did they turn when they needed a confidant?

We interviewed almost every student in the cohort within weeks of the start of their very first semester, then six months later, and again six months later. We interviewed them once more, as follow-up, a year later. We asked both closed and open-ended questions about their social networks and how they used their connections. We probed whom they named when asked the GSS instrument. As I discuss in later chapters, we asked them not only whom they turned to but also how and why, favoring actual events over perception, probing their answers with sympathy or skepticism as appropriate, and recording every aspect of their narrative of themselves and their circumstances, in fully immersive interviews that could last as many as four hours. As part of this project, I developed several new strategies to reconstruct experience as accurately as feasible, to capture their decision-making processes, and to check the students' answers against behavior. (The details behind these strategies may be found in the appendices; the analytical decisions and epistemological assumptions undergirding the narrative may be found in the appendices and endnotes.) We followed the students as, given the new context, they were forced to make decisions about whom to talk to when they needed someone to talk to—they could turn to old or new ties; they could be open or reticent; they could be expansive or limited; they could increase the pool of confidants or reduce it. They could do anything—but implicitly or explicitly, they had to choose. And that choice was an especially clear window into their thinking. Their decision provided the core analytical leverage, the tool with which I pry open the box containing their thought process. To that task I devote the five chapters that follow.

Before I begin, I note an important constraint involving confidentiality. Probing deep, personal aspects of the lives of those we interviewed imposed special constraints (for details, see Appendix A). In a typical qualitative study, no person knows anyone else in the study. In ours, all respondents in a given department know one another. We approached every single student in each of the three departments. Three students overall declined to participate. As a result, no student knows for sure whether any particular classmate participated unless the latter has decided to share this fact. Still, if a student in a department chooses to reveal himself or herself publicly, then there is the risk of identifying other students from that department from the quotations or biographies in the text. A particularly difficult issue involves ethnic background. One of the major problems with PhD programs across the country is the relative paucity of black and Latino students and the associated stresses this paucity creates, and this problem afflicts Hillmount as much as any other institution.[55] Revealing race or national origin would effectively identify individual students. Similarly, a small number of students came out to us during interviews, and at least one of them was not yet out to this person's faculty members. Revealing this fact would be a violation of privacy. Favoring the protection of privacy was an especially difficult decision because some of the problems faced by minority students, and the reasons they sought social support, involved precisely their difficulty fitting in to homogeneous environments.[56] Still, given the sensitivity of the matters at hand, protection of the individual must be paramount. Thus, I present no racial or other physical descriptions of the participants, and give them all common Anglo-American nicknames. The one physical description I provide is gender, because there was a sufficient number of both women and men in our total group of respondents that this particular revelation did not threaten confidentiality. Still, I discuss in general terms throughout the book the concerns faced by students who, because of their background, were numerical minorities in their contexts. Their experiences made clear, as much as those of any, the continuing importance of fulfilling the need to talk.

PART II

The First Year

Weak-Tie Confidants

Whom They Named

Diana felt the call of higher learning just shy of her 30th birthday. A Los Angeles–based freelancer, she had penned stories for years on culture, the arts, and politics. Life had been grand: she had earned a growing reputation, formed deep friendships, completed a one-year master's degree, and even fallen in love. But one aspect of her journalism had begun to wear thin, the inability to probe anything as deeply as she pondered everything, the fact that, attentive to the needs of her market-driven editors, she wrote too much and scrutinized too little, her knowledge of the issues always only surface thin. Years earlier, that itch had been scratched by the MA. But the relief was short lived, disappearing soon after she left the classroom. She longed to write what editors did not care to see. "I realized that the kind of stories I saw myself writing weren't going to really work for that sort of general public audience. . . . I . . . wanted . . . to ask more academic questions."

Hoping for a new trajectory, she had brainstormed ideas with her old MA adviser, now her de facto career counselor. The adviser was blunt about the perils of academia, having endured a grueling odyssey in her own doctoral program. "I get the sense," Diana explained, "that it was a long haul [for her] and then, you know, a tough haul." Graduate training in the humanities can be a notoriously long slog, often 8 or 10 years battling uncertainty, anxiety, and isolation. "[My MA adviser] was really cautious about, you know, pushing grad school generally. And she urged me to consider other options, other channels outside of the academy, because

I'm pretty ambivalent about academia, as is she. Like, I'm not totally an academic. There are other things I'm interested in certainly." But nothing seemed perfect. Eyes wide open, Diana made the leap. She applied to several programs, was admitted to a few, and enrolled at Hillmount University.

Her life would change dramatically. Entering a new organization, in a new profession, in a new town, requires changing habits, negotiating alien rules, and finding one's place in a community of strangers. For those returning to school, it requires readapting to the academy: attending classes, preparing assignments, studying for exams, reading incessantly, and becoming beholden to the whims of an adviser. For anyone changing cities, it requires creating an all-around routine: finding new grocery stores, cleaners, restaurants, and drug stores, and engendering an overall new version of one's now-uprooted life. Such changes, even when exhilarating, create stress. And that stress calls for emotional support.

Diana had a network of support. Just a few weeks into her program, we asked her to think back over the previous six months and tell us whom she talked to when she had important matters to discuss—we asked her, word for word, the General Social Survey (GSS) name generator, as we did with every single student. In response, Diana first named Deirdre, "one of my closest friends." She listed two other intimates, Olivia and Sandy; her long-term, always long-distance "boyfriend"; and her sister. Asked if there was anyone else, she replied, "A colleague," someone in her MA program who had "become a good friend."[1] Her six confidants placed her right above the average of 5.25 for all students.[2]

Yet the ability to count on a network a few weeks into the fall does not ensure support when one likely needs it most. Sure, any of them would listen if Diana called to vent about the dismal music scene or the airs of a professor. The first weeks are by turns fresh, bewildering, exciting, and amusing.

But the kind of distress for which one truly needs support typically arrives later, after the newness has worn off and excitement has given way to routine. It is then, after the first mistakes, missed signals, and unexpected failures, that the anxieties about the change begin to surface, slowly gnawing at the self. At some point, Diana would surely wonder if her wary leap of faith had been a major blunder. After all, she had given up a happy, thriving life for years of little income pursuing a goal of uncertain value. The anxiety might erupt after a trigger, like a fight with her beau over the stress of long distance, or it might bubble up quietly to the surface, like the slow realization that reading, once a joy, had now become a chore. One way or another, after the smell of the new had dissipated, doubt, uncertainty, and anxiety would surely come.

The question before us is whom she—and the rest of the students—would then turn to for support. The six-month mark is an appropriate juncture, since it is long enough for real stresses to begin but not long enough for strong relationships to wither. Six months into the program, after things got difficult, would she still count on Deirdre, Olivia, her boyfriend, and the others, the closest people in her life? The question provides a clear window into how people relate to those they have considered their confidants.

We can broaden the question and render it empirically tractable: after six months, would the students as a whole report the same confidants? A structural view of networks and critical alternatives suggests three competing predictions. A deep probe into the separate lives of three students confirms that each perspective grasps an underlying truth about people and their networks, validating the theories that inform the predictions. But a comprehensive view of the students as a whole belies common expectations about how close people are to their confidants.

STUDENTS WILL KEEP MOST CONFIDANTS

One prediction is that students will keep most confidants. Diana, for example, would continue to confide in Deirdre, Olivia, and her boyfriend, even as she slowly made new friends. The reason: relationships with confidants are strong and strong ties are structurally stable.

The strength of a tie may be defined, following Mark Granovetter, as the "(probably linear) combination of the amount of time, the emotional intensity, the intimacy (mutual confiding), and the reciprocal services which characterize [it]."[3] This definition is intuitive but multifaceted; the thousands of studies that have cited it have applied it in widely different ways. Hoping to bring some clarity to the field, Peter Marsden and Karen Campbell systematically assessed the effectiveness of the most common indicators of strength; they concluded that *closeness* "is on balance the best indicator of the concept of tie strength among those available to us."[4] For this reason, I will use "strength of a tie" and "closeness of a relationship" interchangeably, unless otherwise specified. This use is both consistent with the literature and faithful to the theory that "our core network of confidants" is composed of "people who are very close to us."[5]

Strong ties share several important traits. First, as Granovetter argued, strong-tie networks tend to be dense—one's intimates tend to be strongly tied to one another. Second, the ties tend to reinforce each other—the relation *A* has to *B* and to *C* tends to be strengthened by the bond between *B* and *C*. As a result, strong ties are structurally stable, and not especially susceptible to short-term changes in context. For example, sisters who are close often stay close even if one of them moves away.[6]

The idea is reinforced by the fact that sustaining strong bonds in the midst of major changes has never been easier. People today maintain relations for months and years across oceans and continents through text, email, and online network platforms. While eventually even the strongest ties may well begin to whither, six months is not long among lifetime friends and family, which is why, to my knowledge, no study has shown that people stop feeling close to their intimates after merely half a year. If the students' confidants are their strongest ties, then they will likely still be there for support.

The theory's rationale is confirmed by the experiences of a student, Catherine, whose life, as that of most, was uprooted when she moved to Hillmount. Months into the first year, she began to feel the stress acutely. The importance of the small network of confidants she had arrived with becomes clear upon a careful unpacking of her circumstances.

Catherine entered graduate school with a husband, one toddler, and two master's degrees in tow. After toiling over years in cutthroat companies across the country, she had concluded that a doctoral degree would help her pivot to better roles. A punishing work schedule had often kept her apart from or relocating with her husband—her high school sweetheart—for much of her marriage, while she proved herself again and again and was rewarded with better-paying positions and greater responsibilities. Approaching middle age and having set aside for years the idea of a conventional family life, she was now committed to working efficiently and finishing quickly, no excuses, to regain eventually some kind of balance. She had certainly delayed having a child well past the time she had expected. "I'm really sensitive to perceptions," she explained to me. "Well, one, I wanted to get established and more in my job and go have fun and travel and do all that stuff. And two, I didn't want to be that woman," the one who landed an important corporate job "and immediately became pregnant."

Cognizant of the sexism and double standards of the corporate world, she had been determined to succeed on her own terms.[7] In a later interview she talked about a male work colleague with a similar schedule who was also trying to raise a small family: "it's just very different whether you're the mom or the dad, I think." She described her career as "very high tempo." "So, you travel a lot, and you're gone a lot, and . . . so, it's just the expectation that you're going to do that, . . . and you're going to kind of sacrifice family for it." A kind of solution was to enter the graduate program, since it put the treadmill on hold while not sacrificing her long-term trajectory. "I thought, well, this would actually be a way so I could stay with the family and be there . . . in these formative years. . . . I actually am really happy that I get to spend as much time as I do [with my child]." The clear breadwinner, Catherine asked her husband to quit his job and relocate the family from Dallas for the program. Everyone in the family appreciated the fact that they were now always together.

Six months later, Catherine came to see that balancing work and life would again become a struggle. At that juncture, she felt "guilty": "For example, . . . when I study at home . . . and I'll try to get a little reading done, and my son will come into my study and he'll be like, 'Play with me,' or 'Do' whatever. And I'm like, 'Well, I have to finish this.' And he's like, 'How many pages do you have left?' And I'll be like, 'Uh, five pages,' or 'I have this book,' you know, it just depends on—no matter what I say, that's too many." She continued: "[M]y husband will distract him and everything. . . . But . . . it's impossible not to feel guilty when they look at you with those eyes and be like, 'Play with me.'" Although she could spend time at home, her program, in the first year, was as challenging as any corporate project.

At times she needed to talk. Catherine, at the start of the year, had reported three confidants: her husband, her sister, and her friend Jenny. She was close to all three.

The three had been her confidants in part because they served different purposes. How to maintain a work–family balance gnawed at Catherine constantly. Did she, therefore, often turn to her husband to talk about the issue? "Not like this [like we're talking now]," she told me. "Mostly it's, 'Holy shit, I got a lot to do!'" Over the years, as the demands of her career have ebbed and flowed, "he realized, and he realizes that there's flows." Still, ". . . we don't have a lot of very philosophical discussions, I guess you could say. So, I mean it's there. It's not that it's something we don't talk about; it's just not that, we just don't verbalize it in that way." Family life had always been hectic, requiring constant attention to the many small but important tasks of ordinary household existence. "I mean, we talk about, you know, what's on deck. We have to be thinking about doing, and all the things that are due."

The "philosophical discussions" were reserved for Jenny, a single mother living in Dallas with whom Catherine shared a lot: "Our kids are like the exact same age, and so they play, and so, we just have a lot in common on a lot of the same issues." Jenny and Catherine were both solidly middle class, highly educated, and professional driven. "We talk on the phone all the time. We're trying to figure out [a time to] Skype, so our kids can see each other, because they're really good friends."[8] For Catherine and Jenny, the work–life balance is "kind of one of those things that's always there. . . .

How do we balance . . . our professions and families, and supposedly we're supposed to have 'me time' and all that as well." Jenny has a graduate degree, and "she was a little bit older when she finished. I don't know how long she was in grad school, but she probably finished when she was in her mid-thirties." So, when Catherine vented about balancing career, now school, a young child, and a husband, "[Jenny will] mention . . . her experiences and the fact that probably . . . everybody feels that way. . . . [I]t's just nice to hear that it's not me." With Jenny, Catherine knew she was not existentially alone.

Her sister, though, was a different matter. Neither the task-focused partner on managing a household nor the source of philosophical insight, her sister was nonetheless a kind of best friend. Since their father was a missionary, the girls grew up in a peripatetic household. Today, the sisters checked in often. "We'll talk about just broad [topics] . . . like not making as much as I used to. Or like, 'Wow, rent is really expensive.' We'll generally like that, but we don't talk about specifics, really." What her sister provided was someone who could share a lifelong, ongoing inventory of the activities, worries, and challenges of her life. She was the sole constant in a life of constant change. As Catherine explained in a later interview, "We've just been friends. And so . . . no matter where we live we can call each other and just talk about—it's not really like asking for advice or anything, it's just talking about life and what's been going on."

Close family, safe [handwritten margin note]

A partner, an ear, a rock: the three kinds of confidants Catherine needed. Over four interviews spanning the start of her first through the start of her third year in graduate school, Catherine never reported anything other than three confidants, and almost always these same three.[9] Her experience illustrated perfectly why theorists have believed that strong ties should be stable, and why one would expect the students to keep their core confidants.

STUDENTS WILL DROP MANY CONFIDANTS   *2nd prediction* [handwritten]

A second prediction is that students will drop many of their confidants. The reason: though relationships with confidants are strong, they also require social interaction.[10] And over the course of the first year in a program, students are busy and time is scarce, making continuous interaction difficult. Those students may call, email, or otherwise remain in contact with their confidants; they will have increasingly less time to do so with all of them, even if the students still feel close to those people. The power of structural stability may not be sufficient to withstand a student's inability to keep in touch with every single confidant. If so, after six months, <u>the students</u> <u>should report fewer confidants—with the expectation that eventually,</u> <u>after a year or two, as their newly formed relationships deepen, they will</u> have formed a new set of close friends to confide in.

[margin note: expectation of new friends]

Consider the experiences of Eric. An introverted, "self-admitted nerd" who loved science fiction and gaming online, Eric had yearned to be a scientist since childhood. "So, I started as a research assistant even in my sophomore year. And I sort of just got on to the path." Before the end of senior year he applied to several programs and met with various scientists running laboratories. One of the interviews, with Peter, a young faculty member who ran what struck Eric as a highly innovative lab, was a kind of surprise. "It was relatively informal. Actually they gave us about two hours together which was interesting. So . . . we spent a lot of time talking sort of bigger theory, like theoretical, sort of science in general, and sort of the philosophy of science." Eric knew he was being tested, but he appreciated Peter's approach to science, which combined a clear interest in the details of running good experiments with a desire to think broadly about science. They had other things in common. Both were nerdy, working-class men from a particular metro area in the Midwest, and they found themselves connecting as individuals. By the start of the fall semester, Eric had set up in Peter's lab.

[margin note: Eric more introverted]

[margin note: connection w/ Prof]

Eric had named five confidants: his mother; his father; his girlfriend, Katie; and his best friends from college, Mary and Betsy. He was close to all of them. Katie and Eric had bonded as undergraduates over their love for science and their similar dispositions. She was a year younger when they met, so now they dated long distance, with Katie still finishing her undergraduate degree in chemistry.

A few weeks in, the program actually felt easy. "Well, my adviser's definitely a hands-off kind of [guy]." Peter had recently had a child, so "he basically works from home whenever he can, so he's not always there. . . . So, it's one of those [things:] as long as I'm working and I'm showing progress he's happy." Laboratory meetings were once a week; courses were straightforward extensions of what he had taken back in college only three months earlier. And while an older graduate student had warned him that "my life is going to get harder," he did not see reason to worry.

For his social life, however, the signs were ominous. Eric considered his college friends "probably the best friends I've ever had." He worried: "I'm still in contact with them to some extent, obviously much less so than before. Because they're all spread out. . . . I don't see them anymore." Whereas back in college he was "surrounded by people all the time," in graduate school he only seemed to see the people in his cohort. "It's very

[margin note: don't see friends often]

difficult to meet people outside of the department. And the people in the cohort and I don't have a ton in common. So, I think I'm not forming really deeper relations with anybody, at least not yet." He was, in fact, lonely. "So, it's a little bit difficult and I feel like I have less of a support system here than I did as an undergrad."

Eric typically felt uncomfortable in large social settings. "I don't like going to a party. I don't really even drink, so, I'll go to a party and hang out and talk to people and then leave. It's okay but it isn't like I'm doing any kind of deeper social connections from them. . . . It's just because there are so many people there. It's not like you're going to develop a personal connection." He preferred intimate, deeper conversations. "I feel . . . much more comfortable in . . . smaller social settings." In fact, his largest social settings probably involved the nine other people in his favorite multi-player online game. He and four friends regularly met online to practice and develop strategies to deploy against five other players from around the world. But these relationships were primarily online, and most of these people he never saw in person. A few weeks in, Eric was not quite sure how he would connect to others on campus.

By the time we interviewed him again six months later, Eric understood what the older student meant by "harder." Lab work, class assignments, understanding his new city, and just keeping up—his life had rarely been this busy. One of his major worries, and one he had not anticipated, he explained to me, was "keeping up with the literature." The science in Eric's field has been developing "really, really fast" over the past few years, and "between the classes and the work that I'm doing in the lab sometimes I don't have enough time to do as much reading as I'd like to." Complicating things was Eric's inclination to delve into a literature as he did into relationships—deeply. "And I feel like it's difficult to sort of immerse your-self into a field without doing a lot of reading at one point. I know at one point I'm going to have to do it and it's something that I just haven't really had time for." He had begun to realize, too, that while Peter's approach was laissez-faire, his expectations were not. "I'm always kind of worried that one time he's going to turn around and be like, 'Oh, why didn't you read this paper?'" Eric felt the pressure especially keenly during regular team lab meetings, which, when Peter was stuck on an important or engaging prob-lem, could run to three hours. "[I]t's really overwhelming because then he'll be like, 'Oh, remember [the paper Smith 2004]. The older grad students are like, 'Yeah, of course.' I'll be like, 'Which one is that?'" Things were harder, and insecurities had begun to emerge. He could use people to talk to.

Thanks to Skype, Katie remained his partner, but Eric found less time for long chats with Mary or Betsy. He simply did not talk to them as often.

Pressure in school

Even in gaming, his social life was changing. "Well, I had a group that I played with consistently for a while, but then when I went to grad school I stopped really having time to make the practices, so, I just stopped that." Practice takes time, a suddenly scarce resource. "Some of my real good friends from [college] . . . played . . . for a while but they've sort of slowed down as well, upon entering the real world. So, it's a little bit more difficult to play. . . . This—I haven't spent as much time."

Confidants out of sight became confidants out of mind. After six months, *change in confidants* of the five people Eric had initially named as confidants, only his mother, his girlfriend, and Mary remained. Six months after that, his response to the GSS prompt was even starker: "My mother and my girlfriend." His experience made clear why, in a time of transition, people might have fewer confidants than normal.

STUDENTS WILL REPLACE MOST CONFIDANTS *3rd prediction*

A final prediction is that people will drop many confidants but quickly replace them. The reason: relationships with confidants require interaction, but they may not need to be strong. The notion that social interaction is important may be taken further. George Homans proposed in the 1950s that repeated social interaction increases trust and "positive sentiments" between people. Since then, a large body of research, much of it based on laboratory experiments, has found substantial support for the empirical proposition.[11] In the daily, steady stream of social interactions, people develop ongoing relationships with many with people in many contexts, *quickly find new ones w/a lot* in classrooms and laboratories, grocery stores and drycleaners, gyms and yoga studios, hair salons and barbershops. The students may find themselves confiding in those they repeatedly encounter, the way a client may regularly talk to his stylist at a hair salon or a worker may regularly talk to *who you're* her colleague at the office.

This idea finds support in recent ethnographic research. Anthropologist Frida Furman studied elderly women who frequented a hair salon. She found that new clients soon found themselves sharing deeply personal top- *frequency = comfort* ics, such as cancer treatments, in conversation.[12] In a prior study, I found that mothers who regularly saw one another in their children's daycare centers soon began discussing highly personal topics relevant to children and the family.[13] In both of these cases, some of the women had made close friendships—strong ties—but many of them had not.

In fact, the students' particular form of repeated interaction—one focused on a common graduate experience with other students, professors, and staff—may especially help create trust. Scott Feld has suggested that social interaction affects relationships through its "focus." "A focus is defined as a social, psychological, legal, or physical entity around which joint activities are organized (e.g., workplaces, voluntary organizations, hangouts, families, etc.). . . . [I]ndividuals whose activities are organized around the same focus will tend to become interpersonally tied and form a cluster."[14] When people find themselves in regular interaction around a similar activity, such as the pursuit of knowledge, they may find themselves trusting one another—even if they have not yet become close.

The students' regular social interactions would certainly change upon entering their academic programs. If at work they used to encounter coworkers, clients, and bosses, they now regularly see classmates, administrators, and professors, the latter group replacing the former as the pool of potential confidants. Students may not only drop but also in fact *replace* most of their confidants, not because they make strong ties quickly but because they do not require closeness of their confidants.

Consider Oscar's experience. Oscar approached his PhD program with a mix of familiarity and trepidation. Several years earlier, he had obtained an MA in a humanities field, expecting eventually to return full time to his love of delving deeply into esoteric texts. All of his siblings were either just finished with or currently enrolled in graduate programs: "my oldest brother went to med school. [Another sibling] is currently in med school. And my other brother went to law school." The area was familiar too: he had grown up, obtained both degrees, and then worked for several years in the metro area where he was now enrolling in a PhD program. His parents lived outside the city; two of his siblings lived in town; one of them was his roommate. Still, Oscar worried constantly about "finishing in a timely manner." While he labeled himself "fairly laid-back," he was nonetheless almost 30, unmarried, and entering a field in which students could spend almost a decade obtaining the PhD. "I don't want to be in graduate school forever," he explained. "I want to get out of it what I need to get out of it."

A few weeks into his program, Oscar named five confidants: his siblings, Ned, Ken, and K.C., and his "two very close friends," Benjamin and Corey. Ned was Oscar's roommate; Ken also lived in town. Benjamin was a local friend who happened to enroll in a physics program in the same university; Corey was a high school friend who still lived in the city. Oscar entered the graduate program with a large support network.

Oscar—as Catherine and Eric had—found his program demanding. In his courses, reading lists were notoriously long. In addition to full-time course enrollment, the program required participation in a weekly colloquium, regular meetings with advisers, and customary attendance at departmental social receptions. He needed a new routine.

Over the summer, he began "always coming to campus," so that by the start of the semester it was his daily practice. "So, like, I woke up this morning and came down like straight from home, and was here earlier than I care to think about." The road was bumpy: "I hate being awake early in the morning. I'm just really not a morning person." He had shifted from an 8 AM wakeup time over the summer to 7 AM, which he joked was "gruesome to me." He typically worked at the library, but he also often read books and papers in a departmental lounge with "a little kitchen area and mailboxes for the students." The problem? "[T]here's too many people." It was more of a social space. "And, so, I go there to work when I don't really want to work. It's one of those things where it's like, 'I sort of need to read this, but I also don't really want to.' I'll go there just because there's always people coming in and out." He enjoyed the social interaction.

Over the first few months in the program, he became friendly with ~finding friends in the program~ several of the students, particularly two others, Selena and Benny, both advanced students who worked in the same, somewhat esoteric field that Oscar did. As a result, he saw the two of them often in the advanced reading courses the few students in this field regularly took. Benny had also been Oscar's teaching assistant the very first semester. Oscar could connect with them in ways he could not with others. For example, he had been concerned about the feasibility of his project, but "[n]ormally that sort of an issue I don't normally talk about with other people who" do not work on the topic. But with Selena and Benny, "it's something that comes up just because they're, you know, they're also familiar with the, with like the current state of literature [in this field]."

By the middle of his first year, Oscar was having difficulty staying in touch with some of his old confidants. Among other things, the most conventional means of communication was not really an option: "I hate talking on the phone," he explained. "I just don't like it. I've never liked it. So, people know—just don't." His friend Corey had moved to New York City, which made things even harder. Over the course of the year, he would also spend less and less time with his siblings.

At the same time, Oscar began enjoying the regular visits with his adviser, noticing that he often left Gerald's office with a clearer mind, a sharper focus, and a greater sense of possibility. Oscar's field was esoteric, and he often did not know how to approach his projects. Gerald helped him think things through. At times, they discussed logistical issues; other times, big-picture matters such as "finishing in a timely manner." In a later interview, he recalled one occasion: "[Gerald] was sort of saying, 'You know, when you're working on this kind of a project you have to realize that a lot of your dissertation, like it just can't be very definitive, because of the fact that you're going to be the only person and this is the first time anybody's done work in that area.'" That idea, a kind of revelation, helped. Not every conversation was profound, but most of them were useful. Oscar and Gerald interacted often—at their regular meetings, as he prepared for exams, at the weekly colloquium—and Gerald had heard many of his deepest anxieties. "I've just been talking to my adviser a lot."

At the six-month juncture, he no longer reported Benjamin and Corey as confidants. Ned, Ken, and K.C. remained (though Ken and K.C. would also be gone by year's end, and Benjamin would return). As Oscar would explain in a later interview, since the time he had started graduate school, "I think we just . . . weren't in contact with each other as much." He continued: "I haven't been [to New York] in several years, but [Corey's] family lives here. . . . So, it just sort of depends on when he's around," which, unfortunately, was not often. Out of sight, out of mind. Replacing some of the departed confidants, he now, at the six-month mark, added graduate student Selena, teaching assistant Benny, and his academic adviser, Gerald. His experience suggests that students did not have to be especially close to those they named as confidants.

THE DISTRIBUTION

Catherine, Eric, and Oscar's different experiences illustrated perfectly the three perspectives on the relative importance of network structure versus social interaction. The first assumes that confidants must be close, and thus, are likely mostly to be kept; the second, that they must be close but also regularly encountered, and thus, are likely often to be dropped; the third, that they must be regularly encountered but need not be close, and thus, are likely mostly to be replaced. Which experience was most common across all students?

The results on the whole undermine the notions that people and their confidants are mostly strong ties and that such ties are structurally stable.

The Basic Patterns

First, consider the prediction that the students, as Catherine did, should keep their confidants because confidant networks are stable. Recall that strong ties should be stable because they produce dense networks. For any given student, the density of the network, which ranges from 0 to 1, is the extent to which, for all alter pairs, the tie is present and strong. When every single possible tie is perfectly strong, the density is 1. At the start of the year, the average density was only 0.34.[15] The networks did not have the density that strong ties are supposed to have.[16]

Even Catherine, who largely kept her confidants, had a start-of-year density of 0.24. Her husband and her best friend, Jenny, were only somewhat close; Jenny and her sister had not even met. The finding makes sense. Though the notion that strong ties are interconnected is elegant in theory and certainly applicable in many contexts, there is no reason to suspect some of these confidants to be close to one another. There is little reason to expect Catherine's sister to be close to Jenny, a woman living in Dallas, whom Catherine met over one of many posts in different cities. Similarly, there would be little reason to expect, say, Eric's mother to be close to his college best friend Betsy. Indeed, most students did not have an "inner circle" of confidants, in the sense of a dense or close-knit group; they just had individuals they confided in.

Second, consider the possibility that, though the average network was not particularly dense, the theory that denser networks had more stability could still be accurate. The density of the confidant networks ranged from 0 to 0.69 across students. That is, while some students' confidants did not know one another, as in Jenny and Catherine's sister's experience, others were strongly bound, as when a mother and father were both confidants. That is, the networks at the top of the distribution in terms of density certainly exhibited the expected interconnectedness. Nevertheless, it did not help them. The correlation between density at wave 1 and the number of ties dropped at six months was –0.07, a very weak relationship. Networks with greater density did not exhibit greater stability; having confidants who were close to one another did not keep students from dropping confidants.

[handwritten margin note: higher "closeness" density not always helpful]

Though there was little support for structural expectations, the students might still, on average, have largely kept their confidants, as Catherine did, rather than drop many of them, as Eric did. As it turns out, the students dropped their confidants with impunity. Six months into the year, all but four students (89% of total) had dropped someone they named. The average student dropped 2.8 previously named people, or 52.2% of the network.[17] That is, the average student no longer regularly confided in more than *half* the people he or she had six months earlier. Catherine was unique.

However, so was Eric, since he dropped confidants without replacing them. While 89% of students dropped confidants over the first six months, 84% added new ones, with 2.4 alters being added on average. More than 76% of students replaced confidants—meaning they both dropped at least one and added at least one confidant. Oscar's experience, to drop and to add, was far more common than either Eric's (to merely drop) or Catherine's (to keep them all).

Probing Further

The large number of confidants dropped suggests that, in the absence of social interaction, people will abandon many of their confidants—being close is not sufficient. The large number of new ones *added* suggests that, in the midst of extensive interactions, people will quickly create confidants— being close is not even necessary. Though it is possible that the students somehow managed to become close to their new contacts quickly, it is diffi- cult to imagine that the students were somehow closer to their six-month ties than they were to lifelong friends and family—that Oscar was closer to his first-year teaching assistant than he was to his own brother. Regardless of one's conception of closeness, the students were certainly foregoing stronger relationships in favor of weaker ones when reporting their new confidants.

In fact, the evidence over the course of the entire year belies the notion that students were especially concerned to only confide in strong ties. In Figure 2.1, each horizontal line represents not a student but a tie between the student and a named confidant. The figure exhibits all ties reported by all students at all three waves. It represents how many waves each tie lasted by indicating when it began and ended. If a line spans two waves, the tie lasted six months. (The dotted lines near the bottom indicate ties that were dropped in wave two but added again in wave three.) The longer the line, the more stable the tie, and the stronger the tie.

The figure makes clear that most confidant ties did not last long. Among the 38 students across the three waves, there were 345 ties in total; thus, there are 345 lines. Only 22.0% lasted the entire year, and only 17.1% lasted two consecutive waves. As shown in the bottom of the figure, another 4.3% disappeared in the second wave and reappeared. But the majority of ties, 56.5%, lasted only one wave. Even the new ones, formed in the second wave, typically did not last long. (In separate analyses, I examined whether high turnover could have been due to measurement error; the results are the same.[18]) When students such as Oscar suddenly named their teaching assistants, it was often not because the latter had rapidly become close enough to last as friends; more often than not, these new confidants were quickly dispatched in favor of even newer ones, as students encountered changing groups of people, academic term after academic term, over the

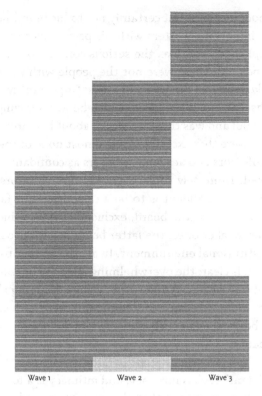

Wave 1   Wave 2   Wave 3

Figure 2.1. How long did ties to named confidants last?

course of their daily interactions. Though people are in theory attached to their strong ties, the students were not especially attached, as confidants, to those they called their confidants.

Finally, all of these findings, which suggest the students confided in a lot of people they were not especially attached to, are consistent with the names they actually reported in the qualitative interviews. The students certainly named spouses, best friends, siblings, and parents. But they also named roommates, classmates, professors, advisers, laboratory directors, and even people they had just met, in response to the GSS instrument.

One student—at the extreme—in his very first interview, just two weeks after the start of classes, reported almost exclusively professors: in addition to his mother and his father, Brandon listed two current professors, his undergraduate academic adviser, one career counselor who had helped him think through graduate school applications, and two high school mentors with whom he kept in touch. Brandon had attended both high school and college near Hillmount, and all of these people lived within a few miles. By this point he may well have been close to his undergraduate adviser or to his high school mentors, but certainly not to his brand-new professors. Did he discuss important matters with his peers? "Not so much with my friends," he explained, "for, like, the serious conversations." Brandon certainly had friends. But these were not the people with whom, as the GSS instrument asked, he had discussed his most important matters over the past six months—the months during which he was applying to and starting graduate school and was thus concerned about his career.

Few students were that exclusive. And almost none of them named primarily their professors and academic advisers as confidants. But the range of people named, from new roommates to administrators, undermined the idea that to be a confidant is to be a close friend or family member. And they certainly, across the board, excluded at least some stronger ties in favor of other weaker ones, the latter being newly encountered people in their new institutional environment. In all, the answer to this chapter's starting question is clear: the overwhelming majority of students replaced their old confidants with new ones—on average dropping about half, and adding about as many—because few confidants were such strong ties that they could not be dropped as such, and new ties did not require strength to serve as confidants.

The term "confidant" evokes intimacy, and intimacy is a form of closeness. It is natural to have supposed that the students would only name their intimates, as Eric did with girlfriend or mother, or Catherine with husband, sister, and best friend. But the GSS instrument does not ask people to name those they were close to; it asks whom they regularly talked to when they had important matters to discuss. And that group, the people students were willing to talk to, included a large number of relationships that both on their face and in their behavior did not function as strong ties.

CONFIDANTS, BUT NOT CLOSE

Diana's own experience, it turns out, was common—over the course of the year, she kept some, dropped many, and replaced several. By year's end, her sister, Deirdre, Sandy, and Nancy—all of whom she was close to—remained among the people she confided in. But she and her boyfriend had broken up, the late-night Skype calls not being enough to sustain the relationship. Another of her LA friends was also no longer listed. Having flown to Los Angeles for a short vacation, she now included two more hometown friends. And she added Oliver, Rachel, and Oscar, the three students with whom she had taken the largest number of courses.

Halfway through the year, Diana reflected on her newfound relations in the program. "I would consider [them] friends, but just barely," she said, speaking of Oliver and Rachel. "[I]t takes time—right?—to become a friend rather than a colleague." Indeed—but apparently not to become a confidant.

CHAPTER 3

Beyond Named Confidants

Whom They Actually Talked To

Words and actions differ. The fact that, when asked to report whom they talked to, Oscar, Diana, and many other students named a battery of newly formed acquaintances does not imply that, when they needed to discuss something truly personal, they actually confided in these newfound ties. The reason is the breadth of the General Social Survey (GSS) prompt. To elicit these names, students were asked to report whom they turned to for "important matters." Many topics, from a national election to global warming, can be "important" without being personal or difficult or otherwise actually requiring the support of others. Broad prompts elicit broad responses—in this case ties of varying strengths. It remains possible that, *in practice*, for truly personal worries the students turned only to strong ties, to the people who had been their confidants for long, as predicted by traditional theories. Was this the case? For their serious personal worries, did the students in fact avoid their newly named confidants and stick, instead, to old ones?

The question turns ultimately on the appropriateness of the GSS instrument to understand what happens in practice. Taking seriously that doubt and exploring the alternatives again creates three competing expectations about what the students did; probing in depth three students' experiences confirms the rationale behind each prediction. Nevertheless, the results across all students suggest that, though the GSS instrument indeed has limitations, there remains little doubt that students, in practice, and for their serious personal worries, regularly confided in weak ties.

The first expectation is based on the idea that strong-tie theory is ultimately correct, and the GSS instrument, merely a weak way to test it. The instrument asks respondents with whom they discuss "important matters." However, that term admits many readings. For an entering student, an "important matter" might be how to make sense of the course catalog, since doing so is required for registration. Yet for theorists of emotional support, that topic is probably trivial. In fact, the idea that many people's "important topics" would seem unimportant to researchers was supported by a recent study by Peter Bearman and Paolo Parigi among respondents in North Carolina. The authors evaluated the GSS instrument by asking respondents to describe the topic they discussed the last time they talked about "important matters." The reported topics included issues as varied as "getting a new haircut," "new traffic lights installed in town," and "the cloning of headless frogs."[1]

assumed convos for weaker ties

If respondents sometimes think of such topics when imagining whom they talk to, then naturally they will sometimes report weaker ties. For instance, the student in our aforementioned example might reasonably think about the course catalog and name a miscellaneous professor. If so, strong-tie theory would withstand the hitherto reported findings. Six months in, the students would not know any classmates or roommates that well, even if they reported the latter as a confidant or discussion partner. When things got truly difficult, they may well hesitate to turn to their newfound "confidants" and instead retreat to their prior, stronger ties. Diana might have named her classmates Oliver and Rachel, but for truly worrisome matters retreated to Deidre back in Los Angeles.

idea of retreating when gets hard

The idea that when "push comes to shove" the students will, in practice, retreat to their long-term confidants is confirmed by the experiences of Kenneth. Kenneth was a social science student who, over the course of the year, added a professor and a classmate to his named confidants, while keeping his mother, his father, and his wife. Kenneth had a restless mind and a facility for math. By the start of his second year, he seemed to have two advantages over his peers. First, he had entered the program with an MS degree and had taken "quite a bit of [the quantitative] methods" that his peers were only learning now. Second, he had taken up a golden opportunity. His department began to allow a few students to sit on the committee evaluating applicants for junior faculty positions, to expose students to the appointment process and get their perspectives. "[T]here was an email [asking] if anyone want[ed] to volunteer as a student rep . . . and I wrote an email that day and got accepted." As student representative, he attended the committee meetings with the faculty, discussed candidates, and wrote reports.

The two advantages, however, were a mixed blessing. Kenneth had breezed through many exams. But in any social science field—especially economics, psychology, sociology, and political science—acing exams and writing good papers require different skills. The latter requires a kind of intuition that comes from doing real research, from trying to make sense of actual data. Perhaps ironically, Kenneth's restless curiosity did not help. "I think my current confusion is that I'm taking a lot of courses in a variety of departments and I know a lot of [math] and I want to use all of them but I don't know how to." As with all first-year students, Kenneth had been assigned a faculty adviser, and the two had a cordial relationship. But this person's strengths did not match Kenneth's need: a kind of intellectual mentor to walk him through the career.

The exposure to how candidates are actually evaluated enlightened him tremendously but deepened his anxiety. "[Serving on the committee is] quite a bit of work, but the good part is we get to sit in all these, all these committee meetings and hearing all these faculty sort of talking about, discussing the candidates and what is his or her strength and weakness and all that. And that's . . . pretty . . . grueling, I will say." He learned first-hand that, if he wanted an academic job, he would need publications. Furthermore, he would need far more than the ability to demonstrate quantitative wizardry: "during meetings they will always emphasize your engagement with literature, the big ideas, your theoretical contribution to literature and all that and that kind of thing." He had to "readjust" to a new way of thinking, a process that had been taxing: "it was kind of hard I'll say at this point. I guess . . . emotional anxiety [which] is greater than sort of physical or, or physical burden."

The process only reinforced his need for a mentor. "And the difficulty in publication sort of related it to [the] problem of finding a good faculty adviser because one adviser I received was like, 'No, there's no way you can do good publication[s] alone.' I mean you have to find . . . someone who you can co-author with who can like give you guidance and, and suggestions about what to write and how to like, how to do that and all that kind of thing." That particular advice may or may not have been appropriate. The end result, however, was a deep, persistent anxiety about the need to find a mentor. "I've always been worried about finding a second adviser. But . . . I guess my world was intensified by being in the search committee. A lot of things were intensified after being in the search committee. Just seeing all these really good candidates that got rejected and, and see the way like faculty discusses about junior faculty candidates and, and you know, the standard's pretty high and you have to work up to that standard and it's, it's a challenge."

Under these circumstances, Kenneth could have turned to any of his confidants to vent his anxiety about finding a mentor and help him think through options. At the time he reported as confidants, in addition to his wife, two graduate students and his assigned adviser, all of whom would *reverted back to fam.* seem appropriate. But when he finally came to terms with the need to talk about his anxiety, he turned only to the single person closest to him. Asked if he had confided in anyone, he was unambiguous: "I talked to my wife after that. Other than that, no."

SERIOUS WORRIES FOR OLD OR NEW CONFIDANTS

The second expectation is based on the idea that the GSS instrument is effective, and the traditional theory, merely wrong. People are probably closer, *ceteris paribus*, to those they have known longer, and one could reasonably infer that students are closer to the confidants they arrived with than to the ones they formed during the year. But the GSS instrument was not designed to measure closeness; if it were, it could have merely asked people to name whom they were close to. Instead, it asked them whom they talked to regularly about the matters they considered important. The idea that people "do not tend to discuss important personal matters with [any friend], but only with those they really trust" was a later interpretation.[2] Such interpretations notwithstanding, the named confidants need not be intimates.

To be sure, students will probably be closer to the average person they named than to a random person in their total network; they probably are closer to the classmates they named than to the ones they did not. But students seem unlikely to report as confidants people who were not actually confidants. Thus, the traditional theory might just be wrong—people may be willing to trust more people than researchers suggest. If so, in practice, even when they have real concerns, the students should be no less likely to turn to newly-added confidants than to the ones they have known for long. *supposedly closeness shouldn't affect who they talk to*

Robert's experiences certainly confirm that proposition. Robert was a thoughtful, perceptive immigrant with a complex set of concerns that took a full year to develop. Having worked in laboratories as an undergraduate, he knew that advisers would be key to his success. When deciding among graduate programs, the weight of that issue tipped the scale toward Hillmount. "[In] the other schools there was only one person I could work with, whereas here there are potentially three or four people I could work

[with] if the relationship with my adviser did not work out as expected." His intuition was prescient.

Just a few weeks into his program, Robert felt the pressure. "[T]he school is very challenging," he told me. "They keep us very busy. One thing I did not expect is to have as much course load as I do, but it's good, because it's stimulating. I mean, we read a lot of papers for classes, and we're keeping busy with classes, and on top of this we have to do research." He had been accepted at the laboratory of a professor he liked. "So, it is stressful but [at] the same time we got to a lot of lab meetings, because we're expected, and this is a lot of fun."

His previous laboratory experience had taught him the value of good relations. "I mean, we're part of the lab. And I see research is a completely voluntary effort that's driven partly by the enthusiasm and intellect of people and partly by the relationship between them. So, if two people don't get along, I don't think those two people can do the research. Because it's a challenging process; it involves challenging each other. It involves contradicting each other. It involves arguing about ideas." He worried specifically about the student–adviser relationship. "So, this is . . . what I'm concerned about. So, if something were to go wrong that means we can't do research together. That means I either have to find a new adviser, start a new path in research, which slows things down—meaning that that would result in fewer studies run, ultimately fewer publications and job prospects, not to mention the reference issues."

[handwritten margin note: need to get along to be successful]

By the start of the second year, Robert was concerned about his progress, facing his own version of the "imposter syndrome" that afflicts many: "sometimes I feel that . . . my productivity in the research is not up to par with what some other people are doing or perhaps what the professors are expecting." This anxiety was deeper than the low-level concern he had expressed a year earlier: "I think earlier when we first met and before coming to graduate school it was sort of like, 'Yeah, I've heard it's tough so I'm worried' kind of thing . . . but then not losing sleep over it. But now that I've been through a year of it . . . it's a real threat. It's not just something that people talk about because they like to appear that they're going through toughness." Part of the "real threat" was the perception of his professors. "[S]ometimes I wonder if implicitly they think, 'Oh well, that's really not working out as well as I expected.' . . . [I wonder if] they're kind of being frustrated with my performance without explicitly telling me that they are."

Robert's fear was not mere paranoia. Since he had not seen his family for some time, he "spent a significant chunk of the summer" after his first year back in his native country. As a result, he "wasn't terribly productive," he explained. "I spent about six weeks there. But I hadn't been home for two years, so, I was due for a visit. And after coming back we've been trying to analyze data that [my adviser] had collected before my coming here." Things were going "very slowly." Robert had many questions, and his adviser's approach was a mix of laissez-faire and to encourage learning by doing. "So, there's some things that I wish could go faster but he says that's a Socratic approach to where it's training and teaching, so, I have to be partly frustrated in order for me to really learn it—and hit my head against the wall for a while until he helps me out with things. So, I understand . . . but at the time it is happening I am very unhappy with it." It was not always working for him. "I felt like we had a few disagreements [this year] over things like data analysis or like that I needed a little bit more guidance that he wasn't there for, that he had greater expectations than I was hoping to have, or that I wanted to continue work on [our original project] because I felt like we were starting a lot of things and not finishing things." His deepening anxiety was not aided by his adviser's biting sense of humor. "So, for a long time he jokingly referred to me as 'slacker.'"

anxious about progress in school (handwritten annotation)

Eventually, Robert objected and the teasing ended, but the long-expired joke, in the midst of everything, still stung. A statement of this kind by an adviser can tap into deep existential anxiety, the kind that seems to prove every doubt a person has about oneself. By the start of his second year, Robert was consumed by fear of "failing altogether." He needed to talk.

Like Kenneth, Robert had replaced his named confidants over the course of the year. He had kept his dear mother, dropped some college friends, and added two classmates, Monika and Camille. Yet when asked whom he had spoken to about his fear of failing, he did not mention his mother. In fact, he said he had spoken only to two people, his new classmates Monika and Camille. Robert's concern was not politics; it was not the cloning of head-less frogs; it was serious, deeply personal, and emotional in nature, and he felt no qualms about approaching his new confidants.

dropped old but feared (handwritten annotation)

SERIOUS WORRIES NOT RESERVED FOR EITHER OLD OR NEW CONFIDANTS

The third expectation is based on the idea that both theory and instrument may be missing something crucial. The GSS asks people to ponder the previous six months and to name those they typically talked to. But the students may actually be wrong about whom they named. Recall H. Russell Bernard and Peter Killworth, who remarked, after many exhaustive studies, that "[p]eople do not know, with any accuracy, those with whom they communicate."[3] While some researchers suggest that people are more accurate than the authors claim, the broad conclusion seems clear—people's representations of their own social networks are suspect.[4]

In fact, an important tradition in cognitive psychology would suggest that the students will remember strong ties more than weak ones. In the 1970s, Amos Tversky and Daniel Kahneman proposed the influential "availability heuristic" hypothesis, which suggests that "a person evaluates the frequency of classes or the probability of events by availability, i.e., by the ease with which relevant instances come to mind."[5] When asked to recall others, students will likely think first of those who are cognitively available—who, for whatever reason, are easier to remember—and these will probably be people who are closer. The students in practice may well have turned to many weak ties that did not come to mind when prompted by the GSS instrument.

Finally, even if students had perfect memory, their representations of their networks would still be precisely that, representations, lists of named alters whose composition depends on the survey's choice of words—and on how the students interpreted those words. When asked to look back over six months, the students may well have believed they were being asked about those they talked to most *often*, rather than everyone they talked to. And the list of everyone they talked to may contain a large number of weak ties, such as miscellaneous classmates. Even when faced with their most serious worries, people may have turned, in practice, to many people they would not even bother considering a confidant.

confiding w/out even considering

Consider Faith, an intellectually creative social science student who began her program with a large set of confidants: her mother, father, sister, and boyfriend, and two friends, Nancy and Barb, who were graduate students at the university where Faith had obtained an MA. Perhaps not surprisingly, six months later Nancy and Barb had been dropped (along with her boyfriend) from the list of named confidants; they were replaced by five new people. Six months after that, Faith had replaced all but two of the newcomers, Evan and Pamela, both graduate students. Her mother, father, and sister were named once again. A new graduate student, Charlie, was added; Barb reappeared. Her seven confidants gave her a robust discussion network with a mix of recently formed and lifelong confidants.

Early in her second year, a seemingly small event would trigger a set of anxieties that would call for the ear of a confidant. Faith had expressed that by the end of the summer she was concerned with "finding a way to be happy day to day here." The sentiment derived from her sense of her social environment: "some of that is loneliness and how much time to spend with friends, and who to spend that with." The loneliness was recent. "I think part of it was that I was here all summer and there weren't a lot of people around. But I think part of it is also feeling more academic pressure, so more pressure on my time and to make sure that I'm . . . spending time with friends that [is] actually rewarding." The academic and social issues were inextricably linked. On days she was social, focusing on work seemed easier, so she started spending time with peers to both avoid isolation and become more productive. "[I]t did feel like I worked better when [I] sort of got me out of my own head a little to be around other people. And getting out [rather than working at home] also helped me focus on the work and just helped me feel more stable." Still, avoiding loneliness took work. To make matters worse, she split up with her boyfriend, and had failed to find new love. And in a bit of cosmic overkill, several of her confidants, over the course of the year, proceeded to get married, including Nancy (in her starting core discussion network), Tom (in the six-month one), and Charlie (in the twelve-month one).

Weeks into the second year, Faith saw her ex at a gathering. The encounter was unpleasant, quickly degenerating into what she called "melodramatically" passive-aggressive behavior on his part, since he remained unhappy she had left him. The situation dissipated but triggered larger questions: "it threw me back into thinking . . . how I feel like I made a pretty poor decision in dating him in the first place." The relationship had been short. "Just about three months, but pretty intensely for those three months. I mean not really enough to justify his reaction. But . . . it's sort of thrown me back into thinking about . . . partners and the bad decisions I've made in the past—but also like how I make those decisions and whether I'm sort of looking for the right thing."

She began to ask why she, unlike many of her friends, had no long-term prospects. "I don't feel like I want to be married, but it does make me wonder if I . . . want to be in a relationship or not, or why I'm not. The ones I have been with recently, they've been weirdoes." The situation made her wistful, particularly nostalgic for her most successful union, a long-term partnership in college. "I feel like I miss him a fair amount. I feel like I made the right decision not staying with him when I left [to get my master's degree], which is not what he wanted. But I do sort of think back to that decision a lot." Perhaps it had been one of many poor decisions that had now resulted in profound isolation.

Faith's concern was <u>not acute but existential</u>; it was the fear that, having bungled her social life for years, she was now—when it was crucial to her school success—suffering the consequences. She needed to talk, and did so—several times over several weeks, but only to three people. One of them, Charlie, was a named confidant. But Charlie was not the person she talked to most—in fact, he was not even the first person she approached. The two people she talked to most about this issue were Nancy, whom she had not considered a confidant for a year, and Uma—a classmate with whom she shared research interests—whom she had not named as a confidant at all. People may often confide in people they do not even consider confidants.

THE PREDOMINANT PRACTICE

variety

The experiences of Kenneth, Robert, and Faith make clear that, when faced with their own most serious worries, the students turned, respectively, to old named confidants (stronger ties), to new ones (weaker ties), and even to people not named at all (probably the weakest). However, any of these outcomes, especially the last, may be rare. If what Faith did were rare, it would be no less scientifically important, since uncommon events often prove theoretically informative.[6] But if it were not rare—if students often talked to people *other* than their named confidants—then we would need to examine whom people turn to and why from an entirely different perspective. What did the students typically do?

To answer that question, I developed an approach that departed from standard solutions, which would not have been effective. One standard approach would be to ask students more precise questions about the people

approaches to find typical actions "actual"

in their networks. For example, they could be asked whom they typically discussed "truly serious matters" rather than just "important matters" with and, separately, whom they were close to. But students may still be wrong about whom they typically turn to with serious matters; the availability heuristic and other biases might still be at play. Another standard approach would be to observe them ethnographically, eliminating reliance on their memory.[7] But an ethnographer cannot actually observe a private conversation between two people, since, as Georg Simmel and many others have shown, when a dyad becomes a triad, all dynamics change.[8] People may be shier, more competitive, or less rash, or may decline to confide in the other at all. As per the Hawthorne effect, the presence of an ethnographer inherently alters the situation, turning it into something other than a private conversation.[9] When studying people and their confidants, the observer effect is insurmountable.[10]

To determine whom students actually talked to about what truly worried them, I used interviews, but differently. I developed an approach based on three principles: begin with the conversation, identify the concrete event, and focus on serious worries. Rather than asking them to either remember whom they usually talked to or imagine whom they might confide in, we began with the event—the actual, concrete conversation during which they confided in others. In essence, we used the conversation to identify the network tie, rather than the network tie to infer what students were willing to discuss. In addition, rather than inquiring about general matters that might or might not be important, we specifically focused on serious worries.[11] And since different people worry about different things, asking all students about, say, their financial worries might not yield what is needed. Students not worried about finances (e.g., some because they have a fellowship) might either not need a confidant or easily talk about the topics with anyone they know. Thus, we asked students to focus on their own most serious worries.

The resulting process was deceptively straightforward and more powerful than expected. After students completed the structured portion of the interview—including naming their core discussion network—we asked the following: "What are the three things that worry you most regarding your graduate experience?" We recorded their answers verbatim. Then, for each issue they worried about, we told them, "Think of the last time you talked to someone about this issue." After allowing them time for reflection, we asked whom they spoke to on that particular occasion. We then repeated the entire process, but asking about what worried them most in their life outside of graduate school.[12] When asked of all students, the method produces the distribution of the last serious discussions, and the confidants involved; thus, it identifies whom students actually talked to when they most recently confided their own most serious worry in someone.

Since a student's last experience may have been atypical, the approach cannot be used to capture what a *given* student usually does. For example, while Faith might have approached Uma during the very last conversation she had had about her social anxiety, it is possible that, most of the time for most of the issues that worry her, she typically only approached Charlie and other people she had named as confidants. It would thus be folly to conclude that Faith typically talks to nonconfidants. However, it is perfectly appropriate to aggregate the responses of all students and make an inference about what happened during the last conversation of the statistically average student in our study.[13]

While the approach produces the answers we need, like any, it has limitations. Just as people may be mistaken about their networks, they may be mistaken about their conversations. They could be wrong about which conversation was the last time they talked about the issue that worried them or about whom they talked to on that particular occasion. The former is not a problem as long as the reason they were wrong about which conversation was the very last is not systematically related to the characteristics of the particular person they spoke to. The latter could be a problem if people's recollections tend to systematically favor alters with certain characteristics. That bias, if present, would likely result in the overrepresentation of named confidants. It is likely that people will tend to remember those they are close to more than mere acquaintances, and also that people will remember those they had named as confidants more than others, since every interview began with the GSS instrument. The fact that these particular alters have been primed means that the students are probably more likely to remember those they have called confidants than others. If so, the results would be biased in favor of reporting core discussion network members. That potential bias may be unavoidable, and we should consider the results a conservative estimate of the number of people students talk to who are *not* named confidants. Students likely talk to more people not named as confidants than will be reported.

[handwritten margin note: Who more likely to remember]

WHAT THEY WORRIED ABOUT

Before discussing whom they talked to, I briefly examine their worries, which are the basis of the names elicited. Consider the third wave of the study, the start of the second year, the point at which they will have developed enough new confidants for the question of which confidant they chose, old or new, to be meaningful. This section of the interview was open-ended, and interview data are naturally messy. Students did not report their worries in simple categories meant for analysis—they simply talked about what concerned them.[14] After extracting each response from the interview transcripts, I first coded each response openly, noting the general category or set of categories to which it seemed to refer. For example, one student reported that the main thing he worried about was "timelines in general, in terms of progressing through the program at a reasonable rate." I first coded this entry as "maintaining timeline" and "making expected progress." I then revised all the initial coding categories and recoded all responses again, ensuring consistency. Next, I grouped the initial codes into more general classes and took a third pass at the raw transcripts, this time categorizing the initial responses into these classes. For example, the student's aforementioned passage was classified under "fulfilling requirements" and "time management." Other general codes were "fear of failure," "fit with program," and "productivity."

The resulting codes are listed in Tables 3.1a and 3.1b. The tables list responses for worries about the graduate experience and about life separate

[handwritten margin note: 2nd year]

Table 3.1a. STUDENTS' WORRIES ABOUT THE GRADUATE EXPERIENCE

Worry	Percentage	Examples
Fulfilling requirements	47%	"I'm worried about writing my MA"; "I'm worried about comprehensive exams that I have to take in . . . less than a year"
Time management	15%	"I'm worried about managing a lot of different things at once"; "I think I'm most worried about the lack of time"
Relation to faculty	13%	"Trying to improve the relationship with some professors that I want on my side"; "[My] adviser may retire"
Productivity	10%	"Generally I'm worried about getting published"; "Developing a coherent line of research"
Long-term career	8%	"What type of work I'm going to find after graduation"; "The anxiety of potentially committing to a big project . . . that could be . . . defining of my early career is pretty daunting"
Fear of failure	8%	"I think the top one will really be the fear of not completing the program"; "Failing [altogether]. That's a pretty persistent one"
Fit with program	5%	"One, that [graduate school] is not right for me"; "That I made the wrong decision by coming here"
Relation to peers	5%	"I guess my relationship with the [other students] in the department"; "I don't know how to be . . . friends with American people"
Finances	4%	"I would tie inadequate health care and inadequate funding together"; "I'm applying for the NSF [National Science Foundation]. So that's high on the list of things that I'm thinking about"
Health care	3%	"I had . . . surgery and I spent the summer . . . reaching the diagnosis, and there were so many tests and everything"; "I, sometimes I think I am depressed little bit"
Social life	2%	"I guess I'm concerned about the gravity of the social situation here. . . . It's pretty dire"

Notes: Third wave, at the start of the second year. Students were asked to name the three things that worried them most regarding their graduate experience. Among students we interviewed in wave 3, all reported at least two worries; all but four reported three. Figures indicate percent of all graduate worries reported that involved the topic.

Table 3.1b. STUDENTS' WORRIES ABOUT LIFE IN GENERAL

Worry	Percentage	Examples
Love and family	59%	"[Hillmount] has no dating scene"; "Marriage"; "The distance in my relationship"; "Figuring things out with . . . my girlfriend"
Social life	17%	"I'm worried about that I don't really have too much of an outside life"; "I wish I had more female friends"; "Having enough time for friends"
Finances	10%	"Financial trouble"; "I think probably just money . . . kind of am I going to be able to afford rent this month"
Miscellaneous personal issues	10%	"With the visa issue, not being able to go back home for two years"; "I feel like [this town] is very much a . . . at least for the people of my age, is not really . . . a destination"
Time management	7%	"Well, I'm the president of [an association]. I don't know what I got myself into, but it's just a lot of work"; "Having enough time for friends"
Long-term career	3%	"Future plans . . . when I began graduate school . . . I thought I had really gotten used to the fact that I never know where I'm going to be in . . . seven years. . . . But now that I'm a bit older . . . now that you and your partner want to talk long term [I'm not so sure]"
Fit with program	3%	"It's a bit disconcerting inuring yourself to the life of an academic, firstly because it's a, really like, test tube strange kind of life to lead, right? You really are outside of the box in many respects"

Notes: Third wave, at the start of the second year. Students were asked to name one thing that worried them most about life beyond graduate school. All but eight reported having a major worry. Figures represent percent of all life worries reported that involved the topic.

from the graduate experience, respectively, and present the codes, the percentage of all reported worries involving the topic, and illustrative examples. Please note that, as in the previous example, some of the students' responses could be categorized under two or more labels. Thus, the percentages will not add to 100. Among the students interviewed, all reported at least two issues they worried about involving their graduate experience, all but four reported three issues, and all but six reported an issue they worried about regarding life in general.

The concerns clustered strongly, such that, in both tables, four or five issues covered the bulk of students' worries. Consider the worries about the graduate experience, Table 3.1a. When Kenneth was concerned that his extensive mathematics background was insufficient for him to do well in his required papers, he was manifesting his own version of the most common concern among students at the start of their second year—fulfilling course requirements. Almost half, 47%, of all reported worries consisted of fulfilling requirements. The next most common issue was time management: "I'm worried about managing a lot of different things at once." Students often discussed their time concerns in conjunction with other worries, particularly fulfilling requirements: "Immediately, I am worried about refining the contours of my MA project. And thinking about whether or not I should use that as kind of a fun experimental one off to try on different ideas, or should I use that as a departure point for my dissertation? So that's pressing right now because I want to finish that this year." *connecting worries*

An almost equally common concern among students involved, as in the case of Robert, their relation to professors, which was reported 13% of the time. Typically, students worried about finding advisers or remaining in good standing ("maintaining a good . . . relationship with my adviser"). One student was concerned with "trying to improve the relationship with some professors that I want on my side." Almost as common was a set of worries that may be classified under "productivity," a general category that captures a battery of concerns not necessarily tied to fulfilling program requirements. Of these, the single most common was getting their work in print: "generally I'm worried about getting published." One year in, students across the board seemed to have adopted the "publish or perish" mantra all too well. Others, however, expressed their concerns about productivity in broader terms, such as the student who expressed preoccupation with "developing a coherent line of research." *common worries*

Two other concerns are worth mentioning. One involves the long-term career prospects students would experience after graduation. The concern was in some ways surprising, given that students were still at least four years from completing their programs. Still, the responses reflect the fact that universities produce far more graduates with PhDs in any given year than tenure-track or otherwise attractive academic positions in which to employ them. *key worries*

Another notable worry involved the possibility of failure. This concern, which often led to deep anxiety, was especially poignant, given that, while some such worry might well be expected at the start of any new professional endeavor, the students were by now in the second year of their program, well seasoned by the local context. One student made clear that "failing altogether" was a "pretty persistent" worry. Another expressed bluntly that "the top [worry] will really be the fear of not completing the program." Students' fear of failure was often accompanied by the broader *failure* sense, in spite of any evidence to the contrary, that they were somehow not up to par, a pattern sometimes described as "imposter syndrome."[15] This fear was often coupled with the anxiety that the student might somehow be "behind," that in the set of unstated expectations about where one should be to eventually succeed in academia, the student might be less accomplished, less respected, or less thought of by faculty and peers as a promising scholar. Some version of this sentiment was common. In graduate school, it seems, everyone thinks everyone else is doing better.

The worries about life outside of graduate school clustered around four or five topics, with social issues at the top (Table 3.1b). Family, love, and romantic relationships were among the students' most common concerns, resulting in more than half the reported worries. Their nonromantic social life was second. Finances was third, which is unsurprising given the economic burden that a graduate career places on many families. Even those students fortunate enough to receive both scholarships to cover the costs of tuition and stipends to provide living expenses rarely received much support. Students in the humanities can consider themselves fortunate for receiving a living stipend of $25,000 a year; those in laboratory sciences, perhaps $32,000. Most stipends are not that generous, and many students must manage the full-time commitment of a graduate program with no stipend at all. And stipends rarely last the extent of a graduate career. Further, if students are the primary breadwinners and are supporting a family, circumstances may be quite dire. In fact, the US poverty level for a family of four in 2014 was $23,850, and most experts believe that this level is too low, as families begin experiencing difficulty at much higher incomes. Among students, acquiring a heavy debt burden is a common experience.

Note that the idea of worries "about life outside of graduate school," while useful as a tool to capture the breadth of students' concerns, can be misleading. Students only have one life, and all their worries are often intertwined. We can see this fact in the tables in two ways. First, note that several of the codes in Table 3.1b, such as "time management," "fit with the program," and "long-term career," were also present in Table 3.1a. That is, even when asked about concerns independent of the graduate program, professionally related questions such as time management emerged. Second, note that the issues that ostensibly were not, such as love and family or social life, often revolved around their new professional context, such as "the [long] distance in my relationship" and "having enough time for friends." Indeed, even one year in, the move to a new professional and institutional context can be so overwhelming in both challenges and opportunities that all of a person's concerns become tied up with the institution in one way or another.

In all, these concerns help explain the high prevalence of stress-related mental health problems in graduate programs. A recent study of more than 3,000 graduate students in a large western university found that "[a]lmost half (44.7%) of the respondents reported having an emotional or stress-related problem over the previous year. Another 57.7% reported having a colleague with an emotional or stress-related problem" over the same period.[16] The study found that the predictors of such problems were many of the same worries our students reported: "Self-reported mental health needs were significantly and negatively related to confidence about one's financial status, higher functional relationship with one's advisor, regular contact with friends, and being married."[17] Each of these is among the top three of either graduate school or broader concerns among our students. They also help understand the student's frequent need to talk. Worrying day after day, and week after week, about the possibility of failure or the prospects of isolation, or facing persistent anxieties about one's intellectual worth or ability to pay the bills, will eventually take its toll.

[handwritten margin note: mental health]

[handwritten margin note: the need to talk]

The particular issues students worried about deserve more attention, and later chapters return to this matter. First, however, I address this chapter's driving question, whether—when discussing their serious worries—the students in practice approached old confidants, new ones, or people they had not named as such.

WHOM THEY ACTUALLY TALKED TO

When we asked students whom they talked to when they last discussed their worries, we sought to open a window to delve deeper into their thought processes. Thus, this portion of the interviews was open-ended, and conversations at times meandered, as they should, heading wherever the students took them. Some students talked to us with equal expansiveness about each of the three worries reported; others spent an hour discussing a single worry; still others became engrossed in an aspect of their personal relationships that veered far from the specific issue of which individual they spoke to most recently about their major worries. As a result, any effort to quantify their responses must be wary of potential pitfalls, and even the most robust results possible must be interpreted not as final estimates about the distribution in some larger population but as general tendencies calling for further in-depth analysis.[18] Thus, I stress that the only point of the figures in the paragraphs below is to capture a very broad picture.

To determine whom the students had talked to most recently, I performed two calculations, both of which approximate that number, based on the third wave of the study, the point at which they will have developed sufficient relationships for the question of whether they preferred long-standing named confidants to be meaningful.[19] One measure focused on the very first topic the students reported worrying about. My team and I extracted whom they talked to during the most recent conversation they had about that topic. If the transcript was unclear about whom they had spoken to, we extracted the name of the first person they mentioned talking to in the context of this topic.[20] Then we recorded whether the alter was someone they had earlier in the interview, when asked the GSS instrument, named as a confidant. There were three possibilities: they talked to an old discussion partner (someone named in the current and one of the previous two waves), they talked to a new discussion partner (someone named only in the current one), or they talked to someone not named as a discussion partner at all.

If the first measure centered on the first worry reported, then the second centered on the last discussion recalled. It focused on the most recent conversation they had about one of the three issues they reported worrying about. We extracted the name of the person with whom students had the most recent conversation about the first worry reported. If it was not available, we extracted that name for the second worry reported. If that was not available, we extracted it for the third. We recorded whether the alter had been named as a core discussion partner, as earlier.[21] Please note that several of the students' conversations involved more than one person. If so, we recorded the alters under all relevant categories. For this reason, percentages will add to more than 100.

Regardless of measure, the results were unambiguous. During their most recent discussions about their most serious worries, students had spoken to old and new confidants in roughly equal measure, suggesting the students in *practice* did not distinguish meaningfully between stronger and weaker ties. By the first measure, the figures were 23% for both old and new confidants; by the second, 20% and 29%, respectively, showing a very slight preference toward old named confidants. Nevertheless, the predominant trend was clear: Depending on the measure, either 63% or 60% of the students had actually confided in someone they had *not* named as a discussion partner.[22]

With respect to worries about life independent of the graduate experience, the number of available responses is smaller, making the figures more difficult to assemble. My original intention with this question was to capture those aspects of their life that were somehow outside the graduate experience. As noted earlier, however, we learned during the interviews that this idea was something of fantasy. As one student put it, "That's a strange question. Um . . . in my personal life? Well, I can't think outside of this rubric of academia now."

A major transition of this kind at a key point in the life course can affect so many aspects of one's experience that few of a student's preoccupations can be described as unrelated to their graduate experience. People come to understand their health problems as the result of work-induced stress, their relationship problems as the result of work-induced neglect, and their social problems as the result of poor fit with one's new colleagues. They worry about finances because their stipend is too small. Thus, their graduate school worries were often, in fact, their worries about life in general. In these and other ways, the first year resembled elements of a total institution.

So, it is not surprising that several students did not offer any additional issues they were worried about when asked about worries in life outside of graduate school. In all, for only a bit over half of all students (20 out of 37 in this wave), we have both a worry they described as being independent of the graduate experience and the name of at least one person they talked to. The numbers, therefore, are less reliable.[23] With this caveat in mind, it is still informative to assess whether a similar picture emerges. I obtained the name of either the person they last discussed that worry with or, if it was not available, the first person mentioned. In this set of cases, 15% of the time they actually talked to new core discussion members, 50% of the time to old members, and 35% of the time to people not in the network. Named old confidants appear more often; nonconfidants remain highly prevalent.

Because of the large number of nonconfidants, I sought confirmation by pursuing an alternative way of calculating the figures that maximized the use of the available data. I still focused on the third wave of data, the start of their second year. Given that the students' answers undermined a too-strong distinction between graduate-school and non-graduate-school worries, I pooled all responses. In addition, my team and I identified and noted every single issue students cited as a major worry and every conversation that, over the course of our long and open-ended interviews, they reported having about it. We thus produced a list of all the conversations they reported about all the issues they most worried about and all the people they reported talking to about such issues, a total of more than 300 intimate conversations. The result confirmed the picture: in 48% of all conversations they had had, students talked to someone they had not named a confidant.

BEYOND NAMED CONFIDANTS [61]

I stress that with qualitative data such as these, making too much of particular percentages is an inferential mistake, because the fluidity of the interview process itself makes such numbers suspect.[24] In a later chapter, I use national survey data to assess these distributions on a large sample. The only point of the current analysis is to determine, for the students we interviewed, whether conversations with particular classes of people were rare, something that, in fact, we can do well. Given that the different approaches suggest that students talked to people outside of their core discussion network between roughly 4 and 6 times out of 10, there is little question that this network does not capture many of the people students actually talked to about those issues they most worried about. Faith's experience—to confide a personal worry to someone not considered a confidant—was common.

IN PRACTICE, WEAK TIES

The findings say something about the GSS instrument and something about strong-tie theory.

First, though the GSS instrument might capture a network well, it does not accurately capture practice—whom students actually turned to and why.[25] In either a large minority or a majority of the cases, it missed whom the students actually confided in.[26] This fact does not necessarily make the GSS a weak instrument for its original intentions. Though it is possible that, as with Bernard and Killworth's respondents, the students were often mistaken about whom they confided in, that conclusion is not quite demanded by the data, since, strictly speaking, we would need to reconstruct their previous six months—an exercise that would undoubtedly produce noisy data.[27] An equally plausible alternative is that, even if the students reported their networks accurately, their answers did not mean what many would take them to mean. Students may have talked to their named confidants more regularly than they did to any individual who was not, while still carrying out most of their conversations with people who were not on that list. That is, they may find themselves talking to many different people—a bartender, a random classmate, another passenger on a plane—only once or twice, but only to the few they call confidants repeatedly. If so, then focusing on the latter at the exclusion of the former would lead to the wrong inference that students were reluctant to confide in weak ties.[28] Later interpretations notwithstanding, the GSS instrument was designed to reproduce a network, not practice. And in this book it is practice, what they have actually done, that we seek to understand.

[handwritten: limits to GSS instrument]

Second, the previous and current chapters, together, also make clear that strong-tie theory as it is normally applied cannot account for the students' practices. Students certainly talked often to their spouses, parents, and others to whom they were obviously close. But they no less often confided serious matters to classmates, former roommates, old and new professors, miscellaneous administrators, a manager at work, and others— people they had just met, or only now considered confidants, or did not even consider confidants at all.

can't fully apply strong-tie theory

In sum, the oft-repeated notion that people confide "only" in those they are close to is not supported by the data. The students confide in weak ties, and they do so often. The question is why.

CHAPTER 4

Incompatible Expectations

Why They Avoided Strong Ties

Carver was pressed. An earnest student of working-class roots, he committed equally to scholarship and family. Born, raised, schooled, college educated, and currently residing in the same hometown, Carver loved Hillmount's proximity to home, his parents, and especially, it seemed, his mother, to whom he was particularly close. Even the 60-mile commute from home to Hillmount barely seemed a bother, content as he was to start life as a newlywed with a newborn. But things were difficult. When asked, 12 months in, to describe his major worry, he was blunt: "Money."

Carver took pains to distinguish greed from necessity, being broke from being, in fact, poor, though he studiously avoided that term. "I'm not . . . materialistic," he explained to me. "I don't need a lot of things . . . to live. But [given] my family, now you have to worry about . . . '[Am] I going to be able to afford rent this month?' And . . . we've got some savings, but it's not where [we would be OK] if something catastrophic happened." A persistent worry was the cost of insurance. "You know . . . insurance for the baby . . . is like 450 bucks a month. And the thing is, you know, I'm insured [by the university] but it's still 450 if I [add] a dependent here. [My wife's] insurance is through her mother. And she can't have the kid on the policy because it's under mother. . . . So, it's a huge problem. So, we're trying to get . . . Medicaid."

Pursuing a PhD on Medicaid may seem an incongruity, but it is not too far from the reality for many. While elite programs may support students with four- or five-year scholarships, most students across the nation must balance their pursuit of ideas against their need for food, shelter, and health care. And since the years of graduate training match the years of family formation, the demands of the profession often clash with needs at home. Health care costs are especially common across the lower end of the income distribution. For Carver, perhaps the most elusive problems were the unexpected crises. "If the transmission goes out on my truck, I mean, that's a thousand dollars easy, and it is really going to eat into our savings." As he explained, in a phrase that echoes across American dining tables: "we're just one problem away from being screwed."

Carver worried about $

Clearly, Carver needed cash. But at times he just needed an ear, someone to vent to about the stress of handling first-year boot camp while managing the taxing strains and sleepless nights of a firstborn child—all with no money to spare. The stress of poverty is as much emotional as it is financial, and talk is therapy. Carver was fortunate to have a strong support network, of whom the most important person was probably his mother. She was one of two people who, over the course of two years, he consistently named as confidant; she had listened to and supported him through everything. But not this. With her, Carver studiously avoided discussing money: "I don't tell my mom," he explained. For this topic, he went to other people.

didn't talk $ w/ his mom

Sometimes, students approached weak ties because they were avoiding strong ones. This avoidance was pervasive and important, one more fact of their relations that seems absurd in light of the theory but intuitive after the fact. People steer clear of many topics with family and friends, out of embarrassment, fear of gossip, general discomfort, worry that they might not understand, and countless other reasons. But people may find the strength of a tie to be precisely the reason to avoid it, a natural aspect of interpersonal relations that fails to square with how strong relations are theorized. Making sense of this predicament is critical for a theory of support.

reason for avoiding convos w/close ties

Though a simple version of strong-tie theory cannot explain the predicament, a structural version could. If strong-tie networks are dense, then any information learned by one member should quickly travel to the others.[1] Thus, students could avoid confiding in strong ties out of fear the information might spread. Carver might worry that his mother would quickly tell everyone in the family about his problems with money. This structural explanation is elegant, intuitive, and probably correct in many circumstances.[2] Nevertheless, the worry about the spread of information did not seem to motivate most of the students who reported avoiding strong ties. In fact, the issue was rarely mentioned. This fact is not surprising, given the low density of their networks of named confidants. The structural account, though powerful in general, cannot be the entire story.

Why, then, did students avoid their strong ties? The answer will require us to examine in greater detail the students' relationships, since their decisions in each case were shaped by the particular way they conceived of the strong tie. How they conceived of their ties depended on which institutions mediated the relation, and the complexity of the ensuing expectations gave rise to the irony that the stronger the tie, the more sensible the decision to avoid it.

DIFFERENT TYPES OF CONFIDANTS

It is easy to think of strong ties as free and open relations unencumbered by boundaries or expectations. But strong and weak ties differ in their closeness, not in the degree to which they are so bound—all relations carry implicit expectations of appropriate and inappropriate behavior.

Such expectations profoundly affected the students' behavior. The students maintained different kinds of strong ties and confided in people with whom they had different kinds of relationships. The former can be classified by their degree of *institutional mediation*; the latter, by the extent of *emotional reciprocity*.

Two Factors

Institutional mediation

The students were close to many people whose relationship was nonetheless institutionally mediated. Institutional mediation is the extent to which the norms or rules of an organization, profession, or other formal arrangement governs the expectations underlying the relationship. Examples are the ties between two coworkers, two church members, employee and boss, or parishioner and priest, all of which differ from purely personal ones in that, no matter how close, they are subject to formal expectations of behavior either commonly understood or codified in rule books or the law.[3] In such relationships, the parties must always manage institutional expectations, a process that may affect the issues they feel comfortable discussing.

Institutional expectations derive from at least two sources: (a) the organizational context in which the two parties interact and (b) the formal positions that characterize the relationship.

(a) Many relationships are institutionally mediated because they are *organizationally embedded*, arising in offices, college campuses, churches, political clubs, hospitals, and other contexts where the norms and rules of interaction dictate what may or may not be talked about in that context. For example, coworkers, no matter how close, must avoid sexist, racist, or homophobic comments while talking to each other at the office, lest they violate local rules and create a hostile work environment. Since social interaction must always occur in some context, either physical or virtual, many relationships are mediated by the rules of the formal organizations in which people encounter their confidants.[4]

norms set by organization (handwritten margin note)

(b) But not all institutionally mediated relationships exist between members of the same organization. Some are bound by the expectations of their professional positions, such as those between therapists, coaches, doctors, professors, priests, teachers, lawyers, and others, and the people they serve or work with. For example, regardless of where they interact—even if they chance upon each other at a bank—a priest and a parishioner must manage expectations about appropriate topics of discussion. For example, parishioners throughout history have been known to fall in love with their priests, but most will feel special trepidation about confessing the fact to their religious father figure.[5]

set by expectation (handwritten margin note)

Emotional reciprocity

Reciprocity generally refers to the extent to which one actor's provision of goods or services to another is returned in equal measure. The foundation of exchange models of social behavior in psychology, sociology, and anthropology, reciprocity has long been theorized to be fundamental to social interaction.[6] As Peter Blau argued, "A person for whom another has done a service is expected to express his gratitude and return a service when the occasion arises."[7] Reciprocity is particularly common in social support. A provision of goods or services of one form need not be returned in exactly the same form—in fact, it often is not. In a classic study, Carol Stack examined support among low-income women and found that people offered services depending on what they had access to, on the expectation that the reciprocal provision would, in turn, help manage their own deficiencies.[8] People received a car ride, for example, and later offered babysitting. Since reciprocity may occur in some different form, one of the tensions that may emerge in reciprocal exchange is whether the resource, service, or good offered has been returned in equal measure.

Such tensions can emerge between potential confidants. In this case, the relevant form of reciprocity is emotional; it is what researchers who think of confidants as close relations expect the relationships to have, what Granovetter referred to as "mutual confiding" when defining the strength of a tie, wherein each party confides in the other, as Simone De Beuvoir did in her partner Jean Paul Sartre and vice versa.[9] Emotional reciprocity is the extent to which the person in whom an actor confides would regularly confide in the actor.

But relationships may be reciprocal in general while not being reciprocal emotionally, such as that between a patient and a therapist. When a patient reveals personal matters to her therapist, she does not expect him to reciprocate *in kind*, with the therapist's own emotional unveiling; on the contrary, the therapist's role is to listen, and the expected reciprocal gestures are to communicate attention by nodding and asking probing questions with sympathy and sensitivity. The support provided by the therapist is reciprocated by financial payment. Relationships between people and their confidants may differ in the extent to which they are emotionally reciprocal—they may resemble that between two lovers, or that between patient and therapist. When a relationship is not emotionally reciprocal, *ambiguity* may arise about what constitutes proper reciprocity.

Types

These two conditions resulted in different kinds of relationships between the students and those they were close to and considered confiding in, as seen in Table 4.1. Consider the top left cell. Unmediated, emotionally reciprocal relations are what come to mind when many conceive of strong ties. These are relations between best friends who confide in one another regularly.[10] They are mutually confiding relations, and their dynamics have been covered in countless scholarly and popular works, particularly those on

Table 4.1. TYPES OF POTENTIAL CONFIDANTS, WITH EXAMPLES

		Institutional Mediation	
		Low	*High*
Emotional reciprocity	*Reciprocal*	Best friend, spouse	Colleague, lab partner
	Nonreciprocal	Grandmother, mother	Adviser, therapist

friendship. It is the kind of relationship that lab science student Michelle had with Betty, her lifelong friend, one of the closest ever, with whom she regularly chatted electronically.

But many of the relationships—and most of the complications I discuss later—arose in the other three categories.

Many were emotionally reciprocal, mediated relationships (top right cell). The majority of these relations were to other graduate students, people who were both friends *and* colleagues. When Sarah was asked to name her confidants in the first interview, she explained immediately that she had "met several good friends. I mean very close friends." One of her "best friends here," she insisted, was Bryce. "She is kind of like my soul mate. Yeah. I think I can tell her almost everything in my mind." Bryce was slightly older, in the same department, and of the same ethnic background, evidence of what Paul Lazarsfeld and Robert Merton termed the principle of homophily, the tendency of people to associate with people who resemble them.[11]

Sarah and Bryce confided in each other. But unlike ordinary best friends, they were also unavoidably members of the same organization, and thus subject to the same institutional context and expectations of behavior. They faced the potential of a competitive relationship in light of the expectations of advisers and, later, the academic job market. As a result, though each could understand the other's professional difficulties more than most, they also faced a form of professional competition that unmediated friends like Michelle and Betty did not.

The bottom row of Table 4.1 identifies relationships in which the students confided in people who did not typically confide in them. Many of these relationships were mediated. Interestingly, many of these confidants were *also* students—that is, many students confided in peers who did not regularly do the same. For example, while Sandra twice over the first two years reported Pamela as a confidant, Pamela never listed Sandra. Some students appeared to be the confidants of many, essentially excellent "listener-friends" who were also colleagues. Halfway through the first year, four students in the laboratory sciences department listed Camille, whose welcoming personality invites confidence, as one of their core discussion partners; Camille listed only one of them. In fact, by the start of the second year, across all 37 students, 76 of the confidants listed were other graduate students, of whom 26 were students in the same cohort. Of these 26 confidants, however, only 4 (two pairs) were reciprocated. The overwhelming majority of confidants who were students themselves were not emotionally reciprocal—it was not the "mutual confiding" of which Granovetter spoke as indicative of a strong tie.

Students often confided in others who did not reciprocate emotion-ally, people such as miscellaneous staff members. Layla often confided in Barbara, who was not exactly a friend but also not quite an adviser. "She's our lab manager and we just have a lot in common. So she's like a very easy person to like come to and every, I think everyone in our lab goes to her. She's like . . . the therapist in our lab." Barbara's paid role was to administer the laboratory, not to listen to students vent. Yet the course of everyday interaction, coupled with her vast experience over the matters that con-cerned students, made her a natural confidant for many of them.

(I must note that the examples in Table 4.1 are only illustrations; they are not exclusive archetypes. For example, a boyfriend is often an unmedi-ated relation. But if a boyfriend happens to be a coworker, the expectations of the workspace mediate the relationship, and the tie would be classified in the right, not left, cell of the top row. Being clear on this fluidity matters.)

Because relationships can be institutionally mediated, and because they may lack emotional reciprocity, three important issues come to the fore: hierarchy, family, and multiplexity.

Hierarchy

Institutions affect relationships in many ways, and when the relationship is organizationally embedded, one party may lie above the order in the institutional hierarchy, whether by authority or general seniority. Students often developed close relationships to those above in the academic hier-archy, such as teaching assistants and especially faculty advisers, people who, in turn, were expected to listen to students vent or to help students talk through problems. These were close yet hierarchical and nonreciprocal relations. Charles, a social science student who described himself to me as "very spunky [as an] undergraduate" and whose work had long been his primary life devotion, began confiding primarily in his advisers as early as the start of his career. His first undergraduate teaching assistant, Nellie, quickly became a confidant: "some of our first interactions were—she was my TA, we'd have discussion group and her office hours were right after. And I would go and I'd be like, 'I think you're wrong about [the topic of the class]' and I would . . . argue with her, and she was great." He continued going to Nellie's office hours, because "professors are . . . busy and like have all this stuff and [are] like important, but I found that . . . advanced gradu-ate students are way more like giving with . . . their time." However, Charles was intense, devoted to his work, constantly in need of an intellectual fix. Most of what he talked about when he talked about what mattered to him was his scholarship. By the time he enrolled in graduate school, he had found a way to carve into professors' time. In his first semester, he reported one of his new professors, whom he had met before graduate school, as his most important confidant.

These relationships were naturally not emotionally reciprocal. Recall Oscar, the humanities student who found himself replacing many of his old discussion partners and who added Gerald, his academic adviser, who, after countless meetings and encounters at a departmental colloquium, had come to know him more than most. Oscar often vented to Gerald. For Gerald's attention, Oscar was expected to remain in good standing, participate actively in the workshop Gerald helped organize, and generally perform the role of graduate student as effectively as Gerald performed that of an adviser. But the relationship was free of *emotional* reciprocity—at no point would Gerald vent back to Oscar. In fact, such an action would violate the norms of the professional relationship. As a result, many of the emotional obligations Oscar felt toward his peer discussion partners were not part of his relationship with Gerald. The tendency to confide in advisers was common. At least two students in the laboratory science department listed an adviser for multiple consecutive waves. And of the students in the humanities and social science departments, roughly *half* reported confiding regularly in academic advisers at least once across the four waves.

[handwritten margin note: benefited from one-sided; some to look up to]

Family

I have defined institutional mediation as the extent to which a formal institutional arrangement shapes a relationship's expectations. The family may not be a *formal* institution in the sense of the previous examples, but it remains an institution nonetheless, one in which people's membership in and position within the group shape behavior.[12] Though kin-related expectations may vary across cultures and class backgrounds, they remain perennial aspects of interpersonal relations, the source of phenomena as varied as the family feud, the dowry, the arranged marriage, and the filial obligation.[13] All of these reflect practices that people feel compelled to engage in that, had they not belonged to the family, they otherwise might not. Family norms are strong, and people are inclined to follow them. For this reason, though kin relations are often not formally institutionally mediated, they are never *un*mediated; they exist somewhere between the formal relations of colleagues and the unmediated relations of childhood friends.

[handwritten margin note: family in the middle]

Many students were close to family members in whom they considered confiding. And such relations were sometimes emotionally nonreciprocal, and even hierarchical. Isaac's closest confidants were his "dad and mom," followed by his "girlfriend" and a few others. For Kenneth, the main one was his "wife, who [he had] just married a couple of months ago," and four of the five others were family members—a grandmother, a grandfather, and both in-laws. Kenneth had grown close to his in-laws, who had taken him on as they would a son. But whereas Kenneth confided in his grandparents and in-laws, they did not, in turn, confide in him. Emotional asymmetries of this kind created ambiguities, making some topics inappropriate for discussion.

Multiplexity

Multiplexity may be defined as the extent to which relations between two parties are characterized by two or more roles.[14] As network anthropologist Jeremy Boissevain has proposed, a role is nothing more than a set of "norms and expectations that apply to the occupant of a particular position."[15] Robert Merton defined it as the "behavioral enacting of the patterned expectations attributed to [a] position."[16] Some roles, as we have seen, are attached to formal professional positions, such as therapist, coach, and lawyer; others are not, such as neighbor, parishioner, and coworker.

But the roles that will matter most to our discussion are not *titular*, such as "therapist" or "coworker," but *behavioral*, such as "listener," "evaluator," "competitor," or "supporter." The "listener" role is expected of every kind of confidant, including best friends, priests, therapists, and professors. But institutional expectations can imbue these confidants with additional behavioral roles, such as "evaluator" in the case of a priest, "invoicer" in the case of a therapist, and "grader" in the case of a professor. When relationships are mediated by institutional expectations, multiplexity of this kind will often arise.

Most of the students' strong ties were multiplex in this particular, behavioral sense.[17] Since many of these relationships were either formally or informally mediated, the classmates, mothers, husbands, lab directors, and professors who were potential confidants played multiple roles in light of the student, not only listener but also competitor, evaluator, boss, provider, and even help seeker. This kind of multiple relationship is what Layla referred to when she half-jokingly called Barbara, the laboratory manager, "the therapist in our lab." Barbara was listener and advice giver, but also supervisor, staff member, and rules enforcer. The multiple expectations implicit in such relationships would prove thorny.

AVOIDANCE IN PRACTICE

I have proposed that students turned to weak ties at times because they were avoiding strong ones, and suggested that their avoidance turned on expectations about the nature of their relations. Since these relations, as we have seen, took radically different forms, categorizing those forms was an important first step. But our central focus is what they did in practice, an inquiry that requires us to determine whether, as Carver did, they in fact avoided their strong ties.

To this end, I adopted an approach all too rare currently in either formal network analysis or the behavioral science that has been used to understand human motivation—I asked them. Among the most conspicuously missing data in recent social network analysis has been discussion of what people say motivates their decisions to seek others. In the 1970s and 1980s, a period that witnessed an explosion of creativity in sociological network analysis, several researchers took care to introduce people's representations of their own decisions into the analysis. For example, Granovetter's work on how people found jobs made extensive use of his respondents' own thoughts about why they approached whom they approached.[18] Occasional studies in recent years have done the same. For example, Peter Bearman and Paolo Parigi studied people's discussion partners and asked people who did not report any partners why they did not talk to anyone. However, such studies are surprisingly rare.[19]

My research assistants and I used the open-ended portion of the interviews to probe the students' motivation. Recall that students were asked to think of the last time they talked to someone about the specific issues that worried them most and to report whom they talked to on that occasion. Then, we discussed the people whom, based on the prior conversation, they might have approached but did not—core discussion partners, mothers, fathers, spouses, advisers, roommates, other graduate students, and others. I believe that the scientist learns as much about how people understand themselves by their account of their inactions as one does about their justification for their actions, and that this approach—probing the counterfactual conditions—will yield valuable insight. Naturally, these were open-ended interviews, with all their advantages and disadvantages, including the fact that we did not ask every person this question precisely this way about every conversation. Had we mechanically listed every single person and probed why they were not approached, the students would have fallen into short-answer responses, the conversation would have been stilted, and the naturally creative process of the interview would have suffered. Instead, we probed as often as we could, then let them speak, and

learning from the inactions [handwritten marginal note]

followed them to the places the interviews seemed to take them. The details behind our interviewing technique are discussed in Appendix A.

INCOMPATIBLE EXPECTATIONS

The interviews made clear that the heart of the students' reservations lay in the possibility of *incompatible expectations*, in the potential discordance between different roles that those they were close to might expect to perform. The most important role of a confidant is to serve as listener, supporter, or sounding board. But most of the students' strong relations were behaviorally multiplex, characterized by multiple roles whose expectations at times conflicted with those wanted of a confidant. These expectations were sometimes affected by institutional norms. And they had the potential of being especially ambiguous when relations were not emotionally reciprocal. The students avoided strong ties when the topic they would broach might elicit any other unwanted behavioral role, a situation likely to produce uncomfortableness or awkward disjuncture at best, and the deterioration of the relationship at worst. The stronger the relationship, the greater the consequences of being wrong, and the more likely students were to avoid the interaction.

Incompatible expectations undermined the possibility of approaching others in many ways. At times, students feared eliciting a hurtful or unhelpful response, as might happen if the confidant is also an evaluator. Other times, they were not so much afraid of the wrong response as reluctant to create an awkward encounter, as might happen if the confidant had once been a provider. Still others, they simply hesitated to bring to light a role, such as competitor, that was an uncomfortable part of the relation. Consider the following situations, which depict the many behavioral roles with which those of a confidant—listener, supporter, or sounding board— may be incompatible.

Layla and Her Classmate: Listener Versus Competitor

By the start of her third year, Layla had established her reputation as a strong member of her laboratory, a student with several interesting projects in the works and a couple of papers on their way to publication. Yet early in the semester something happened that gave her pause. She was scheduled to present the results of a recent study to a group that included many faculty and graduate students and other members of her laboratory.

It was one of the first formal presentations she had given that was based on a line of research primarily of her own design, and it did not go especially well—she was more uncomfortable and unsure of herself than she ever expected, nervous, and seemingly ill-prepared. "I thought it was so bad. . . . I was embarrassed by it." Others she had confided in did not necessarily agree that she had underperformed, but that belief did not matter. She tried to explain her frustration, particularly about performing this way in front of her laboratory colleagues. "I think that I'm comparing myself to other people, and other people's talks are sometimes just . . . better. . . . They were just smoother . . . and everyone seemed to agree [with the presenter] and there [weren't] too many of these questions . . . like, 'I have no idea what you are saying.'" She got to the crux of the matter: "I think most of the competition maybe from our labor group is . . . probably a good kind of competition." She continued, "You want to do your best if possible but . . . at the same time you're comparing yourself to people [in the lab]."

One person, another high performer in her cohort, particularly came to mind. "So . . . often I find myself comparing myself to [Andrea] because we started at the same time." Feeling competitive, she explained, "is very easy to do . . . when you think that other people are doing it." In fact, early in their training, when they had both joined the lab, their adviser gave them both an assignment that inevitably had an undercurrent of competition, even if the sense was unintended: "within . . . the first week or two of grad school, our adviser . . . gave us the same assignment. . . . She's like, 'You know, look through a bunch of readings and . . . come up with an idea that you have and . . . come back to me.'" It was a simple way to motivate budding researchers to pursue independent thought, but it was given to both of them, at the same time, with the same purpose. Layla and Andrea had been friendly from the beginning, but the undercurrent was difficult to avoid given that the similarity of their situation occurred in the context that it did. Layla happened to finish that assignment first, which meant her peer had to work harder to catch up with a more impressive study. "And it just became like really competitive" over the short and long term: "it just became this . . . constant [issue]. . . . We literally sit right next to each other in our office. It's . . . very clear who's doing what."

The sense of competition was never overt, antagonistic, or openly confrontational. Indeed, although their _positions_ were competitive, their _relationship_ was not, instead evincing an admirably collaborative demeanor. Layla often confided in Andrea, and by the start of her third year described herself as closer to Andrea than to anyone else in the cohort, while Andrea did the same.[20] Furthermore, Layla found Andrea "very supportive. I mean, she's supportive of everybody." Although they worked in the same lab, the lab's interests ranged widely, and independent researchers within the large laboratory can and do work on topics with little relation to one another. So, they often discussed work. "We would read each other's papers all the time. . . . Our research is different enough that like that's not a realm that we would compete in."

But I asked Layla a question I posed to all students, which is whether, in a scenario where she was considering leaving academia, she would then talk to Andrea, and the answer was different. On that particular topic, she would not, for the confidant's role as listener would be clouded, in Layla's mind, by the role of competitor: "I think that in some ways we still sort of compete and . . . telling her about leaving academia would be . . . like forfeiting the completion or something." A confidant shares; a competitor does not admit defeat.

Diana and Her Classmates: Supporters Versus Applicants

At times, the competition with peers is explicit. The first six months for Diana had been difficult. Managing a long-distance relationship, she missed her friends and her boyfriend and her life as a writer back in Los Angeles. Recall that she had been "pretty ambivalent" about the academic career track. Hard-working, imaginative, and gifted, she had initially decided on an academic career when her work as a journalist did not allow her the depth of investigation she yearned. But an academic career, she was discovering, required more than just depth; it required a commitment to spend hours and days and years buried in esoterica in pursuit of a dissertation that, in the end, would be read by far fewer people than the substantial audiences she commanded as a successful writer. She also felt far more radical than some of her peers and many of her professors, with politics and a lifestyle uncommon in what she saw as the self-seriousness and "conservative" environment of academic institutions such as Hillmount's.[21]

Recall that, over the course of her first year in her program, Diana had expanded her core discussion network, keeping her old confidants from Los Angeles but adding graduate students she had begun to meet in courses and public talks. Six months in, she had added students Oliver, Rachel, and Denton. Diana made clear that she was only beginning to know them: "I have a few friends here . . . people who I would have, were colleagues, right, and now I would consider friends, but just barely. . . . It takes time . . . to become a friend rather than a colleague." But they were clearly kindred spirits. For example, when Diana and Denton were discussing their dissatisfaction with several aspects of the program, she felt a sense of "solidarity." "I think we're both pretty ambivalent about academia in a grand sense. So it's nice to, uh, you know, to find a sort of kindred spirit. We have other interests." Diana and her colleague-friends had begun to develop an emotionally reciprocal, institutionally mediated relationship, one in which, at least for some issues, each confided in the other while being a relationship in which the norms of expectations of budding scholars shaped some of their topics of discussion.

[margin note: confiding still w/ some barriers/limits]

That relationship would soon be tested. Diana needed financial support. In many universities, students are expected to apply for national or internal fellowships as early as the first year. At Hillmount, one well-endowed, internal fellowship provided at least a year of stipend support and was offered to multiple students in a given year. She and two of her student confidants applied, and all three knew that the others had applied.

[margin note: needed $]

When students first enter a program, faculty and other evaluators have little information on which to make a judgment. Many faculty members can recall students who were deemed brilliant early on but who eventually dropped out of programs, or students who had appeared average who instead went on to excel as scholars, teachers, and leaders in their fields. But little is known with certainty in the first year, and, for students, applying for funding is a crapshoot.

The odds were not in her favor. When awardees were announced, Diana's two friends received the scholarship; she did not. In institutionally unmediated friendships, such differences may not matter. Many friends in other contexts know that they differ in salaries, and even if money is a sensitive topic, a writer or an artist, say, does not necessarily lose sleep over the fact that her lawyer or doctor friend makes substantially more. Indeed, any given pair of friends is unlikely to make exactly the same salary. Among a pair of unmediated friends, while the topic of money may be studiously avoided, the knowledge that their incomes are unequal is often not a problem. But Diana's relationship with Oliver, Rachel, and Denton was not an unmediated friendship. It was structured and shaped by the norms and expectations of an institutional environment, one in which students are implicitly evaluated against one another, in which they may eventually vie for the same limited number of jobs, and in which therefore colleagues are inevitably, even if only minimally and not overtly, a source of competition. Peers in unmediated relationships are not competitors; in institutionally mediated ones, they often are, vying for money, positions, attention, or prestige.[22]

[margin note: # not big problem to talk about]

This competition makes comparisons inevitable and relationships sensitive. Diana worked hard—she prepared for classes carefully while maintaining a taxing job. She knew full well that she was at least as smart and committed as others who had gotten luckier in the grant application process. "I see other students . . . ill prepared, . . . don't take it seriously, don't bring their readings to class, and ask to borrow my readings when I've been up till 3:00 in the morning reading, working on [my other job] so I can finish my work." Diana was brilliant, professionally accomplished, and dedicated to her work. Resentment was inevitable. Indeed, the experience had been "psychologically damaging."

The particular nature of Diana's humanities field deepened the problem. Like many professional institutions, academia places a premium not merely on outward measures of success but also on perceived innate ability, on "brilliance," an elusive quality that, as Pierre Bourdieu has argued, those with high cultural capital may embody to their advantage but which ultimately depends on subjective, rather than objective, evaluations.[23] Many a prep-school graduate of average ability has been deemed brilliant by mere virtue of their manner, strategic deployment of cultural knowledge, and astute silence in the midst of ignorance. In context after context, knowing how to seem smart can be as consequential as actual skill.

However, the predicament of first-year humanities students such as Diana depended even more on subjective evaluations than might be true in other professional contexts. To be sure, by the time Diana and her peers are ready for job placement or tenure, there will be several objective indicators by which to measure their success—papers published, manuscripts under contract, teaching evaluation, and the like. But over the course of the first year, when students are forming relationships to their peers, developing new confidants, and finding out how much to expand or transform or retain their safety net, such objective measures are scarce. A police officer in his first year out of the academy can count how many arrests he made; a first-year investment analyst can see by how much she beat the Dow Jones Industrial Average; a first-year law associate can see how many hours she logged. Even a first-year student in mathematics and engineering, fields that depend on exams to test knowledge of the subject matter, might have grades as an objective measure. But a first-year PhD student in many humanities fields has little to go on—grades are poor markers, since many students consistently get As and Bs. The measure of ability, of supposed brilliance, is expected to come later, in the insight and originality of MA-level papers and dissertation chapters. As a result, class sessions among the first-year students were often filled with attempts at signaling ability and competence through intellectual one-upmanship. As Diana put it, there was a "whole competitive, performative . . . project that people are committed to in classes"—one she wanted no part in and found, in part because of her long professional experience, "easy to laugh at."

Yet even in that context, in the midst of meager external measures of success and a hypercompetitive signaling environment to which she did not want to contribute, Diana was performing well. A star student throughout her career and committed perfectionist, she had to get used to the idea that "if you get an A minus, like that won't destroy you." All of this background made the discovery of the difference in fortunes from her no-smarter, no-better-prepared, no-harder-working peers a bitter pill to swallow.

I asked if she ever discussed the situation. She had vented, yes, to her many friends back in Los Angeles, and even to other students in the program who were not in her cohort. "I speak about it to older students . . . in the program. . . . A few of them have been in similar positions." But what about her own peers, her confidants, like Rachel or Oliver, who she had named just an hour earlier in our interview? "No. There's . . . an absolute silence. . . . No one speaks about it."

Michelle and Her Professor: Sounding Board Versus Project Director

But not all role conflicts are in fact social conflicts. At times, they are mere ambiguities about the scope of appropriate domains of conversation. Ultimately, role conflict in the kind of multiplexity we have discussed results in ambiguity, an ambiguity that produces uncertainty that loss-averse actors are likely to avoid.[24] Consider the experiences of Michelle.

Michelle had always thought she wanted to obtain a PhD, to work in a laboratory and attain renown as a scientist. But by the time she had finished her undergraduate training at another university, she had begun to hear many "horror stories" from acquaintances of one of her best friends, Tommy, who, at the time, was in a graduate program. She often heard about would-be scientists who had begun PhD programs directly after college—bright but professionally inexperienced men and women who later realized, often only after accumulating substantial debt, that an academic career was not a good fit. "I had several friends who were PhD students in astronomy, and computer science, and all that. . . . [And many of them] said the same kind of things to me, that they were really excited to start, but one thing they all had in common was that they started right after undergrad. And then they [realized] that it was not for them. So, a bunch of them quit and went and got real jobs." Their experiences gave her pause.

Then there was the matter of her transcript. "I think a lot of people who start PhDs came right out of undergrad and they are just like top-notch genius kind of people. They're type A, like did their homework, did the research, all that, from a very young age. And, you know, just really smart, well-rounded students. And I really wasn't [*laughs*] all the time. Like in high school I was kind of mediocre. College, not great." Michelle realized she could use the break, and some growing up, and the chance to experience life in a new city. So, rather than pursue a PhD immediately after college, she enrolled in a master's program that provided training for scientists interested in industry.

In the program, she began working with Cameron, a professor who ran one of the laboratories. Cameron had high standards, an open personality, a collaborative spirit, and the willingness to delegate. He gave Michelle a lot to work on, and the experience began to change her understanding of herself. "I started to realize more and more that [my undergraduate performance] doesn't really matter because the way that you study in undergrad, or especially high school, really doesn't correlate to how you're supposed to be in grad school. And grad school really is more research-centric. . . . And that's really what I love. Not so much the memorizing and taking tests and all that." She loved her environment. "I just [had] never really envisioned myself as being one of the smart kids," but in a research laboratory, working on questions of scientific import and participating in the process of discovery, she thrived. She was such a strong performer that, upon completion of the master's program, Cameron hired her as a full-time researcher in the lab. Cameron was an immensely helpful mentor. "Right before I applied for PhDs . . . he asked me, like, what I wanted to do, what my plan was and volunteered advice." They talked at length. She applied to several programs, but mostly as backup options. Over several years, she had developed a strong working relationship with Cameron, and preferred to stay at the university. She was admitted and she immediately accepted. By the start of her program, she and Cameron, she explained, were "tight," and he was the first person she named as confidant.

Michelle had a general problem with what she described as her "shyness" and difficulty speaking in front of others. "I'm just like terrible at . . . speaking in front of people. . . . I just get really, really nervous. Like I just get . . . a really bad physical reaction to it. There's nothing rational about it. . . . I mean even talking in class is stressful." In one of her classes during her first year, "we had to like give a six-minute presentation on our research . . . and I was like having a seizure up there." It was among the issues she most worried about. She clarified the point, trying to find the jest: "Yeah, it's specifically standing in front of a group of seated people facing me . . . oh, my God, I'm getting freaked out just thinking about it." But the worry was unambiguous: "This is going to be a terrible, crippling problem." Related to this problem was her difficulty in making connections to other scholars who might be relevant to her work. "I'm worried I'm not going to make as many connections outside of my lab as I should. You know, networking and getting other professors to know me."

We asked whether she ever discussed the matter with Cameron, who might seem a natural outlet. "No, I have not mentioned that yet." She explained why, pointing to the very different role that, over their period working together, he had come to occupy, struggling to explain the ambiguity she felt about broaching the topic. "I don't know. I guess, I don't know, I'm not sure why. I just feel like, well, for one thing we don't talk very much about things other than our particular projects. So, it'd feel kind of awkward to all of the sudden interrupt him and be like, 'Hey, so, big picture.' . . . But that and I guess it's not really his problem. You know, I should be the one who is kind of facilitating these connections and finding threads that my adviser would be interested in as well as another professor and kind of bringing them together. I think that's what a lot of the times is the grad student's job, you know? So I don't want to be like, 'Hey, help me,' you know?"

Michelle might well have been unable to articulate her thoughts until we had asked her. Yet, the issue was clear. Though Cameron was her adviser, he was also her laboratory director and, as such, would have reason to expect—in her mind—that finding collaborators was her job, not something for her to vent about. Michelle may well have been wrong about how *may not be personal* much Cameron would care. But in her mind, the ambiguity about the role *but still* was sufficient for her to avoid an "awkward" interaction with someone with *close* whom she had gotten close.

Queenie's Adviser: Listener Versus Advocate

Similar kinds of ambiguities can be far more difficult to handle. Consider Queenie. For her, the conflict between two different roles an adviser might occupy were bound up with the complications of loyalty and ambiguity about the nature of reciprocal expectations. Her situation deserves discussing with some care.

Queenie was a philosophical, independently minded social science student who tended to confide regularly in a small set of people that nevertheless turned over frequently. The two exceptions, the two people who were consistently on her list of regular confidants, were her father and her boyfriend, who over the course of our study became her fiancée. In spite of her natural gifts as a scholar and love of her field, Queenie spent most of her first year deeply conflicted on whether she had made the right decision in attending the program. As she told me halfway through the year: "I worry that I shouldn't be an academic and that I'm here for the wrong reasons."

Queenie had attended Hillmount as an undergraduate, and before the end of her senior year—at a time when she did not yet know what she wanted to study but felt compelled to remain in a university environment—she had applied to a small number of graduate programs. Her uncertainty showed in her submitted packets. "I didn't get into the four schools I applied to."

Despondent, she moved out of town and took a research job in a different city, where she lived with her boyfriend. Throughout the period, she kept in touch with her BA thesis adviser, Hans, and a few other faculty members who had been supportive of her work. Two years of experience in research and life later, she applied again. "And then the next time around, I think with his, with their, not just one blessing, letters—that was really the variable that changed in terms of the responses. Um, they kinda pushed for me hard." Queenie was convinced that Hans and one or two other faculty members had made the difference by making strong cases for her. She was admitted to Hillmount and to another university, a top-five program. The top-five program seemed like an exceptionally good fit, a dream. Had her advisers pushed her to attend Hillmount? "I mean, they told me it was better for me to come here," she explained to me. Still, "[my adviser] never said, like, 'You have to come to [Hillmount]' or anything like that, but . . . I just felt indebted and very loyal and very appreciative."

Queenie was conflicted. And that sense of conflicted loyalty was common among students. One of the characteristics of the adviser–student relationship is that, while institutionally mediated in multiple ways and governed by well-understood norms, it can also be deeply personal, confounded with the feelings of loyalty and obligation that friends and family instill.

That deep feelings may arise in such circumstances may same strange. The fact that her adviser provided a strong letter of recommendation is not special; it is explicitly part of his job. References are required in academia and standard across many industries. And even if he had somehow written nicer things than warranted given her record, the fact is that, across the humanities and social sciences, letters of recommendation are increasingly filled with hyperbole and exaggeration, a text and narrative version of grade inflation.[25] Strong references are provided by former advisers and former employers as part of the course of doing business—it is expected in the hierarchy between student and adviser or employee and boss.

However, the differences between this pair of roles are instructive. An adviser—like a coach, a guru, or a mentor—is institutionally expected to invest far more time and effort in the intellectual and professional development of a student than an employer is typically expected to invest in an employee. Advisers listen to their students vent, work through intellectual problems, and discuss students' frustrations with a project; they are confidants. They provide professional, intellectual, and personal advice; intervene on behalf of students in professional disputes; provide personal references for research grants or teaching fellowships; and more. A good adviser can pave the way for emotional catharsis, intellectual epiphany, and personal growth.

engaging relation w/ mentors
more personal

Advisers can choose to invest much of their time in a given student—and time, being a zero-sum resource, can only be spent more on one student at the expense of time on another. A student, in turn, is expected to reward that investment. Because a good adviser can provide so much that is not merely professional but also personal, what a student will often feel is not just gratitude but also debt, a sense of obligation much more personal than the kind articulated in formal contract.[26] An adviser is personally vested in the success of a student. The student's personal success is also the adviser's personal success, in a way an employee's success is not necessarily the employer's personal accomplishment. Therefore, students' sense of reciprocity can feel personal. Furthermore, advisers need not make the extent of their investments, and expectations of reciprocity, known explicitly. The interactional dynamics of the context make such practices clear: other students in the same class or cohort or field are not getting the same attention from a given adviser (and they might get it from another).[27]

expectation of success

However, that very fact—the fact that an adviser's decision to invest more time in one student at the expense of another need not be stated openly—makes possible for other unstated expectations, real or not, to emerge in the relationship. Recall that the adviser–student relationship is not emotionally reciprocal, a fact that can engender ambiguity. In an emotionally reciprocal relationship, each knows what to expect of the other—a husband knows that in return for venting to his wife, he must be ready to let her vent at some future time. But when a student has vented to an adviser, what she must do in return is unclear. Do well in her classes? Work hard? Try to complete her assignments in a timely manner? All of those tasks are surely part of it, but how should a student know that the debt—the emotional debt—has been repaid? That answer is not known. And this ambiguity is, in fact, an important source of control on the part of the adviser, even if a benign adviser decides to never exercise it. Perhaps the deepest form of obligation is to know that one is indebted while being unsure exactly how the debt must be repaid.[28] This particular form of obligation, in the context of the support of a confidant, is a state of *reciprocal*

obligation

ambiguity. The result of these dynamics is that students may feel not only a deep sense of loyalty but also a fundamental and at times debilitating uncertainty about how that loyalty must be exercised.

That was Queenie's predicament. At the time of her decision, she and her boyfriend lived in a city near the other top-five department to which she had been accepted. And that department had offered a substantially larger grant. The optimal decision from the perspective of her future family, her personal finances, and her professional success was to decline Hillmount and enroll in the other university. Queenie, an exceptionally intelligent thinker, was clear on the most rational choice. "But primarily because I felt an intense loyalty to, beholden to professors at [Hillmount] even though they didn't say that. . . . But I got that feeling and I cared too much about my relationships with them. . . . I didn't realize that I was, could have, it would have been okay if I didn't come." Queenie was not particularly paranoid in being unsure whether "it would have been okay" if she had attended another school. In the economy of emotional and professional debts she had incurred, even benign statements by her advisers—for example, that "it was better for me to come here"—could reasonably be interpreted as a creditor calling for payment of an emotional debt. And whether or not that was the adviser's intention, Queenie did feel a debt was owed, and there had been no other discussion about the proper form of reciprocity. She did attend Hillmount. And that sense of loyalty "was really the only, the primary motivation" behind her enrollment.

Now, six months into the program, she was struggling with a long-distance relationship and an intellectual environment she had come to find uninteresting. "I'm kind of bored, bored as in the sense like I wish I had a new adventure academically." She had found herself taking graduate versions of the same undergraduate courses with the same faculty she had learned from three years earlier. "It's staid, I guess. . . . It's not because the work is any less rigorous or anything like that. I just mentally felt that I would have been challenged more by somebody new and something else, like a new style. And I regret that a lot." In fact, she regretted the decision altogether: "across the board . . . personally, professionally, and mentally [the other university] would have been a better place. And it's a very strange feeling because I usually don't regret things."

Her regret led to deeper worries about academia. Queenie's growing ennui was a contrast to what she thought was important to succeed in her career. "The most successful graduate students, I believe, feel as though the business of it is more existentially rewarding for them than anything else. And I don't feel like this specifically is existentially most rewarding to me." Queenie had come to wonder not only whether she had made a terrible professional mistake but also whether, in the end, this multiyear invest-ment of time and energy during the prime years of her adult life were worth the trouble, whether an academic career was her calling. "My intense regret about not going to [the other program] makes me think that . . . I maybe should reconsider academia, because if coursework here hasn't done it for me, hasn't assuaged that regret, then maybe I'm not as committed to the academy as I thought."

Many students worry about their fit with their programs, but Queenie's consternation was far more existential, primordial, and sustained, a sense of betrayal with herself of which she was reminded every time she sat in a seminar that failed to stimulate her thinking, every day she awoke in a bed far from her future fiancée. "I . . . wake up in the morning crying about it." I asked her to explain: "I mean it's weird. You shouldn't wake up and start crying the first thing you wake up. But I really have. It is a huge regret of mine and I have to move past it, but it just feels like I gave up something that I really wanted for [the sake of] somebody else, for some—you know, other people as opposed to myself. And that's what really bothers me." The anguish was relentless. "I mean, I'm constantly thinking about it. There are very few moments when I don't feel, even in the background, a pain, a regret. . . . It's probably the most consistent thought I have."

Earlier in the interview Queenie had reported three people as confi-dants: her boyfriend, her long-time friend Marla, and her adviser Hans. I asked her if she ever talked about her predicament. Her situation was so all-consuming yet so personal that I could imagine either extreme scenario—she might consistently feel the need to vent to anyone who would listen or might instead develop a deep sense of privacy about a sit-uation that, to her mind, was all of her own making. Her response was unambiguous: "All the time." While she may have talked about it all the time, she did not talk about it to everyone. And whom she avoided reveals a great deal about why the people we are close to may be the worst people with whom to discuss our problems.

Queenie certainly talked to her boyfriend, which was not surprising. The problem involved her boyfriend, who had a stake in whether she decided to leave and how she talked about the process. He also was genuinely con-cerned about her mental and professional well-being, and hoped to be near his future wife but wanted, above all, for her to achieve realization in a ful-filling vocation.

She also had Hans. Hans was better suited than anyone else she trusted to brainstorm with Queenie in an informed fashion. "I don't know my options," she had explained. Hans would know them.

But Queenie explicitly avoided Hans on this particular topic. "I don't really feel comfortable at this stage talking to my adviser about wanting to leave." What is notable is that Queenie saw, worked with, took courses from, and confided in Hans regularly—they were by now close. In spite of the fact that this was her "most consistent" thought and preoccupation, she never broached the topic. Yet it would be difficult for Hans to miss the signals. "I mean, I think he knows." I asked her to elaborate. "I mean, he knows I'm constantly traveling [out of town] to see my boyfriend, but that takes a toll on me. I think he's aware that my boyfriend— . . . the writing's on the wall in that sense, you know? So . . . I'm speculating here but I think he does know."

Monika and Her Mother: Listener Versus Protector

The relations I have discussed so far are strongly mediated by formal institutions. But the complications associated with incompatible expectations also arose in less formal family relations. Two brief scenarios document the point. One is Monika's.

A budding science student with strong professional ambitions, Monika was close to her mother, whom she named as a confidant in every single wave we interviewed her, and usually first. In a long-term relationship, Monika was concerned that she and her boyfriend were reaching a critical juncture. "He's very like reticent to talk about like the future or like he pretends we're on this, a day by day [relationship, but we are] not at all like that. I mean we live together." A recent and otherwise trivial event had brought these matters to the fore: "here's my anecdote to illustrate what I'm trying to describe. . . . So, we decided, we took care of [a friend's] cat for a week, and he's the best. And before we had been talking about maybe getting cats. . . . But being with [our friend's] cat was great so we decided that we are gonna get cats." Though she preferred dogs, her boyfriend loved cats, and was eager to acquire them. "And I was asking [him]—because he really wanted to get kittens—and I was like, 'Okay, so are we gonna be together for ten years while these kittens are growing up?'" The gauntlet had been thrown; the reaction did not inspire confidence: he was "very . . . defensive [, saying,] 'I didn't think getting cats meant like talking about ten years from now,' which . . . I think it's a reasonable conversation to have . . . if you're adopting animals that live longer than . . . a year. It's . . . not unreasonable." Though she insisted the issue in general was not "a major stressor," she still found it "frustrating." It is "something that . . . comes up every once in a while."

Though she vented her frustration to her peers on occasion, and also to her sister, with whom she was close, she avoided her mother. "I don't talk to my mom about that stuff a lot." The reason made clear that, in her mind, the mother would have difficulty playing the role of listener, rather than protector: "in the past, like my mom gets very quick. . . . I think my mom's just always . . . looking out for me . . . so if I give like any negative information about a boyfriend, she's very quick to . . . judge that person." Mothers are expected to take their children's side, and in the complicated contexts of interpersonal relations, negative news may take long to be forgotten. "So . . . I usually try not to talk to her about that stuff just because . . . I feel like it gives any boyfriend I have an unfair chance. . . . I think sometimes she . . . would blow it out of proportion."

didn't talk to mom about bf problems

＊common w/ fam → detached listener

Carver's Mother: Listener Versus Provider

Recall that Carver did not talk money with his mother. Though Carver's concern was finances, not relationships, his reticence had similar roots, the worry that his mother would have difficulty playing the simple role of listener. His father and mother together barely made subsistence wages, and thus faced their own financial strains. In fact, they always had, since Carver's childhood. "And I don't know how they did it. Her and my father both make, between them, forty thousand dollars a year. And they raised three kids. I'm like, 'I don't know how you guys did it.'" Carver avoids talking to his mother precisely because they are so close that she would intervene, unable to play the role of detached listener. In fact, Carver considers the topic completely off limits. "So, I can't even joke about it with her. Or even if I broach it with my grandma, she'll put two hundred dollars in an envelope and give it to me, and I'm like, 'Look, you guys need your social security money. I don't.'" In fact, it would not stop: "I'd hear about it for the next month. And I'd get my grandma calling, 'Are you sure you have money?'"

It would be easy to imagine the opposite, that Carver's family members— mother, father, grandmother—are the primary sources of emotional and financial support in what is clearly a difficult situation. For Carol Stack, friends and family are always the best source of information precisely because they are close. And in a certain sense, Carver's situation does resemble Stack's families, in the willingness of the people to offer help. Yet a mother plays too many roles that an adult child might find incompatible with his own expectations. Ironically, the very fact of their strong willingness to help with finances makes them terrible sources of help as listeners. At times, people do just need to talk.

CONCLUSION: THE AVOIDANCE OF STRONG TIES

When seeking a confidant, the last thing anyone wants is the possibility of a difficult interaction.[29] The role of the confidant requires a person to listen, to provide advice if asked, to help brainstorm if appropriate, and to offer a shoulder if called for. But few confidants occupy only that role. In practice, confidants are mothers, siblings, coworkers, professors, wives, husbands, therapists, staff persons, priests, and many other actors with whom relations are partly bound by formal and informal expectations, wherein alternative roles, such as provider, protector, evaluator, critic, competitor, and even boss, create the space for the wrong topic to create a difficult interaction. The students seeking a listener avoided a close relation when they risked getting an evaluator, provider, protector, or competitor.

Many have complained of a spouse who needed to be a listener but instead became a problem solver. "I do not need your solutions," they have said; "I just need you to listen." In such cases finding fault in the confidant is easy, but they may ultimately be a matter of incompatible expectations, the kind that, across many kinds of relationships, even the best listeners face when their relations are behaviorally multiplex. People do not always know which of multiple plausible roles to enact when a particular topic has been broached.

These dynamics may arise among both strong and weak ties alike. Yet two conditions help them account for people's avoidance of strong ties. First, when ties are multiplex, they are more likely to be strong. As Boissevain has argued, and many have shown, "where multiplex relations exist, they will be more intimate (in the sense of friendly and confidential) than single-stranded relations."[30] The reason is that multiplex relations typically arise when people share multiple contexts of interactions (work and church) or kinds of relationships (student–teacher, research assistant–boss), and this multiplexity expands the number dimensions through which people know one another. Though strong ties need not be multiplex, multiplexity tends to strengthen ties. Thus, when people face the complications of behavioral multiplexity, they will often be facing strong ties.

Second, when ties are strong, there is greater risk involved, because the potential loss is greater. People are inclined to avoid uncomfortable situations. Exposing one's worries and receiving the wrong reaction—one wrought by a plausible but incompatible expectation—can lead to awkwardness, disappointment, betrayal, and even anger at the actions of a confidant. The fear of incompatible expectations can be a powerful deterrent. The stronger the relation, the more there is to fear, since the consequence of being wrong is emotionally greater. For this reason, people may find the strength of a tie to be a reason to avoid it when the topic may elicit that uncertainty. Relationships can weaken, wither in their intimacy, and at the extreme become undone. The stronger the tie, the more it can withstand, but the more there is to lose.

CHAPTER 5

Relevance and Empathy

Why They Approached Weak Ties

Why would anyone confide personal matters to people they are not close to? While students may at times be avoiding their close friends and family, that cannot be the sole reason—after all, they could just decide not to talk about what is worrying them. In this chapter and the next, I suggest that a decision that seems irrational in the abstract becomes comprehensible when people are conceived as pragmatic in orientation, responsive to institutions, and ultimately hopeful of being understood.

To understand the students' predicament, consider briefly the relation between risk and expectations that the book has assumed to this point. Recall that students often avoided their strong ties when they had reason to expect that broaching a given topic might elicit the wrong behavioral role—a problem solver, competitor, evaluator, or some role other than what they sought, a listener. That decision reflected an assessment of risk based on their expectations about how the potential confidant might react.

To clarify the point, consider a simple decision-making model. Confiding something personal to another always carries some level of risk. It involves some probability of gaining a benefit (feeling relieved, understood, etc.) and some probability of suffering a loss or harm (feeling judged, embarrassed, etc.).[1] The expected gain is a product of the probability and the magnitude of the benefit; the expected loss, the product of the probability and the magnitude of the harm. The risk lies in making a decision wherein the loss turns out to outweigh the benefits. In the context of strong ties, the possible loss the students reported was creating an uncomfortable, difficult, or even hurtful interaction with someone whose expectations about the proper role might be incompatible with their own. In that context, the risk, at the extreme, was the loss of the relationship.

In the context of weak ties, the risk is different, since, *ceteris paribus*, the weaker the tie, the less regret there would be to losing it.[2] Here we must return to the basic fact that confiding in anyone involves exposing one's vulnerabilities, a risky act. Approaching a weak tie heightens the risk, because, unlike family, close friends, or regular discussion partners, such people are untested. There is less certainty that one will not feel judged, embarrassed, demoralized, or worse. Revealing one's weaknesses is especially risky in professional contexts that place a premium on demonstrating competence. Because of this uncertainty, a person who stopped to think about it would only talk to an untested potential confidant if he or she had reason to expect great benefit and minimal harm.[3]

risk of weak ties

How did the students' assessment of that risk convince them to approach weak ties? What benefit made the risk worth it?

HOPING TO BE UNDERSTOOD

To answer that question, we begin by returning to the importance of topics. Recall that we used the open-ended portion of the interviews to probe the students' motivations. After the students reported what they worried about and, then, with whom they last talked about it, we asked them to explain why, mindful of people's natural tendency to represent themselves as rational and deploying strategies to address that tendency (see Appendix A).[4] Every situation differed, and just as they avoided strong ties for multiple reasons, they too approached weak ones at different times for different reasons.

Different Topics, Different People

Nevertheless, just as before, much of the matter turned on the particular topic they hoped to talk about. The students rarely reported talking to an acquaintance because they could trust the latter with anything; instead, they typically explained their motivation to do so as a function of the topic at hand. This form of trust is what Russell Hardin has described as a "three-part relation," and philosopher Annette Baier, as a "three-part predicate":[5] "A trusts B with valued thing C."[6] Adapted to our question, whether A took the risk to trust B depended specifically on whether the topic was x; it depended on the match between the person and the topic.

The general idea that people trust different individuals with different things has been confirmed by research on social support. Barry Wellman and Scot Wortley studied multiple kinds of social support—such as services around the house, emotional aid, financial assistance, small services, and companionship—among residents of a Toronto suburb; they found that people tend to get "different strokes from different folks."[7] For example, they tend to get emotional support from strong ties and services from physically proximate ones.[8] Peter Bearman and Paolo Parigi studied the discussion of important matters among North Carolina residents and found a distinct pattern of "topic-alter dependency," wherein people talked to different alters about different topics. For example, "conversations about life and health are [often] between spouses," they reported, and "conversations with relatives are more likely to be about relationships than anything else."[9]

While these studies confirm that people sort confidants by topic, they stop short of explaining why: it is not clear why conversations with, say, relatives would involve the topic of relationships more than the topics of life or health. Discovering heterogeneity is not synonymous with uncovering its causes. A clearer answer may be found in the studies of Brea Perry and Bernice Pescosolido, who have examined whom people approach when discussing their health problems. The authors have proposed that people "selectively draw on ties and their diverse resources depending on who is most likely to be useful for a particular purpose at any given point in time."[10] People, they suggest, are motivated by usefulness.[11]

But that idea still has its limits. Determining whom people will find useful is straightforward when they are pursuing a concrete task: when people need a job, a useful person is one who could help them find it; when they are trying to treat an illness, it is one who might know what to do. But when people are seeking emotional support, determining who is useful can be far more elusive, since the help seeker's aim is often less tangible—it is not to find a job or manage an illness but, ultimately, to feel better. Certainly, as we will see, people may see information as a vehicle to that end. But more often than not, whether by venting or brainstorming, the ultimate aim is not instrumental but emotional. The notion of usefulness can only go so far. If not usefulness, then what?

Empathy

Students sought confidants when worried about many kinds of problems—sick relatives, visa requirements, a coming baby, a broken bone, a growing sense of despair, and more. But I argue that underlying many of their decisions was a <u>desire to talk to someone who would understand their pre-</u><u>dicament as they themselves saw it</u>. That is, the students sought people from whom they could expect what psychologists have termed *cognitive empathy*, the ability to understand one's predicament from one's perspective.[12] Confiding in such people, even if weakly tied, was often worth the risk.

Empathy and sympathy are not the same thing. The latter is the feeling of pity or sorrow for the troubles of another; the former—specifically in the cognitive sense—the sense that another's predicament is understood as they understand it. One can understand why a coworker yelled at another during a meeting without necessarily feeling sorry for the coworker—for example, while still believing he was rude. That understanding merely reflects the ability to see what another sees. Conversely, one can sympathize with a malnourished child in the midst of famine without understanding the sensation of prolonged hunger. Feeling pity does not require empathy. In fact, <u>pure empathy is often difficult to achieve, even among well-meaning or sympathetic people, because life experiences differ so dramatically.</u>[13]

People can seek empathy or understanding without necessarily hoping for pity or sympathy, and students far more often sought the former than the latter. Furthermore, they often did not find pure empathy. The more unique a person's worry, the more difficult it will be to find a truly empathetic listener. Often, they found people who could only approximate a truly empathetic understanding. How did they find empathy?

Whereas sympathy derives from kindness, <u>empathy, in its purest form, derives from sameness.</u> The person who can certainly understand another's predicament is the one who is experiencing it herself. Students approached others because they had similar difficulties, concerns, positions in the program, backgrounds, and more. Indeed, among the two most common words in the students' answers about why they had talked to others—strong or weak ties—were "similar" and "same." As we shall see, the hope that the potential confidant either had or could approximate this similarity of experience lay at the root of students' motivations to take the risk to approach others. Consider the following cases.[14]

COGNITIVE EMPATHY

Recall Layla, an intelligent, energetic, highly organized scientist whose natural skills and exceptional performance in a large laboratory had earned her the praise of her adviser and a concomitant increase in duties and responsibilities over the course of her first year. Layla was thrilled by the new challenges, which provided the confidence boost that anyone starting in a field appreciates and gave her a focus, clear goals, and motivating deadlines. The summer after her first year, Layla's adviser, a highly demanding and accomplished scientist, had sent her as the laboratory representative to a different university, where collaborators were working on new methodological techniques that could lead to new grant applications and an expansion of the Hillmount laboratory's research agenda. "So, I spent two and a half months in [the other university's] lab just learning the method and running a couple of studies." She returned with a pile of new work and a new role in the laboratory. "No one in our lab is doing [the work involving the new technique]. Maybe one other person will start but . . . I would be the only person in our department doing [it], which is really scary." Indeed, for all the promise involved in the new work, the responsibility was also great, and she was beginning to feel the burden, the anxiety about maintaining her performance and the sensation that, for all her new techniques, expertise, and authority, she was still just beginning her second year in the program—that she was a budding researcher still in the early part of her 20s with much of her life uncharted. Layla was feeling overwhelmed. "I'm starting on a bunch of new things. So, . . . I guess I'm worried about . . . managing a lot of different things all at once. So, I guess that's one of the major things, like having so much stuff happening at once and like making sure that everything is . . . progressing."

She had a strong group of confidants, naming her boyfriend, her mother, her sister, and a childhood friend at the start of her second year in the program. But none of them had the experience or knowledge to empathize with her circumstances, regardless of the fact that they could offer honest sympathy. Instead, the last time she had talked to anyone, it was to three students, Melissa, Andrea, and Marie, who worked in the laboratory. When asked why, she expressed being motivated by their similar circumstances. "Because [Melissa] knows a little about [the techniques in my] study. . . . But mostly because she has that experience. And [Andrea] and [Marie] like usually are [also] just overwhelmed in the office. We talk to each other about . . . feeling overwhelmed." Just as Layla was, Melissa, Andrea, and Marie were budding scientists with similar interests in the same research group, they were all women in the sciences, and they were all buried in mountains of work.

Professional concerns were commonly addressed with people in similar circumstances. Sandra had been concerned that, though by now she was starting her third year, she had yet to develop a relationship to an adviser. She explained that she lacked "the kind of adviser relationship that

[handwritten margin note: confidants couldn't offer what she needed]

I see . . . other students having. . . . [T]hat's probably the biggest worry. And I guess two is closely related which is like not being sure I have a chair for my dissertation. The person who is most likely to be my adviser is not a candidate for chair, so it's a separate question kind of, but those are sort of the two, which is that I'm going in a direction with my research that I didn't really anticipate when I got here. And I'm not sure who is well set up to sort of advise me on that." Comparing herself to her peers, as many students did, did not help: "it feels like a lot of people who are at a similar stage in the program have like four member committees already kind of like signed on, and I don't have anyone yet signed onto my project." Her department had, at best, four faculty members in her area, "one of whom doesn't do anything even remotely related . . . and one of whom with I have . . . a personality clash, not professional clash—. . . we can have discussions about my work, but in terms of that person being like a guiding force in the next several years, I don't see that being . . . productive." Without an adviser, and a committee, guiding her work early, she would likely linger in the program for many years.

We asked whom she had to talked about the issue. "I have been talking with [Theo] about it because he's in a very similar position." Theo also had not settled on an adviser, and was anxious about it. She continued later: "we're both in this dissertation proposal workshop together . . . and . . . with these . . . impending deadlines where you have to like say to a group of people, including one of the faculty members of the department who runs the workshop, 'This is my project.'"

Theo, for his part, explained separately why he often talked to Sandra about his related, major concern, which is to get published: "so I've talked with [Sandra] about it, because the two of us, both of us have MAs that we don't think we would publish uh and, and we are both aware that we probably should get something published. So I have talked with her about that. We have the same worries and concerns." *share concerns*

By the middle of her first year, Kaylee had begun to develop a deep sense that she did not quite fit or belong in the department. She explained: "I guess the way people sort of succeed in academia is when you work with a person and when your research really clicks with that person's research. And I don't feel like that's happening [for me] with anyone because, you know, for the most part because they don't have [a specialist in my particular area]." The department, in the humanities, had particular camps with different orientations toward the field. "And then I don't really know where I sort of belong." The issue had nagged her when she was deciding. "I think that honestly I keep thinking, 'Oh, I should have gone to [the other university].' " It was a debilitating feeling. "I think I was screwed over big time."

In some senses, Kaylee was careful whom she shared this with. She especially did not share it "with the faculty. . . , because . . . you don't want to advertise that you're having a breakdown. I always sort of like pretend that everything is going well, my research is going tight, and all that." Instead, she talked to many in a loose network of people of her own ethnic background around campus who are facing similar circumstances. For example: "I have this swimming group with two girls and one other guy. So, after the swimming we talk quite often and how I feel this way. One of the girls is from [another department] and she's actually trying to change her program. She really feels that way, too." She had found random people to talk to and, upon learning of their similar circumstances, shared her frustrations. "I also talked to one girl from [another department]. I met her in the seminar and we've been sort of having these coffee conversations, because she also . . . comes from a women's college and she did women's studies there and I did women's studies. We're both first-year PhDs. She's [of a given ethnicity] and I'm [of the same one], so, we have a lot of shared common ground. . . . So I've been [talking] to her and it's been helpful."

But not all concerns for which students sought people who could understand were academic in nature. By the start of her third year, Annie had agreed to serve as president of a student association, a decision that seemed rational when she made it but increasingly was a source of regret. The work consumed her every free minute, cutting into time for academics. "I don't know what I got myself into, but it's just a lot of work." Quitting altogether was not an option, given the social reprimand she would likely experience. Though Annie had a long list of regular confidants—her boyfriend, her roommate, her mother, and two close friends—she tended to avoid them. She had once confided her insecurity to a friend: "And she, she tells me, 'I think [if I were in your shoes] either I would screw up the job and do well at school or screw up with course work and do well with the job, or screw up both.' And I'm, like, [sarcastically] 'you are really nice.' Because there's no option of like, oh, I can do both well." Rather than providing solace, her friend had reinforced the worry that Annie would "screw up both. So, I just didn't mention anything [after that]."

Eventually, however, she found a good outlet, the former president of the same ethnic association, someone who had similar interests, the same leadership abilities, and experience in the same situation. The simple validation, born of true cognitive empathy, was in a way cathartic. "He tells, he tells me that he understands that I don't have time, because he didn't have time when he was doing the job. And, uh, I think he's the only one who actually understands how much time it takes and efforts. So I lean on him a lot."

Though they differed in circumstances, Layla, Sandra, Theo, Kaylee, and Annie used a common language—"the only one who actually understands," "shared common ground," "very similar position," "similar stage," "same worries and concerns," and so on—that makes clear what they sought: someone they could expect would understand a worry that others might not.

Homophily Everywhere

The proclivity to find people facing similar circumstances is related to one of the most important concepts in social network analysis, what Paul Lazarsfeld and Robert Merton termed the principle of "homophily," or people's tendency to associate with others who resemble them.[15] The tendency has been documented in thousands of studies across a variety of attributes: people are more likely to associate with those of their own gender, race, sexual orientation, nationality, socioeconomic status, and many other factors. They are more likely to choose friends, pick husbands and wives, and even hire those who resemble them in many well-documented personal characteristics.[16] Homophily is everywhere.

And that is, in fact, the problem—the tendency is so prevalent that it threatens to become a nonexplanation when used to account for people's decision to confide in others, a teleological tool easy to lift from the conceptual drawer in service of any network-related task. Any decent researcher can easily find homophily after the fact, since one can usually uncover at least some attribute that any two persons share. Consider Layla and Andrea: Both are women. But if they had been of different genders, we might have focused on their status as colleagues, rather than women; if they had been at the laboratory where Layla spent the summer, on their status as researchers, rather than laborers in the same demanding workplace; if they had been in a different discipline, on their status as graduate students; and so on. A researcher can always find some similarity between two observed actors, allowing one to take uncritically people's accounts of their motivations as based on similarity.

One way to avoid this problem is to consider plausible forms of similarity that people could have employed in making their decisions and ask, in the end, why they did not pursue those. That deeper examination helps clarify what kind of similarity matters in a given context. Consider Kenneth, whose decision making makes clear that an easy association between demography and interest fails to capture the complexity of motivations in practice. By the start of his third year, Kenneth had become consumed with selecting an appropriate dissertation topic, an issue he described as one of his core concerns. Recall that he had received excellent training in quantitative methods and had a number of possibilities at his disposal but was unsure about his prospects. His named discussion partners were his wife, his mother, his father, his adviser, and two graduate students. Indeed, Kenneth was explicit that similarity was a primary reason he often confided in one of the students: "[W]e are [of the same ethnic origin] and we all have a wife here and uh, our wives are . . . both carrying babies, so, you know, we have a lot of similarities in terms of lifestyles."

Given these circumstances, I asked Kenneth what any social scientist expecting homophily to play a role would have asked—whether he talked to Matthew about his concerns regarding his dissertation. Matthew was male, of the same ethnicity, recently married, a father to be, and a graduate student in the same discipline. "[N]o, we don't talk about that." At all. I asked why. "I consult him on a lot of life issues, I mean it's not life issues, but . . . life convenience sort of issues: where to buy groceries, where to fix my car, something like that, but . . . academic [issues] no." I asked why not, and he was clear, echoing Wellman and Wortley: "you talk different things with different people." I asked him to elaborate: "it's probably because we don't have the same interests . . . we don't have the same interests substantively or methodologically." They had similar attributes but were not faced with similar situations.

Or consider Theo, who explained why, when he needed someone to talk to about his concerns about his research agenda, he rarely talked to Steven, whom he considered a confidant, yet had often talked to Noreen, whom he did not. "I do [a given topic], [Steven] does [another], and we were good friends because [we] met on our very first day here at [Hillmount], because it turns out he was also from [the same public university in a different state], and I had met him when we did previews when we were both prospective students. And in that sense, obviously because I didn't know anyone else at the time, I spent a lot of time talking to [Steven], so I viewed him as a good friend." Same university, same age, same department. However, he explained, "it became very, very clear very, very quickly that he and I had very, very different interests in the field." I asked Theo to elaborate. "While he is capable of waxing philosophical about [his topic] for several hours on end, I for one, do not even remember what I read about [his topic] as an undergrad, so not a whole lot we can talk about in terms of coinciding interest, so it's usually going to be about something else that is not very academically related."

Indeed, Theo's relationship to Steven is similar to Kenneth's relationship to Matthew—in both cases, the similarity of life experiences and their early connections as graduate students cemented a bond that made each think of the latter as a regular confidant. At that juncture, homophily was clearly at work. Yet in both cases, that natural tendency was trumped by the absence of another kind of similarity, the one needed for Steven and Matthew to be empathetic, not just sympathetic, for the particular concerns they had. For those particular topics, Theo and Kenneth sought people who, because of their similar situations, would likely prove rewarding confidants. Relevance as similarity matters. But multiple types of similarity are at work.

Three Types of Similarity

In effect, the students described being motivated by one of three different kinds of similarity, none of which necessarily implies the other and each of which would signal that the student could anticipate cognitive empathy. One was *attribute similarity*, the commonality of race, gender, nationality, sexual orientation, or other personal characteristics that an actor might see as a likely source of cognitive empathy. This kind of similarity often underlies homophily.[17] It is what Kaylee alluded to when she explained talking to an acquaintance "because she also . . . comes from a women's college" and "[w]e're both first year PhDs" and were of the same ethnicity. The common attributes served as signals that the confidant would have relevant experience.

A second kind was *situational similarity*, the commonality from presently facing the same problem or predicament for which a person could use a confidant. It is the kind of similarity Sandra alluded to when she explained that she talked to Theo because "we're both in this dissertation proposal workshop" and facing the same "impending deadlines." Someone facing the same problems can clearly empathize, making situational similarity a quite common and powerful motivator.

A third kind is *structural similarity*, the commonality facing people who are in roughly structurally equivalent positions within a network.[18] In network analysis, people are in structurally equivalent positions to the extent they have the same relations to all other members of a network. In the hypothetical set of actors A, B, C, D, and E, if A and B are both friends with D and E and with no one else, they will be in structurally equivalent positions (regardless of the other connections among C, D, and E). One can reach precisely the same people in the network through A as through B, and the two are in this sense interchangeable. In the real world, perfect structural equivalence is rare, but actors may have similar sets of relations to the members of a larger network. Sociologist Ronald Burt provides a good example: "You and I are equivalent professors to the extent that we are expert in the same specialty, our work is popular with the same constituencies, we teach the same courses, and try to place students in the same jobs."[19]

Similarly, two graduate students in the same cohort who are both high achievers, technically skilled, and in the same laboratory may well have structurally similar relations to the members of the program: they will likely have the same adviser, share dissertation committee members, and probably be the two primary sources of technical advice for other students.[20] Most important, they may feel themselves to be in similar positions (and I will use the term to refer to those who do[21]). The key is that structurally similar actors can empathize with one another's positions, when faced with a particularly complicated set of relationships. At the same time, structurally similar actors will often be competitors.[22]

Structural and situational similarities may overlap at a given moment, but their differences are important to keep clear. The latter refers to a predicament, the particular problem the student is experiencing and an inherently temporary condition; the former, to a state, the particular position in a network of relations and an inherently stable condition.[23] A broken bone, an imminent divorce, the death of a loved one—these are situational, not structural, conditions. But one's set of relations to an adviser, three committee members, and eight graduate peers is a structural, not situational, condition. A student may share with a peer one condition and not the other. When Layla and Andrea saw themselves as two top students in the same cohort with the same adviser, they experienced a structural similarity, one likely to last well into their graduate school and their year on the job market.

In spite of their differences, the three forms of similarity may overlap. We saw that Kenneth commiserated with a man who exhibited similarity in attributes (ethnic origin, age, marital status) and situation (beginning their training while preparing for new fatherhood). Layla commiserated with three women who exhibited similarity in attributes (gender, age, career stage) and situation (working in a demanding laboratory and buried in responsibilities). When overlaps in kinds of similarity were related to a student's concern, they substantially raised the odds that making the leap and approaching a person they did not know especially well would pay off. A potential helper who was both attributionally and structurally similar, or structurally and situationally similar, would likely provide a lot more insight and true cognitive empathy than one with only a single type of similarity or none at all. And when that potential confidant was facing either the same particular problem or structural condition, that empathy might itself be a mitigating factor, since few would betray a vulnerability that they are themselves experiencing. In that sense, both situational and structural similarity can provide buffers in themselves.

PROBING FURTHER

Understanding from Direct Experience

Cognitive empathy, or something close to it, may derive from a different source. Students did not merely confide in people facing self-evidently similar circumstances; they also found others with direct past experience with such such circumstances. Students often took advantage of former *experience* professors, who were likely to have gone through many of the issues that the students, now embarking on their own academic career, were likely to experience.

David was a generally level-headed laboratory scientist who had pursued graduate school with a clear sense of purpose. Admitted at his top two schools, he was interested in Hillmount primarily because of the well-known, highly influential, senior faculty member who had essentially created David's field of interest. Two weeks into the program, he explained to me: "I interviewed at both schools and other professors I had applied to work with, and [this senior scientist] was very, very encouraging of the research I had discussed with him in my interview, and sounded very excited at the prospect of having me come here. It sounded like a good environment to work in." Loyal and reserved, David was not the kind to have large numbers of friends or develop networks quickly. Two weeks into his program, he named four discussion partners: his girlfriend, his mother, his roommate, and an old friend he had met while working in a laboratory as an undergraduate. He was clear that "those are probably my major confidants." Six months later, all four remained but his mother, who was replaced by a graduate student who worked in his laboratory. Six months after that, the revised network remained intact. David maintained as steady a set of confidants as we saw.

By the middle of his first year, David had begun to wonder, not acutely but in a low-level yet persistent way, whether he still wanted the trajectory he originally saw for himself. The issue was not second thoughts about an academic career. "I think it just comes down to—I know I would like to stay in academia. I'm very much set on that. But I'm less set on whether I would like to go on an environment like a small liberal arts school where it's teaching based, or go somewhere like an R1 institution and have pressing deadlines for publishing and competing research." It was a common concern among people who had entered a PhD program more for the love of knowledge than in pursuit of a career, and missed the sense of intellectual purity of their undergraduate experience. At issue was the fact that preparing for those two tracts during the graduate training phase requires making some decisions about focus early on—for example, whether to apply for fellowships that allow students the time to dedicate themselves solely to their research or to begin developing a teaching portfolio by serving as a teaching assistant on the path to develop independent courses. Since he had spent part of his undergraduate career at a research institution and part of it in a liberal arts college, he had "seen the pluses and minuses" of each path. Furthermore, still in his first year in graduate school, David did not need to make any decisions. But the worry lingered.

David approached his former undergraduate adviser, who had started his own career at a "very large research lab and enjoyed his research, but enjoyed teaching," and had "moved to a liberal arts school." The former adviser was good to talk to, as he had great experience in the issue David was debating. It was not as if he provided David much information. The benefit, as David seemed to see it, was more the benefit of brainstorming with someone with experience. At the school, his former adviser "still enjoys his teaching, but . . . he's almost discouraged from doing research to focus on teaching. And I know he's very frustrated with that at times. So, yeah, it's interesting just to see that conflict," since David had served as a teaching assistant as an undergraduate and "really enjoyed the teaching aspect of it. But I don't know that I want to be in a situation where faculty or administrators are actively discouraging me from completing research."

Understanding from Indirect Experience

Some of the people students spoke to could not exactly empathize, since they were not and had not experienced the students' particular concern. Nevertheless, because they had repeatedly listened to others experiencing the same circumstances, they could reasonably be expected to understand the students' worry. These people had not necessarily experienced the problem but had heard, many times, the concerns of others who had. This indirect experience was enough to put the students at ease, the way some married couples feel at ease discussing their problems with priests—the latter may not have experienced marital strife, but they have listened to many who have.

Halfway through his first year, David experienced his own version of imposter syndrome, worrying deeply that others were far more advanced than he was, and perhaps also feeling a not-uncommon tinge of paranoia. "I worry I'm not being productive enough, or at least not on the right time scale. I guess to some extent I worry that the other graduate students are doing things that I should be doing and I'm unaware of it. And I don't really know." He was particularly concerned about the timeline for his first-year project. He was having some trouble with his experiments. And though he had gained enough experience as an undergraduate laboratory assistant to know that such problems were par for the course, he still did not quite see himself, rightly or not, as measuring up. The very last time he talked about his concerns was not a conversation with his adviser, or his girlfriend, or his three confidants—not even the laboratory mate who was also in his cohort. "I was talking to, well, I don't know what her technical role is, because she's not a professor. [Leona] is kind of a departmental secretary and she organizes most of the courses and requirements for the [department]." After many years on the job, Leona had seen generations of first-year graduate students— and the oft-repeated concerns and natural anxieties of people joining an institution anew—many times over. She had seen as much as anyone *providing relief* what David was experiencing in many different forms across generations of cohorts, and thus could be reasonably expected to provide empathetic understanding.

A similar kind of choice was made by Rachel, an immigrant student who had been concerned for several months about her visa status. Having married her long-term partner during her first year in graduate school, she did what many would have done: "I applied for a green card based on my marriage." The stability of permanent residency, added to the stability of a new *immigrant status* spouse, boded well for a productive graduate experience.

There was a problem. "We both wish that we had consulted a lawyer while I applied for the green card, but we just applied by ourselves. . . . [We thought], 'Why not? It seems I'm already here, why not?'" She later talked to an administrator at the office of international affairs and learned that she probably should have first consulted an attorney. "They told me that, well, 'If you apply with a lawyer, if a lawyer helped you to process all these documents, they would have told you not to do so because you now have the'—I now have the F1 student status, and I really don't need a green card. I really don't need it. But we didn't know. We were like, 'Why not? What's the harm? There isn't a harm. Why not just do that?'" The harm was that, by her understanding, waiting for the application to be approved restricts her ability to travel outside the country.

importance of leaving country

While constrained international travel might not be a major problem for most, it was for Rachel. Her graduate program required a master's-level research paper, and for the paper she would have to travel outside the United States to spend months reading and studying archival materials. Being unable to leave the country delayed her progress and paved the way for a long-term stay in graduate school, an outcome she was determined to avoid. She needed someone to whom she could vent and with whom to brainstorm and think through worst-case scenarios.

We asked about the last conversation she had about the topic: "Two weeks ago with [Professor Spencer]," a faculty member who had worked with many students doing international work, and thus, had often experienced this kind of struggle. Rachel had first talked to this professor months earlier, the first time the issue came up, given the professor's experience. At this point, there was nothing the professor could do. "But there is no progress, of course, because this is not, this is actually not something that the university or my professor could help me with. This is actually states and government." At this point, all Rachel could do, and wanted to do, was vent. "So our recent conversation is just a reiteration of the whole figuration, we're just like talking about how sad it is, so it's not about how to solve the problem." No advice? "She had advice in May [several months ago, when this first came up], but not now." There was nothing to do but express frustration.

Support Versus Information

Rachel's experience—of first approaching Professor Spencer for information and then, months later, for support—brings to light an important issue. The difference between seeking support and seeking information is clear in the abstract but sometimes fuzzy in practice, conventional theory notwithstanding. Recall the standard rule of thumb that weak ties provide information while strong ties offer support. Though this book has shown that weak ties can also provide support, I have nonetheless avoided discussing cases when students were pursuing information. The reason is twofold: first, there is no surprise that people may seek weak ties for information; second, there is comparatively less risk in approaching a weak tie for information. Exposure and vulnerability lie in the pursuit of support.

Nevertheless, there were times when students seemed to seek both information and support. Consider Oliver. By the start of his second year, he was deeply worried about the feasibility of his research project, an MA-level study required as part of his program. The project was highly complicated, requiring access to difficult-to-reach materials and special permissions that Oliver was not even sure he would be able to obtain. He was deeply committed to this project, had pondered this set of issues over many years, and realized that it was one of the few topics that both interested him and could set him apart from the rest of the field. Oliver was at a stage where, after months of trying to gain access to his materials, all he could do was wait. No one could do anything to speed up the process; no one could provide any information he did not already know. But the frustration was palpable. At this point, talking the problem out every now and then was useful.

He sought someone who, given his or her knowledge, would likely understand his situation. When we asked him to recall the last time he had talked about this issue, he described a professor in another department, someone who, as he explained, "I've been pondering having added to my committee. He's really young [and not yet tenured], so I'm not sure he's actually going to stay here [at Hillmount], and I don't want to deal with [a] long-distance adviser. But he's really great, and he does [work in the same field]." Oliver went to the professor's office, first getting a sense of him before delving into the topic: "I gave him a very similar spiel to what I just told you with all the anxieties, like, 'What do you think?'" Oliver was quite explicit when we asked him why he decided to reveal his anxieties to that person: "Well, because he's . . . a specialist, and he's . . . the only person—well, that's not true—[this field] is kind of gaining steam right now. And so there are more and more people doing it, but there is not anybody in [my] faculty who does [this particular kind of work]. . . . [S]o he was . . . one of my very few outlets." Oliver's term, an "outlet," was telling—though he sought the professor's knowledge, he also needed a place to release his thoughts.

CONCLUSION: APPROACHING WEAK TIES

Why Weak Ties

I have argued that students often sought to approach someone they could reasonably expect would understand their predicament as they saw it. That motivation, however, does not inherently require them to pursue weak ties, since a close friend or family member, depending on the topic, might empathize just as well. In fact, at least one of the cases discussed earlier, the relation between Sandra and Theo, could easily be described as close.

But the pursuit of cognitive empathy did bear a relation to the probability of approaching a weak tie.

Recall that students listed a wide range of personal worries that I classified into broad categories: love and family, fulfilling requirements, social life, time management, relation to faculty, finances, productivity, long-term career, fear of failure, fit with program, and health care. These categories masked the specificity in the issues the students worried about, from particular problems with a visa to broken bones to personal difficulties with a particular adviser. The more specific and unique a concern is, the fewer the number of people who will likely empathize. In all personal networks, there are far more weak ties than strong ones; in fact, most people have but a handful of truly strong ties. Thus, the more specific a topic of concern is, the greater the probability that those who can empathize are weak ties. Anyone can understand relationship problems, but not everyone can understand why agreeing to head one's local ethnic association might have seemed like a great idea but was in fact a terrible one. The more the students wanted a confidant who could empathize with a particular need, the more likely they were to discover that this person was not a close friend or family member but an acquaintance. Cognitive empathy, or its approximation, raised the expected gains from approaching a weak tie.

But a risky decision is only worth the trouble if such gains surpass the expected harm. Two factors helped reduce the probability of that harm. First, many of the people the students approached were part of a larger network of faculty, staff, and other students in the Hillmount context. In such a context, if a confidant humiliated, demoralized, or otherwise reacted poorly to a student, the news would spread quickly through the network, undermining the potential helpers' own reputation. To the extent the confidant worried about her own reputation, she would be expected to be less likely to cause harm.

Second, many of these relationships were institutionally mediated in the specific sense of being organizationally embedded, and thus, subject to specific expectations relevant to their positions. The advisers, secretaries, former bosses, lab mates, advanced graduate students, and others whom the students approached were subject to both policies and norms of behavior, decorum, and support that dramatically lowered the risk of exposing vulnerability. Professors are required and staff members expected to provide support for students; students and managers in a laboratory, if they hope to keep their jobs, must ensure they do not create a hostile environment. Such expectations substantially lowered the probability of harm. Were Professor Spencer to shun Rachel or the administrator Leona to embarrass David in the context of their respective departments, they would risk reprimand. The importance of institutional norms lies above and beyond the network structure—the network was neither dense nor close-knit enough to be independently effective as a deterrent. Institutional rules and norms provided a crucial buffering role.

Though network structure and institutional expectations both played important roles, it is crucial to not overstate their influence. Not every weak tie was part of a close network or mediated in a way that would substantially undermine risk. The woman Kaylee went swimming with was not even in the same academic department, not part of a dense network or subject to institutional policies that would make a substantial difference. But more often than not those factors played important mitigating roles in the students' experiences.

Expectation, Not Certainty

Mitigating factors aside, I emphasize that approaching weak ties was nonetheless a risk, one that did not always pay off. Sometimes, talking did not help. For example, Sandra did not always get much out of talking to Theo: "our conversations are not terribly productive. It's a lot of feeling sorry for each other and no like way forward." At times, the result was worse, a net loss. When Oliver approached the professor in the other department, the outcome was not ideal. "What do you think?" Oliver asked him, hoping to get some understanding. "And he's like, 'I don't know.' I'm like, 'All right, yeah, I know you don't know. I just wanted to say it,'" to express himself. Rather than feeling validated, Oliver came away a bit embarrassed.

Or consider Isaac, who was deeply concerned about feeling out of place. A student from an ethnic background largely underrepresented in his department, he was disturbed by what he described as "an atmosphere of elitism" in the department. He explained the general message he believed the students were getting from faculty. "They're like, . . . '[W]e're training you to be here.' [But] I don't want to be there. That's not the people I want to be around." He thought his purpose as a scholar was not necessarily to spend his time at a research-focused institution: "that's not who I'm worried about. It's the people struggling to get into a state school . . . those types of communities that really need the people that are coming out of here but don't go to those places." Isaac was serious about the personal politics behind his motives. "You know, if I could get a job at a community college, then so be it . . . because those are really neglected groups that we forget about." He continued: "I went to a community college and

I transferred to a four-year school and then came here. So, it's definitely possible. You just gotta find people that . . . will help you." His long-term career would seem to be something for which an academic adviser would be appropriate. He thus took the risk.

However, it did not work: "my current adviser really does not help at all. He . . . listens and he'll give some feedback but it's not like he's invested in what I'm trying to do to see it go further." The empathy simply did not materialize. It is not surprising that, by the end of the first year, Isaac almost studiously avoided the topic with any of his academic advisers. At the extreme, such situations are dire. The inability to find an empathetic ear—someone who can truly understand one's experience, or get close to understanding it—is a difficult form of loneliness.

Worth It

Most students, for most of their worries, ultimately found themselves confiding in others. The need to speak to someone who would understand, and the scarcity of such people for some kinds of topics, repeatedly made approaching a weak tie well worth the risk. The students needed empathy more than they feared being hurt. The decision was not irrational; it reflected a reasonable assessment of the gains relative to potential harm, given the topics they discussed and the people they approached. Indeed, the students often thought carefully about whom to talk to before they did so.[24]

But sometimes, as I discuss next, they did not.

CHAPTER 6

Because They Were There

Why They Did Not Always Deliberate

By the end of her first year, Camille had developed deep anxieties about fulfilling her intellectual expectations. She worried, as she explained, "that I won't be able to come up with . . . good ideas." "[W]hen so much of your self-concept is in your . . . intellect," she said, "you . . . start to get down on yourself." The concern, like an aching tooth, was somewhat ignorable but mainly debilitating and stubbornly ever-present. Camille was philosophical about the issue, trying to see it as "part of the package" of graduate school, as she put it, and working to avoid the deep and ongoing self-doubt from becoming paralyzing. She found comfort and relief in Jorge Cham's popular comic strip, "Piled Higher and Deeper," or "PHD Comics," which centers on the everyday lives of graduate students. "Okay, there's . . . a really funny PHD Comic. . . . [I]t's this woman working and she's like, 'Oh, time for my . . . daily five-minute existential crisis.'" The sentiment was all too familiar. "Because the gains are so far off in grad school. Like, they're so, so far off. And so it just . . . makes sense that every once in a while you're gonna get stressed out because there's no . . . really immediate reward."

Camille also found comfort in talking, often with her classmate Robert or with her boyfriend. We asked her to try to remember the last conversation she had experienced. "Mm, I can't actually. I don't know." Could she remember any recent conversation? "There's actually a conversation that sticks out in my mind. . . . [It is] one I had with [Cesar, a classmate], but I don't normally talk to him about that." She remembered the talk because it was cathartic: "we . . . talked about how . . . we're at the end of our first year and . . . we have nothing exciting to show for it and no good ideas to . . . go forth with 'til next year. But it was . . . really reassuring to know he was also in that state." Though Cesar was not someone Camille regularly talked to, she found comfort in venting with someone who, by virtue of the similarity of his circumstances and position, could easily empathize. Given what we saw in the last chapter, there is little surprise that she would decide to approach Cesar about this issue.

Nevertheless, describing what she did as "deciding to approach him" would be misleading, for it implies far more deliberation or even reflection than she undertook. Camille had not sought Cesar for a conversation or invited him over for a chat. She explained: "He just . . . happened to—he left something at my apartment so he came over to pick it up and I . . . happened to be in . . . that state of mind and he was luckily there." Camille talked to Cesar about her anxiety not because she was avoiding her boyfriend or because she had concluded that Cesar would be the best person to talk to; she confided in Cesar because, when she happened to be ready, he happened to be present. The decision, that is, was spontaneous.

I have hitherto discussed the process of seeking help as a deliberative decision, wherein people weigh the pros and cons of approaching a spouse, or a parent, or a peer, or a counselor, or an adviser before deciding. We saw that students may avoid spouses because they fear incompatible expectations or seek lab partners because they are likely to be cognitively empathetic about the worries at hand. However, Camille's course of action can hardly be described in those terms. By her own account, she had no plans to talk to Cesar before she did. He just happened to be available when she needed help; she spontaneously opted to ask him. Was this decision a fluke?

I argue that it was not: students often found themselves confiding in others not because they had planned it—not because they had, upon reflection, concluded that a given person would be worth talking to—but simply because the confidant was present and available when needed. They found themselves blurting out confessions without apparent basis, at times even to people they hardly knew. The reasons reveal much about how people approach their network and why their spaces of interaction may affect not merely whom they confide in but also the very process through which they make the decision.

DELIBERATION

An Important Assumption

A standard assumption in theories of purposive action across the social sciences is that deliberation precedes action. The assumption informs the classic version of the rational actor perspective.[1] Economist Gary Becker argued that "people rationally evaluate the benefits and costs of activities" before deciding on a course of action.[2] Becker believed this to be true across many contexts: "even intimate decisions such as marriage, divorce, and family size are reached through weighing the advantages and disadvantages of alternative actions."[3] People weigh their options, then decide to act. Sociologist James Coleman seemed to express some ambivalence about the issue, but nonetheless was willing to assume that "different actions . . . [have] a particular utility for the actor and . . . the actor chooses the action which will maximize utility."[4]

[margin note: maxe. utility]

But many researchers who reject the strict rational actor model still assume that deliberation precedes action. Some experts on social support are explicit about this fact. For example, sociologists Brea Perry and Bernice Pescosolido argue the following: "Our networks are composed of many different relationships that vary in type of connection, intimacy, frequency of contact, proximity, and other characteristics. . . . People selectively draw on ties and their diverse resources depending on who is most likely to be useful for a particular purpose at any given point in time."[5] Therefore, when people need to talk to someone about, say, health, they think about who would be more useful before drawing on the tie: "individuals appear to evaluate support needs, identifying the best possible matches among a larger group of potential health discussants."[6]

[margin note: trend of analysis]

In fact, the assumption is present in any theory of motivated behavior, such as Max Weber's broader model of motivated action, Robert Merton's view of purposive action, or their many contemporary derivations.[7] When theorists argue that people are motivated to act because of factors such as value rationality, institutional norms, or the belief that someone has valuable information, the theorists are usually making the same core assumption. In fact, I have made this assumption throughout this book: to understand what motivated Diana to avoid Rachel or David to approach Leona, we presumed that they thought about their actions before they pursued the latter, that Diana first considered Rachel and then decided not to approach her or that David assessed his options before deciding that Leona would be able to cognitively empathize. This assumption is prevalent across many social science models, because it is difficult to propose that a factor motivated someone to act without also proposing that the person thought about it before acting. Otherwise, a critic could argue that the presumed motivation did not precipitate the action and was merely, instead, a *post facto* rationalization. Theories of motivated action must typically presume deliberation before action.

Critiques

But researchers in philosophy, sociology, and psychology have questioned the assumption that people necessarily reflect on their options before acting. Pragmatist philosopher John Dewey rejected the idea that deliberation necessarily precedes action, instead proposing that much action derives from "habit" and "impulse."[8] He believed action is often best thought of as behavior or conduct, in the sense that most of what we observe are the mere expressions of accumulated habits, rather than the calculated consequences of conscious decision making. Furthermore, he argued that even when an action has an aim or purpose, that aim is not necessarily clear in the mind of the actor—it may be a "mere tentative sketch."[9] Without a clear aim, a motivation cannot be clear. Dewey thought implausible the notion that people consistently calculate courses of action and their respective advantages and disadvantages.

Philosopher and social theorist Alfred Schutz agreed. "It is erroneous to assume," he argued, "that consciousness of . . . alternatives and therefore choice is necessarily given before every human action and that in consequence all acting involves deliberation and preference."[10] Schutz believed that action "does not necessarily . . . [presuppose] reflection, volition, and preference. When I walk through a garden discussing a problem with a friend and I turn left or right, I do not choose to do so. I have no alternative in mind."[11] As he explained, he would not turn left or right because of an interest in maximizing utility or even a drive to accommodate an institutional norm—it would merely be a spontaneous action, one in which there was no deliberation at all. By extension, it makes little sense to think of this action—the decision to turn left versus right—as motivated. The importance of spontaneous action of this kind has also been noted by sociologists such as Pierre Bourdieu, Hartmut Esser, and Clemens Kroneberg, as well as recent sociologists of culture.[12]

In recent years, cognitive psychologists have developed similar ideas, though few commentators on this new "behavioral economics" have taken stock of the work of the earlier philosophers and sociologists. Researchers have proposed that people make decisions through at least two dramatically different processes or "systems" of thought. As Daniel Kahneman has written, system 1 decisions are made through a cognitive process that is "typically fast, automatic, effortless"; system 2 decisions are "slower, serial, effortful, more likely to be consciously monitored and deliberately controlled."[13] The latter involve deliberation; the former do not. He has referred to them as "thinking fast and slow."[14] Dual-process theory, as the perspective has been called, does not disagree that people often deliberate before acting; it merely posits that they do not always do so, in part because of the enormous cognitive cost of reflecting on every decision before making it. Much intuitive thinking involves relying on heuristics or mental shortcuts to avoid having to think carefully about every decision.[15] Since the mind has multiple ways of making decisions, an all-encompassing, one-mode model such as classical rational choice theory is likely to fail under many circumstances. It is not merely that people decide on an action based on different factors at different times; it is that the very decision-making process may differ, at times involving little or no reflection on the actor's part.

This perspective may help account for Camille's behavior. The overwhelming majority of studies in dual-process theory have taken place in the laboratory, where scientists can carefully control the conditions under which subjects are tested and reasonably activate one or another form of thinking. Outside the laboratory, in the messy interactions of the real world, it is impossible for a researcher to know what mental process a person applied when merely going about their daily business. The fact that few if any sociologists studying support networks have studied how these processes may affect support decisions is not surprising.[16] Yet understanding whether students' actions were deliberative is not impossible, at least within a clear yet significant scope, if the question is approached with caution.

An Approach

In a previous chapter I suggested that people have a bias toward rationality, toward explaining their actions in ways that represent their motivations as rationally sensible. People probably also have a bias toward *intentionality*, toward explaining their actions as motivated, rather than reflexive, as the result of willful decisions.[17] Psychologists Eldar Shafir, Itamar Simonson, and Amos Tversky put it well: people "are sometimes unaware of the precise factors that determine their choices, and [may] generate spurious explanations when asked to account for their decisions."[18] If we had asked Camille to explain why she approached Cesar, she probably would have given us an answer. She might well have told us that, as a classmate, Cesar understood her problems more than most. Or she might have told us that Cesar was a good listener. Yet, even if she were being fully honest, her answer would not necessarily represent the process through which she ended up discussing her problems with Cesar. Indeed, it would have given us the wrong impression that her decision was highly deliberative.

Consider, for example, Andrea, who had been worried, as many students are, about whether her research project would yield intellectual fruits. Her last conversation about it was with her own mother. When she was asked, "Why your mom?," Andrea dutifully provided an answer: "Just because she's nice and likes to comfort me. I don't know. And it's . . . nice to have an outside perspective. . . . So, it's nice to . . . first hear words of encouragement from someone." Given these circumstances, it would be easy to stop at this juncture and conclude that Andrea decided to approach her mother after first thinking about the matter and then concluding that her mother would be comforting and encouraging.

But that is not what happened. When Andrea was asked to simply explain how the topic came up, she elaborated: "I called her. . . . I typically call her a few times a week, so it wasn't like I had necessarily called her because of that, but we talk about things and it came up." They talk, it came up, and she confided.

The point is not that people are always wrong about how they make decisions. Sometimes, decisions clearly result from willful actions that people understand perfectly. The point is that people may or may not be right, and the researcher must avoid an interview process wherein theoretically-convenient assumptions about how people arrived at an action will unwittingly be reinforced. Answering our question, therefore, required a different approach to the interviews, an approach discussed at length in Appendix A. In a nutshell, the approach required asking students not necessarily to tell us what motivated their actions but to reconstruct the events themselves where they confided in others, to describe the circumstances under which the events took place. Indeed, their answers made clear that, quite often, to ask what motivated them was to ask the wrong question—the how, not the why, was what mattered.

THREE DIFFERENT PROCESSES

Decisions

Before turning to their answers, disentangling the process will be useful. When a person mobilizes her network, she is actually making not one but three decisions: to *seek* help, to *select* a confidant, and to *activate* the tie. Being clear on the differences among them will help our discussion.

The seeking decision is the resolution, in one's mind, to confide in another person, with no necessary determination about who that might be. Given any emotional need, people may or may not decide to seek help, and many people with deep preoccupations simply decide not to do so. For example, this scenario is what worries health providers about people who suffer from HIV but who do not seek help, or what worries teachers about students who have been bullied and are contemplating suicide.[19]

The selection decision is the process of opting for one potential confidant as opposed to another. Selection, for the purposes of our discussion, is also strictly a mental process. It is the moment at which considerations such as the ones we have discussed—whether someone will have incompatible expectations or be cognitively empathetic—play a role in the process.[20] Much of the research we have discussed, including the "different strokes from different folks" proposition, wherein people select different members of their network for different kinds of support, is ultimately about the selection decision.

The activation decision, contrary to the other two, requires interaction between the actor and another. It is the specific act of confiding in another. It is possible to have both decided to seek help and selected whom to approach while not yet acting on those two decisions, as when a shy student has not yet mustered the courage to ask an intimidating professor for help or when the ideal confidant, already selected, is nowhere to be found. Researchers do not typically distinguish activation from selection or seeking, but they have used the term "mobilization" to emphasize this activation process.[21]

Reflective Activation

Keeping the three elements of the process in mind helps clarify the aspects of deliberation to which the interview data can speak. The interviews cannot tell us whether students made no rational deliberation of any kind whatsoever before a given action. But they can tell us whether the standard model about how people mobilize their networks accounts consistently for the students' experiences. In that model, the process of mobilization is highly deliberative in the specific sense that each decision succeeds its prior one in sequence: a student would first decide to seek someone to talk to, then select a confidant from their network, and finally activate that tie.[22]

That model characterizes perfectly how some of the students behaved when needing a confidant. Recall Oliver, who had been working on a highly complicated project for which, after months of background preparation, all he could do was wait. He was frustrated, and decided he needed to talk to someone. After some reflection, he turned to a young professor in another

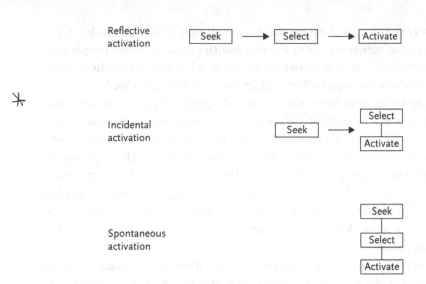

Figure 6.1. Three types of decision making when activating a tie to a confidant.

department, because the professor was a "specialist" and might serve as a useful "outlet" to vent his frustration. He had been thinking about this person for a while; as he explained, he had been "pondering" adding the person to his committee. By the time Oliver found himself in front of the faculty member asking for help, he had long decided to seek help and from whom he would seek it (Figure 6.1, top).

This kind of reflective activation represents schematically the position of much of the research—and hitherto, of this book: first, you decide to seek help; then you decide whom to ask; finally, you go and ask. It is an elegant and systematic way of accounting for the process, and the general way many existing theories operate. For example, a rational actor theory of whom in their network people mobilize for support may require people to weigh the benefits or costs of selecting particular members before asking the chosen one for help. Reflective activation is also how at least some of the avoidance of strong ties for fear of incompatible expectations or pursuit of weak ones in search of cognitive empathy would work. People reflect, select, activate. As Oliver's experience shows, that model of activation sometimes works.

Incidental Activation

However, the experience of Camille suggests that students did not always reflect on their decision in the particular sense of not necessarily making each decision in the sequence shown previously. In fact, some students had decided they needed someone to talk to but had not selected anyone from their network until they found themselves unexpectedly confiding in someone in the midst of a social interaction. The reasons differed. Some had not found the time to think about who might have the experience or expertise to be appropriately empathetic. Others had decided, finally, that they needed to talk to someone but had not mustered the courage to take what would seem the logical next step, to figure out who that person might be. In either case, the decision was incidental, in the sense that they did not select someone before approaching that person (Figure 6.1, middle). In a real sense, the opportunity presented itself.

"just happened"

Consider Robert, who had been wondering whether academia was right for him, a nagging issue given the opportunity costs involved in this pursuit. He talked about it often, finding comfort in venting. The last time he had talked about the topic had been with two of his peers. But he had not approached them for that purpose. "We kind of talked about it . . . because we were working [on] homework together for one class." It happened to be one of the classes where they receive training in research methods, one of Robert's strengths. "I was talking about this friend . . . who got a job in consulting and she doesn't even have half the statistical experience we do and she's getting paid probably three times as much as we are." In fact, a common concern among today's graduate students is seeing their peers earn substantially higher incomes with fewer years of education and none of the particular anxieties of a PhD program. But the conversation itself was not planned. "So . . . we just . . . because we were doing stats homework . . . that's why I was talking about it, and that's when we talked about, 'Oh yeah, maybe we should think about doing something else instead of this.'"

Early in her second year, Diana had been worried for months about her financial situation and the impact it was having on her work, life, and health. As she explained, "it was . . . on my mind," and she knew she needed to talk it out. When asked whom she talked to the last time she had talked about the problem, she reported, "an older graduate student." She was asked why. "It just happened. I had just met him for coffee . . . so it was . . . you know, on my mind." As many students did, as she continued to talk over the course of her interview, Diana, when asked to provide a motivation for why she talked to this particular graduate student, provided one: "I guess as an older, a sort of veteran student I thought, you know, I guess I was looking for comparable experience or something." Yet her initial response made clear that, while she was seeking someone to talk to, she had not decided on this particular student. That decision "just happened" while they were having coffee.

Victor had been concerned about his required MA-level paper. "I didn't get enough done over the summer, but this is my first summer of not getting enough done in this context. So, it [has been] present in my mind." It was one of his deeper preoccupations, an ongoing concern, and one he needed to talk about. As he explained, "It's on my mind, so I bring it up." He was asked to reconstruct the last time he talked about it. He was at the library, where he "ran into" Gaby, and they sat together to read. How did the topic come up? "Um . . . she got a text message, or an email that she was reading . . . and then she showed it to me, which caused her to comment about . . . regretting . . . having dropped another course in favor of the one she was taking and studying for at the moment." The conversation turned to courses and faculty members, and Victor ended up talking to Gaby incidentally. "I brought up that I just met with this professor [who is helping with the MA]. And that's . . . how it came up."

Victor talked about this concern often—it was an issue he needed to work through in conversation. When asked about the prior time he had talked about it, he had no trouble remembering. He had been auditing a course, and one of the people was "another person in the . . . department that I'm friendly with." After class, "I walked home with her partway." The topic had emerged so organically over the course of the conversation that he had trouble recollecting who broached the topic. "And I think it was her who brought it up, or I don't know how it came up, but . . . I think I expressed a little bit of anxiety." Later, he corrected himself: "Oh, no . . . actually no. I totally asked her advice about part of the MA thing."

Victor wanted to talk to others about his stresses regarding his MA, but it is not as if he selected Gaby or this other classmate after deliberating on whether they would be able to cognitively empathize. He certainly did not assess whether these people were among the two or three people he would call himself emotionally close to. The desire was on his mind, and he simply responded to opportunities as he ran into plausible discussion partners.

A few researchers have seen evidence of this process in how people use their networks for reasons other than social support. One little-noted finding in sociologist Mark Granovetter's *Getting a Job* reflects this fact.[23] The book examined how white-collar professionals found jobs and probed how they decided whom to ask for information about available positions. Granovetter discussed the experiences of one respondent, Carl Y, who was unemployed and had been looking for help in finding a job. In the interim, he began driving a taxi until he could find a job in his regular field. Once, while on a fare, he ran into an old friend at a train station and asked for a job on the spot. Carl did not select this friend to then go out and find the person; Carl decided whom to ask (selection decision) at the moment he decided to ask (activation decision). Some version of this situation was common. Granovetter explained that many of his respondents were, in a sense, "always looking" for a job, but not explicitly aiming to ask a particular member of their network for help. They simply responded to opportunities as they saw fit.

Spontaneous Activation

Still, there were times when approaching a confidant involved even less deliberation than the cases of Victor, Diana, and Robert suggest. Consider that as people go about their lives, they often talk to others with no objective in mind. Georg Simmel referred to this tendency as sociability, a form of interaction in which there is no instrumental purpose—wherein the purpose of interaction is the interaction itself.[24] When two friends sit together on a park bench to talk or two coworkers share lunch in a cafeteria, much of their interaction is likely to reflect sociability. Sociable interaction is a common aspect of routine, everyday activity: at bus stops, offices, churches, gyms, barbershops, cafes, hair salons, restaurants, and other organizations.[25] While Simmel would not disagree that people often talk to others for strategic or instrumental reasons—because they want something or are hoping to capitalize on a social connection—people often talk because they like to talk.

It was in this way that several students, having not even decided to confide in anyone, over the course of an interaction decided to do so on the spot, making all three decisions—to seek, select, and activate—simultaneously. I refer to this as a kind of spontaneous activation[26] (see Figure 6.1, bottom).

Consider Kenneth, who was not a natural worrier, but was concerned that he was having difficulty finding an adviser. He talked about the issue with his wife, but otherwise considered the matter private. Unlike Victor, he certainly did not walk about either waiting for someone to talk to or even expecting it to happen: "it's not worth talking about in a sense." But he had, in fact, talked about it. The last time was with a friend of his who was not part of the department but knew something about his area. When we asked him to recollect the conversation, his reply made clear how spontaneous such actions can be: "I just [ran] into that guy. . . . I think it was on the bus," he recalled. "Yeah, yeah, yeah. And then we . . . start talking about . . . some of the [faculty in my field] in [his institution]." That conversation, in turn, helped him think through the adviser-seeking process.

Sarah had become concerned by what she called her "language issue," the fact that she was a foreign-born student for whom English was a second

language as a social barrier

language. In fact, her verbal English at the time was moderate at best. Her difficulties in communicating with others, in turn, undermined her ability to develop a local community beyond the very few people of her own ethnicity with whom she had begun to form bonds. As a result, Sarah became socially isolated and often lonely. Isolation is common among graduate students, but perhaps especially so among those with language issues. In fact, the language problem was becoming "a real difficulty or challenge" for Sarah, because it was also exacerbating her perceived inability to connect culturally with Americans. Sarah's cultural background differed in norms, lifestyle, and values from those of the native-born, predominantly white, middle-class Americans who constituted most of her program, and she often found little common ground. She just did not understand them. As she explained, "I don't know how to be a friend with—[it's] a little bit weird but I'm just gonna say it, right honest, honestly—how to get to be friends with American people. Sorry. Yeah. That is really hard because . . . I don't have many friends [here]."

Although her three concerns, with language, social isolation, and cultural alienation, were connected, she saw the latter two as distinct from the first. Personal isolation and cultural distance are private problems, in the sense that one can hide them from others; an inability to speak English at the level of one's peers is public. This fact made her language anxieties more salient but also, in a sense, an easier topic of conversation, because her difficulty was self-evident. "The language issue is less private than the social issue or cultural issue," she explained, "so I talk about it more often." She particularly talked about it, and often, to people of her own ethnic background who easily understood her predicament, who could cognitively empathize. In this sense, Sarah, as Kenneth did, was not walking about looking for people to talk to. However, it was for opposite reasons: Kenneth, because his problem was too private; Sarah, because she had talked about it plenty.

Yet the last conversation that she had was equally telling about how spontaneously people often made social support decisions. It happened in a restaurant. "I went to the birthday party of one of my [coethnic] friends and we went to [a restaurant of a different ethnic background] and it was really hard to order in English, even though we was in [the ethnic neighborhood]. So every time we [ordered] something we [had] to be very short and quick." They could utter the name of the dish and point to the menu, but nothing else. At the table, Sarah remarked that, when they ordered a meal back home, they could engage in conversation with the server. "I mean, orders should be really clear so that they can understand and, yeah, that is why the language issue came up on the table." The trivial difficulty with ordering from the menu triggered an extended discussion of the perils of language isolation for a foreign migrant. It "is hard for [my friends], even [though] they spend like five or even eight years here in the United States, but they are not native speakers of English." Sarah vented, at length, finding the conversation at once "gloomy," as she explained, and cathartic. "So, it's good when I talk about it with my [coethnic] friends because they have something in common with me and that makes me feel I'm not a, not an only person here that [is] having some trouble."

The nature of the open-ended interviews made it at times impossible to discern whether a discussion was incidental or spontaneous—whether a student had or had not consciously decided to seek help at all before the interaction where it happened. Part of the issue is that decisions rarely operate in the straightforward way that social science must posit to make them tractable for quantitative modeling and analysis. People may decide on an action, hesitate, then proceed; they may think they have decided on an action, only to realize they do not fully understand the problem; they may entertain two sides of an issue simultaneously, waiting for circumstances to dictate one or another path.[27] The decision process is messy.

hard to distinguish

In addition, students are likely only able to reproduce the messiness of the process imperfectly. Consider, for example, how Anthony recounts the last important conversation he had about his research topic, a discussion with one of his acquaintances: "I was just talking to her after class one day and I don't remember how it came out, but I was somewhat worried about it I guess." When probed about why he spoke to her instead of someone else, he made clear that, though at the time he would have appreciated talking about the issue, he had not exactly decided that he would do so. "I don't know. It was probably just the nature of the conversations—and it's not a conversation I'm going to force. So, if there's an opportunity for it to come up, maybe, but otherwise, it's like with my friends who either are not grad students or grad students but not in the field. I'm less likely, or in the department I should say, I'm less likely to bring it up." The issue is on his mind, and not exactly something he has decided to talk about, but also not something he is opposed to discussing.

Another student, Faith, when recounting one of her own most valuable conversations, which happened over dinner, put it well: "Yeah, I think I was sort of asking her how things were with [her friend], and how her quarter was going. And . . . our conversation sort of branched. . . . [I]t's hard to trace exactly how the conversation goes." Hard to trace, at times, indeed.[28]

Regardless of the difficulties in discerning where on the spectrum between incidental and spontaneous their thinking was, the students repeatedly made clear that, one way or the other, many of their most valuable discussions were unplanned—a lot of the time, to paraphrase several of the students, "it just came up."

Asking Without Asking

Indeed, many of the conversations were so unplanned that the students did not, strictly speaking, ask for help. For example, Pamela recounted the most recent time she vented to someone, Queenie, about her difficulties with her research. Pamela was not the one to bring it up. "Um, we were kind of bitching about people's . . . topics and how some of them are really kind of crazy. And she was like, 'Oh, by the way, what's yours?' So then we started talking . . . about mine." Sometimes, it is the helper who brings up a topic that, having heard it, makes a person realize it would be something good to talk about, at that moment, and with that helper.

Sometimes, students were not going to bring up a topic that came up anyway. When Oliver was still weeks into his very first year, he had been worried about the high-stakes environment he realized he had entered. He was regularly concerned about not "sounding stupid in class." It was a rather private concern, but one he had talked about recently with a friend from law school. I asked him how the topic emerged. "Well, I wasn't going to bring it up, except she started talking about how much she hated law school." "So, she brought it up?" I asked. "Hilarious," he continued, nodding. "And I was really surprised, too, like she only started law school this year. . . . So, it's just, I was trying to make her feel better. So, I was like, 'Well, you know, I mean I don't feel very bad about myself here, but it is a concern I have.'" She brought it up, for her own sake, and, in the process, as he tried to convince her he could empathize, Oliver ended up confiding his own worry to her.

not always bring to bring it up

Oscar had a similar experience, when he found himself talking through his worries about his research with his teaching assistant, an advanced graduate student who was helping the professor conduct one of the courses Oscar was taking. The assistant had invited the class to a bar for drinks. "I was half an hour late and everybody else was like two hours late." Oscar and the teaching assistant found themselves alone at the bar, waiting for the others. "And he's currently working on his dissertation. And he made the comment that, 'I'm doing all this writing but sometimes I think that it's not actually that interesting.'" It was an issue that, over the course of their careers, scholars will often face, but one that a first-year graduate student might only be starting to hear others articulate. Oscar was motivated to reply. "I was like, you know, I've been thinking about my own project a lot lately and thinking whether or not it's actually . . . doing anything different than we already knew." He explained, "I think it was like a mutual support thing."

Both Oliver's and Oscar's experiences demonstrate that people may find themselves confiding in others with similar concerns not merely because they are reflecting on their predicament and deciding to approach others who resemble them. They sometimes end up doing so because the people who in the end become their helpers, concerned with the same topics, have brought these up on their own. A person's mobilization of one's network is profoundly embedded in the actions, and mobilizations, of the network members themselves. *[handwritten margin note: when it just comes up]*

This notion is supported by research on personal disclosure, an issue to which psychologists have paid some attention. Researchers have noted that people at times reveal themselves to strangers in surprising ways. As Simmel noted over a century ago, the stranger "often receives the most surprising openness—confidences which sometimes have the character of a confessional."[29] Examining this question, psychologists have shown that people tend to reciprocate the intimacy level of their counterparts. People approached at train stations by study experimenters who have revealed something intimate about themselves are more likely to do the same than when the strangers only discuss impersonal topics; they essentially "model" the behavior of their counterparts.[30] Modeling the behavior of his teaching assistant is very much what Oscar did—the difference is the assistant was not a complete stranger. When the latter began revealing something about his current dissertation anxieties, Oscar reciprocated in kind.

This kind of modeling might help explain why students have discussed a topic even when they did not want to it bring up—only to discover, having entered into the topic because of the actions of their counterpart, that they later found themselves grateful. Ricky was having difficulty with his MA-level paper, on which he had made faster progress than his peers. It was not something he talked about often, because the competitive nature of the environment in his program tended to make people anxious, uncomfortable with the possibility that others might be ahead of them. Still, though he was moving quickly, he was still having trouble with his work. Ricky recounted the last conversation he had, with a colleague he met for lunch, about the paper. "I was just telling him about my paper then." We asked if he "went to lunch with the intention of talking about [the] paper." "No," he explained, "just to catch up in general." How, then, did the topic emerge? "I think he might have brought it up."

But there was more—it was not merely that the topic, already something Ricky wanted to talk about, happened to be discussed by his counterpart. On the contrary: "I actually—this was not something I was gonna [talk about]; I was gonna keep this to myself, because I'm aware that it might be . . . a source for competitive pressure amongst a very competitive, anxious group." Yet even then, the situation made the sharing of confidences natural.

Or consider Faith, who made a point of not talking to peers such as Andre about her anxieties about work. "I feel more self-conscious talking about it with people who are . . . actually . . . the closest to, who are on exactly the same track as me." Andre was on that track. Nevertheless, "it came up with him because he was nervous about whether or not we could actually, he could write his proposal at all." Did Faith seek out Andre, then? "I didn't seek him out specifically. No, he was asking about it." And in response to his query, she ended up having a conversation that helped them both. The calculated decision-making model seen in reflective activation simply did not account for many circumstances.

No Deliberation—Of Any Kind?

When analyzing situations such as these, it is easy to fall into one version of a common but wholly unnecessary debate about the extent of rationality in social action. Indeed, rational actor models incite such strong passions, both in favor and against, that even thoughtful scholars may find themselves unable to accept perfectly reasonable ideas on either side, instead entertaining increasingly particular arguments supporting or critiquing the view.

Consider one version of that debate. A strong defender of this particular aspect of the rational actor model—of the idea that, as Becker put it, people "evaluate the benefits and costs of activities"[31] before acting— might argue that people still deliberate on their options before talking to others; they just do so very quickly. Anthony, one might say, right at the moment after he ran into his classmate, still quickly assessed whether confiding his research anxieties to her was worth it—that is, whether she might at some point betray his confidence or would really help improve his state of mind.[32] Faced with this response, a critic might counter that, had this been the case, Anthony surely would have remembered that fact, and yet he did not. As Anthony quite explicitly and somewhat sheepishly admitted, "I don't remember how it came out, but I was somewhat worried about it I guess." In turn, the strong rationalist might counter that

Anthony's memory is beside the point, since the absence of remembrance does not imply a lack of calculation, and in fact, people may even calculate costs and benefits subconsciously. In response, a critic might argue that such calculations, assuming subconscious calculations were possible, would be so cognitively taxing that it is infeasible for them to precede every single act, down to the decision of placing one foot before the other while walking.[33] Many actions must involve no deliberation of any form whatsoever.[34] And on and on. Though one could continue to volley increasingly clever arguments back and forth ad infinitum, the matter ultimately admits no resolution, because it is impossible, at least given the present state of science, to observe outside of a laboratory how much people are deliberating while making multiple decisions over the course of their ordinary lives.[35]

In this light, I emphasize three points. First, many rational actor theorists today, unlike Becker, remain agnostic on whether people actually evaluate their options before acting. They simply theorize behavior "as if" people were rational in this particular way, and assess those expectations against data. They make no assumptions about the cognitive process. For them, the benefit of the theory is analytical elegance and the ability to make predictions.[36]

Second, though that solution may work when the aim is predicting behavior, the stance is insufficient when the aim, as in this book, is understanding decisions. The decision-making mechanisms must form part of any complete theory of mobilization, and the students' experiences suggest that they did not always evaluate their options in the specific sense of making the seeking and selection decisions before confiding in others. Though we cannot know whether no calculation of any kind whatsoever took place in students' minds, we can certainly know whether every time they confided in others they had approached those people with that intention—and we know the answer is negative.

Third, I neither hold nor believe it is necessary to hold a uniformly pro- or antideliberative actor position. Sometimes people clearly reflect on the matter before deciding whom to ask for help: one cannot pick up the phone to talk to a priest about one's marital troubles without having deliberated on whom to talk to. At the same time, sometimes people clearly do not: one cannot have deliberated on whom to approach if one had not even realized one needed to talk about something that came up unexpectedly in conversation. Instead, I propose a variant of a dual-process model: reflective and incidental and spontaneous activation each takes place often, varying as a function of the circumstances. In sum, the decision-making process is heterogeneous across circumstances.

Students sometimes had decided they needed help but only figured out whom to turn to after this person unexpectedly materialized; sometimes they had not even concluded they needed help but found themselves confiding in someone while talking to them for other purposes; and sometimes they did not even want to talk about a topic but found themselves doing so because the other person brought it up. To the extent they had not yet reflected on whom to talk to, the students were responsive to their social interactions.

Understanding something about those interactions helps place the students' decisions in their proper context. Incidental and spontaneous decisions will be prevalent to the extent that actors encounter (a) many people (b) on a regular basis (c) who are likely to be cognitively empathetic, or at least supportive. In all three respects, the students were aided by the fact that many of their daily interactions were embedded in a formal organization, Hillmount University, which through multiple mechanisms structured the students' behavior, opportunities, and decisions.[37] I believe that four elements of this context placed students in social interactions favorable to the prevalence of incidental and spontaneous activation.[38] The first two elements created the opportunity for students to run into others repeatedly; the latter two increased the probability that such interactions would turn supportive.

The key difference between reflective and either incidental or spontaneous activation is that the latter two did not require the students to find the people in whom they ultimately confided. The confidants were just there. The frequency with which students confided in others unexpectedly was possible due to the repeated opportunities to encounter others as part of their daily routines. Like doctors and nurses in hospitals, analysts in large firms, and police officers in large precincts, students in the university came in regular contact with many people, with other students, professors, staff, laboratory researchers, artists, technicians, and many other individuals of various sorts, people who constituted a very loose, institutionally bound network from which they could draw on potential helpers. There were simply lots of people to talk to.

Two elements of the organizational embeddedness of these networks made such opportunities possible. The first was the set of institutional rules governing students' allocation of their time during the initial year in their programs—they had to enroll in class, and in classes with many other students, and at regular times of the day, and on a continuous basis, or else face sanctions or exclusion. The fact that they were first-year students was

especially important. In many PhD programs, while later years are dedicated to independent research, the early years of instruction are devoted
primarily to coursework, and coursework increases the amount of daily
time that students spend with their peers. A recent study of high school
students showed that taking clusters of courses with others increased the
students' odds of making new friends, and I suggest that something similar happens with the odds of making incidental and spontaneous activation decisions.[39] We recorded every course of any type that every student
took during the first year, the most course-heavy portion of the career in
each of the programs we studied. They could be lectures meeting several
times a week, seminars meeting weekly, or workshops meeting once or
twice a month. Over the first 12 months of their graduate careers, students
took as many as a dozen formal or informal courses of one or another sort,
with many students taking the maximum number allowable. As a result,
much of their day, every day of the week, they spent in a classroom, interacting regularly with other students and with faculty members. (Students
in the laboratory department saw others even more. These students were
typically admitted to that program to work directly with a given professor
in a given laboratory, where they had a workstation and scientific research
materials, and where they were expected to begin collaborating on scientific studies immediately. Thus, during the week, when these students were
not taking courses, they were working on experiments.) For the first-year
students we observed, repeated interaction with many people daily was all
but unavoidable.

But a second element, the space for social interaction, was equally
important. Confiding in someone must always happen somewhere, and
confiding in someone without having planned it cannot happen independent of a space in which interaction is taking place. Though spatial
analysis is not always central to network research today, it was important
to mid-century psychologists such as Leon Festinger, Stanley Schachter,
and Kurt Back, who understood that ostensibly trivial matters such as
the physical proximity of doors in building hallways may affect network
relations.[40] Space matters as much as the rules governing daily routines,
and often in conjunction with the latter. Consider, for example, the
requirement to take courses. Many courses, it turned out, met on overlapping days. Thus, on any given day when students traveled to campus
for coursework, they were often forced to spend hours—as they waited
between the end of one class session and the beginning of another—at
libraries, department lounges, coffee houses, offices, laboratories, student centers, and similar contexts with multiple opportunities to run
into others.

It is no surprise, therefore, that these spaces often turned up in the students' accounts of incidental and spontaneous activation. Victor's, discussed earlier, was at a library; Anthony's, in a classroom. When David, who had become preoccupied with his relative standing in the program, recently had an unexpected conversation about the issue, he described something similar. "I can tell you . . . it was on Tuesday evening. . . . I was in my office. I was working on an assignment with another grad student and we were just discussing it." In a place he spent so much of his time and so often in the company of others, it was no surprise that the activation was spontaneous, as he confirmed when I asked how the topic came up. "I think he brought it up. He just said he kind of felt [that] . . . he's not sure of how much effort he's putting in, in comparison to other students." Pamela, reconstructing the circumstances behind the first time she talked to one faculty member about her deteriorating relationship to her adviser, described something similar: "So, the first time it happened, I spoke to him about, yeah, we just happened—we were walking together. . . . I spoke to him about [an e-mail in which my advisor had said something troubling]. And I spoke to [the other faculty member] at the end of class. We just happened to go together in the same direction and I told him."

Spaces, even in the age of the Internet and mobile technology, mattered. Consider, as a contrast, an online university, wherein students must enroll, take courses and exams, and register for credit. The institutional mandates are similar to those of any university. But the absence of spaces of interaction undermines the possibility of incidental and spontaneous activation. Students may call or e-mail one another when they need someone to talk to, but they have few opportunities to spontaneously vent to someone who happened to bring up a topic that had troubled them.

The third and fourth elements raised the odds that those encounters would turn emotionally supportive. The third was the structured nature of the people they were encountering, which improved the odds that these would understand their predicament. Sociologists as varied as Georg Simmel, Peter Blau, and Lois Verbrugge have made the point that contemporary social life tends to structure the opportunities to meet others in such ways that much of our time is spent surrounded by others who resemble us.[41] To understand the significance of this fact, note that the students discussed in this chapter often confided in people they knew, at least distally. Notwithstanding the willingness of people to reveal personal intimacies to miscellaneous researchers in train stations, most of these students confided in people who, though not close, were also not total strangers. The teaching assistant at the bar, the student at the library, the colleague on the bus—these people were in one way or another part of the broader set of actors students encountered in their routines. Though the context provided multiple opportunities for interactions, these were opportunities to run into not just anyone—random strangers with no connection to them—but people who had good odds of being plausible confidants.

This plausibility derived from their high potential for relevance and empathy. Recall from the previous chapter that when students reflected on whom to talk to, they often sought people they had reason to expect would understand their circumstances. The kinds of problems students faced, while quite broad in range and emotional import, also overlapped with the kinds of issues the people around them either faced themselves or otherwise understood. In fact, these people were likely to be specifically experts or people facing similar circumstances, people with current, direct, or indirect experience. Thus, even when the students did not deliberate on whom to talk to, they repeatedly encountered people whom, had they reflected on it, they would likely have concluded would be useful confidants.

overlapping in experience

In this respect, their experiences differed from those of the commuters at the train station: both, on a daily basis, encounter multiple people as they go about their ordinary activities. But the commuters would have little reason to expect that others will understand their circumstances, except those issues surrounding the difficulty of the commute. (Still, as I discuss in a later chapter, such contextually induced similarities exist in many contexts beyond universities and colleges.)

The final element was the substantive or topical reason motivating the social interaction, what sociologist Scott Feld called the "focus" surrounding the activity.[42] The first three elements are related to the fourth. The programs placed the students repeatedly before others for institutionally-relevant reasons that required some degree of collective activity. Oscar and his teaching assistant were at the bar because his class was meeting there. Victor and Gaby were at the library because they had to study. Anthony and his confidant were both in the classroom because they were taking a class. As such, the focus of their activities created multiple opportunities for situational similarity.

The activities also took place in a space where it was appropriate to talk about institutionally relevant topics. To the extent that those topics happened to be related to their concerns, it was easy for conversations to eventually turn into confidences. In such situations, suddenly sharing their personal difficulties would be, even if unexpected, not unacceptable, because the topics being discussed were appropriate to places they were and to the institutional reasons for being there. Notice that many of the forms of incidental and spontaneous activation not only happened on campus but also involved work-related difficulties. For a student stepping out of an impressive lecture with another, sharing her worries about her own work to him is quite natural, a domain-consistent topic given the particular situation. But discussing, say, her inability to make friends with Americans would be domain-inconsistent and far more difficult. That conversation, in contrast, might be more natural in a place where the language obstacles of an immigrant are domain-relevant, as in the restaurant where Sarah was trying to order from the menu. The students confided easily in others about domain-specific topics in domain-specific places, where such revelations would likely be appropriate and useful.

These four elements of the social interaction—the rules, the space the people, and the focus—both made possible and increased the likely helpfulness of incidental and spontaneous activation. All four were constitutive of the first-year graduate experience, creating repeated opportunities to interact with people likely to be useful listeners in ways the students were not necessarily cognizant of in the moment they confided in others. As Theo explained when recounting a particularly helpful conversation, "I'm not sure how the topic came up. I suppose, being grad students, these topics will come up naturally inevitably to be entirely honest." Indeed, they do—except it was not a mere matter of their identity as students but a consequence of the social organization of their activities. What seemed to occur "naturally" was, in fact, socially structured.

CONCLUSION

The actions documented in this chapter make clear that any view of how people confide in others must accommodate that people may decide differently at different times—not just make different choices, but engage in a different decision-making process altogether. To be sure, when the students reflected on it, they sought either people they were close to or people they were not close to but whom they had reason to believe could empathize. In this respect, they not only deliberated on their actions but also, in fact, behaved in ways a rational choice theorist would expect. But often, quite often, they did not reflect on it. And we must seek a deeper understanding of what makes possible the kind of social advantage of not having to reflect on whom to talk to.

The current trends in network analysis would have us first map the network structure and capture the characteristics of its component ties. But the key to the students' behavior, ~~I believe, lay less in network~~ structure than in the ubiquity of favorable interactions. Consider that in the first few weeks and months of their programs, some of the students, including introverts or those with family commitments, made few or no new friends. They were in this sense isolated from the local network. But all of them, regardless of their natural dispositions or other obligations, were, from the first week in class, immersed in a constant stream of social interactions. Under such circumstances, even a student with no interest in meeting anyone to talk about anything could not help but regularly run into others, finding repeated opportunities to just talk. Incidental and spontaneous activation make clear that the researcher needs to know whether people are surrounded by others—physically, at the moment they are asking, thinking about asking, or mentally open to the possibility of asking—and the circumstances of that context to understand how they decide to discuss what worries them, since the presence of others may alter whom they think they could ask and even whether they think they should confide in someone at all. That epistemological shift, from network structure to network practice, demands serious attention.

[margin handwriting: import. of the social intera spect. ↓ key determing instdy]

The first year in graduate school is special. Some of the conditions that created favorable interactions change naturally as students proceed to the later years of their programs. The number of required classes dwindles, eventually reaching zero as the students write their dissertations. The amount of time on campus follows suit, and thus the number of unexpected contacts with peers, faculty, and others. As these encounters dwindle, so do the opportunities to vent when they did not necessarily expect it.

Thus, I would not be surprised if upper-level students were increasingly likely to rely on a small core of discussants: as the opportunities to talk to many dwindle, the reliance on the limited few will likely rise. That would be the expectation—at least until their new routines place them regularly in other environments with new rules, in new spaces, with new routinely encountered actors, and with new expectations for social interaction. And again, the dynamics of their contexts would likely shape the everyday decisions about whom to talk to when they need to talk.

PART III

Beyond Graduate Students

CHAPTER 7
Empirical Generalizability

Graduate students are unique. The average first-year PhD student is more educated, younger, healthier, more likely to be white, and more likely to be single than the average American. That student is entering an institution that is also peculiar in many of its traits, its particular pecking order, its sets of obligations, and its penetration into the lives of its members. I have argued that the first year in graduate school, like the first year in any new institutional context, provides analytical leverage to the researcher hoping to understand the mobilization of networks for support, because it reveals how much people change, retain, develop, avoid, and make use of confidants as they face the large and small challenges that come with entering a new social, organizational, institutional, and spatial context. And I have argued that a number of decisions about one's confidants, such as the tendencies to replace named confidants quickly and to confide in people to whom one is not close, are inherent to how people mobilize their networks today, among the most fundamental elements of social interaction. Yet graduate students are still graduate students; they are not average Americans. Whether the propositions of this book help explain the behavior of people in other life stages or outside graduate programs remains an open question.

The next two chapters take up that question, the extent to which the findings are generalizable to other populations. This chapter asks whether other populations make decisions about whom to confide in as the graduate students did. The next chapter examines whether they did for similar reasons, a discussion for which I present in systematic form the theoretical ideas about support decisions discussed throughout this book.

In what follows I show that, while graduate students are unique, their decisions with respect to confiding in others are largely not. Both recently released and hitherto unpublished findings from new, nationally representative surveys confirm that many of this book's propositions accurately describe the behavior of not merely graduate students but also, in many respects, average Americans. Consider each of the book's propositions about what people are likely to do.[1]

EMPIRICAL PROPOSITIONS

People Readily Replace Their Named Discussion Partners Quickly upon Entering New Contexts

I begin with the findings about the network elicited by the General Social Survey (GSS) instrument. We saw in Chapter 2 that students' core discussion network changed quickly after they entered their programs, as they came to interact regularly with new sets of people. Contrary to expectations, the most common pattern was not stability but turnover. Nevertheless, the graduate students, who were younger at age 25 than the average American, 37, may dispose of old confidants more quickly than people later in the life course. They might be quicker to trust others, slower to forgive a slight from an old friend, or generally more fickle. As people age, stabilize, and find a new family, their network of confidants may be much more stable, even if they change environments.[2]

Nationally representative data on older adults belie that idea. The National Social Life, Health, and Aging Project (NSHAP) is a nationally representative survey of more than 3,000 adults ages 57 to 85 first interviewed between 2005 and 2006. The same respondents were again interviewed five years later.[3] At both interviews, respondents were asked to report their core discussion networks—using the same question we asked the graduate students.

The most common experience, even among this group of stable adults often well past retirement age, was turnover. As sociologist Benjamin Cornwell reported in a recently released study, the "data reveal considerable change within these older adults' confidant networks over the 5-year study period. . . . Fully 81.6% of the sample added at least one new confidant between waves, whereas 73.5% lost at least one confidant."[4] The average respondent had 3.6 core discussion partners in the first wave, and added 1.9 and lost 1.5 by the second wave. Some of those losses were, not surprisingly, due to death. If we exclude those, the average respondent still lost

1.2 discussion members. In sum, their networks experienced substantial turnover.

Another new survey, this one focused on adults of all ages, reports similar findings. In 2014, sociologists Gerald Mollenhorst, Beate Völker, and Henk Flap published results from two waves of the Survey of the Social Networks of the Dutch. More than 1,000 adult residents of the Netherlands ages 18 to 65 were asked in 1999–2000 and again seven years later to report their core discussion network, as well as the people they turn to for practical help.[5] The authors reported an average 2.31 discussion partners in the first wave and 2.41 in the second. The authors found that "whereas the size and general outline of personal networks of confidants and practical helpers is considerably stable, about 70 percent of these confidants and practical helpers are replaced by other persons within seven years."[6]

These findings, though consistent with those among graduate students, are not dispositive. Although both the NSHAP and the Dutch survey asked their respondents the same question we asked graduate students, they both reinterviewed people after several years, rather than after 6 or 12 months. Furthermore, the two national surveys are not explicitly focused on respondents who have changed the contexts where they regularly interact with others.

Nevertheless, both surveys support the notion that changing the regular context of social interaction contributes to rapid turnover. Respondents to the NSHAP were asked explicitly why their former core discussion partners were no longer in the network. In a new recently released study, Cornwell and Edward Laumann report that the "most common reason respondents gave for why they did not name confidants again at W2 (23.4% of all losses) had to do with physical distance—either the respondent or the confidant moved, or it was determined that the confidant lived 'too far away' from the respondent."[7] The elders, as the graduate students, tended to replace discussion partners because they were no longer interacting with them regularly. The Dutch researchers also examined the reasons behind turnover and also found that contexts of interaction played a role. Consistent with the idea that people's networks change because altered routines change their opportunities to interact with others, the authors found that "52.9 percent of the relationships . . . were discontinued because of a lack of meeting opportunities."[8] Though these findings do not speak to the speed of change, they make clear that the opportunity to interact with others matters as much as how close they are.

In sum, the core discussion networks of people at all ages change most often as people experience transitions that alter those with whom they regularly interact.

People Are Not Close to Many in Their Core Discussion Network

But the more general conclusion of Chapter 2 was that many of those whom students named as confidants were weak ties. Recall that the original designers of the relevant question in the GSS proposed that the name generator would "elicit reasonably strong ties, with prominent representation of kin among those cited," rather than mere acquaintances.[9] Over time, as the survey question gained in popularity, the notion emerged that people will regularly discuss important matters only with those they are close to. As one later set of researchers put it: "While people can have many network members and even many friends, they do not tend to discuss important personal matters with every one of them, but only with those they really trust. We therefore use the word 'confidant' to indicate these core discussion network members."[10] Another set of researchers defined them as "people who are very close to us," adding: "The closer and stronger our tie with someone, the broader the scope of their support for us . . . and the greater the likelihood that they will provide major help in a crisis. . . . These are important people in our lives."[11]

These expectations clashed with the students' experiences. Though students often listed husbands, wives, and best friends when asked, word for word, the GSS question, they also included people with whom they were not close—people such as new roommates, classmates, and professors. Still, most people do not have professors or other professional advisers in their lives. Thus, it remains unclear whether, contrary to the students, adult Americans reserve discussing important matters "only with those" they are close to.

One piece of evidence from the 1980s helps provide an answer. Claude Fischer's survey of Northern Californians contained a precursor of the GSS question—it asked respondents to report with whom they discussed "personal matters," rather than "important matters." It also, separately, asked respondents whether they felt "especially close to" the people previously named in answer to this and other questions in the survey. Ronald Burt examined the survey and found that, of the named discussion partners, respondents felt close to 71%.[12] Stated differently, respondents were *not* close to just under to 30% of those they reported as regular discussion partners.

I asked a similar question of a national population in the new millennium. I recently commissioned the Core Networks and Important Alters (CNIA) survey, a study of over 2,000 online respondents with characteristics representative of Americans ages 18 and over (details discussed in Appendix B). One randomly selected half of respondents of the CNIA was asked to report their core discussion network. Next, the respondents were asked "two questions intended to capture explicitly those alters who are important to them (as opposed to the alters with whom they discussed important matters)."[13] They were asked to name people who were not in their family but important to them, and then, people in their family who were important to them. They could list up to 10 names in total. I then used the results to examine what proportion of the core discussion network consisted of people who were close or important to respondents.[14] I first reported these results in the journal *Social Networks*.[15]

The average respondent reported 1.7 core discussion partners, with a range of 0 to 5, and 4.2 important people in their lives. (Online surveys tend to generate slightly smaller core discussion networks, though they can also be designed to produce artificially larger-than-normal ones.[16]) Since respondents had far more important people in their lives than core discussion partners, there was little possibility that people who were important and also discussion partners were missed from the list of discussion partners.

In spite of this fact, 45.3% of core discussion partners were not people whom respondents considered important to them. Indeed, among core discussion partners, respondents included therapists, neighbors, coworkers, and advisers.[17] In other words, the average American adult is not close to nearly half the people reported as regular discussion partners. People certainly include their spouses and close friends among those they consider regular discussion partners—but they also include many nonintimates, in a pattern consistent with the students'.

The difference between the earlier results (~30% weak ties) and mine (~45% weak ties) may result from any of several factors. The surveys were collected in different eras (1970s vs. 2010s), of different populations (Northern Californians vs. Americans as a whole), and with slightly different question wordings ("personal matters" vs. "important matters"), among other differences. Nonetheless, the differences do not alter the basic conclusion: people report many weak ties as regular confidants.

A clue about why many discussion partners reported were not strong ties can be gleaned from a methodological study by Stefanie Bailey and Peter Marsden of what people understood when they were asked the GSS name generator instrument. The authors conducted cognitive interviews with 50 respondents wherein the latter were asked to talk through their answers aloud, explaining how they interpreted the question. The authors found that 13% interpreted the question as referring to the names of close or important alters, 28% interpreted it as referring to the people with whom they discussed general topics, and 43% interpreted the question literally, as referring to the people with whom they talked most regularly about important matters. The last two groups would include many weak ties for many people.[18]

Regardless, the overall conclusion remains: the existing surveys suggest that somewhere between 30% and 45% of the people in Americans' "core discussion networks" are not close friends and family.[19]

People Actually Confide Often in Individuals They Are Not Close To

Though these results are important, eliciting the core discussion network with the GSS instrument is not the best way to address the main question of this book—whom people actually talk to and why. This book's concern is not reconstructing a network but understanding behavior. Chapter 3 distinguished what students said from what they did. When asked whom they had actually talked to the last time they talked to someone about their graduate school or personal worries, somewhere between 4 and 6 times out of 10 the students talked to people *other* than those they had previously listed as their core discussion partners, and often described people to whom they were not close. Though the specific proportions were impossible to ascertain confidently with qualitative data—after all, that is not generally what such kinds of data are useful for—the proportions were too large to be dismissed as chance occurrences.

The worry is that such a pattern may not be present among other kinds of people. Graduate students, younger than the average adult, may be quicker to confide in people they were not close to. Furthermore, recall that many of the people they confided in were professors, and most people in most jobs do not have to interact with professors and formal advisers, people whose job description includes the responsibility to serve as confidants. The ability to confide in someone not close to them may be greater than in other contexts.

The CNIA survey provided a way to answer this question. In the survey, the other randomly selected half of the sample was asked a question that began as the GSS name generator did: "From time to time, most people discuss important matters with other people." However, respondents were then asked to recall the most recent time they actually talked to someone: "think about the last time you discussed something that was important to you. That time, what did you talk about?" The last question, which prompted respondents to report, in a few words, what they actually talked about, was crucial. It helped ensure that respondents recalled a specific event, rather than attempting to generalize from past experience. Finally, they were asked whom they talked to on that occasion. The result was a representative sample of last important discussions.

The respondents were then, as before, separately asked to name up to 10 people, family members and otherwise, they were close to.[20] The matter at hand is whether respondents had actually confided in their close friends and family. The results were unambiguous: 50.3% of those who had actually talked to someone about something important over the previous six months had done so with someone who was *not* important to the respondent. They had confided in neighbors, friends, professionals, coworkers, and even distant family members they did not feel close to.

That is, adult Americans had actually talked to someone not close to them *more than half* the time.

Does this finding contradict previous results from the GSS name generator?[21] Not necessarily. What this finding and those in the previous section show, instead, is that the old data should be interpreted in different ways, and that new questions about how people use their networks need answers. First, suppose that respondents to the standard name generator were completely accurate about whom they most regularly talked to. Even then, as shown earlier, interpreting the response as representing strong ties would be inaccurate on average for a substantial minority of ties.

Second, suppose that we limited our analysis to only respondents for whom 100% of the core discussion network is composed of strong ties. Even that group may have talked to those not close to them more than half the time they actually talked to anyone. Consider that the "core discussion network" is merely the name researchers gave to the set of people respondents report talking to most regularly—that is, the ones that over the previous six months they had talked to two, three, or more times. It is possible that, more than half the time respondents talked to anyone, they nonetheless talked to someone they had not repeatedly talked to, as would happen if they spend a lot of time in contexts with many different people to talk to about their problems. For example, a relatively chatty man might talk to his wife and to his brother more repeatedly than he talks to any given other individual, while still sharing his problems with any coworker, gym partner, church friend, commuter, barber, priest, or bartender he comes across. The core discussion network would consist of two close family members, but many more people would have served as actual confidants. One can both talk to a few more repeatedly than to most and talk most frequently to people other than the few.

Thus, understanding who people talk to and why requires a shift in focus, not just reconstructing their core network but following their behavior. Chapters 4 through 6 did so among students, and identified three patterns of behavior with multiple constitutive elements—the avoidance of strong ties, the pursuit of cognitive empathy, and the incidental or spontaneous response to opportunity. How prevalent are these patterns in other populations?

People Often Avoid Those They Are Close To

We saw in Chapter 4 that many graduate students explicitly avoided the people they were close to, running counter to the oft-repeated idea that people consistently prefer to confide in intimates. Yet graduate students might be especially prone to experience the ambivalence that encourages them to avoid their parents or closest friends. They might be at an age where people tend to seek independence from their family. Their local friends, often other graduate students, might be potential competitors in ways that complicate the relationships. For these and other reasons, adults in general may be less prone than graduate students to avoid intimate ties when looking for a confidant.

The evidence generally belies these ideas. One suggestive piece of evidence derives from a body of work showing that people feel ambivalence toward close friends and family.[22] Karen Fingerman, Elizabeth Hay, and Kira Birditt asked 187 adults across the age spectrum to name, separately, the people who mattered to their lives and the people "they considered problematic."[23] Each could vary in degree. Using a diagram, they asked respondents to classify the former into three categories: those "to whom they felt so close that they could not imagine life without them," those "to whom they felt close but not quite that close," and those "to whom they felt not quite that close but who were still important in their lives."[24] They asked respondents to classify the problematic relations into those "who bother them quite a bit," those who "bother them somewhat," and those "who bother them occasionally or slightly."[25] Importantly, people could be listed in both categories. The respondents separately identified each person as a "spouse," "close friend," "roommate," "acquaintance," and the like.

The average respondent reported about 20 names, which the authors classified into three types of relationships: close, problematic, and ambivalent (i.e., in both lists). Twenty-two percent of names, on average, were ambivalent. Most important, the bottom line was unambiguous: "closer relationships were *more* likely to be considered ambivalent than were less close relationships."[26] In fact, "tests revealed that relationships with sons or daughters, spouses, siblings, and parents were all more likely to be considered ambivalent than friendships and other family ties. Indeed, ties to spouses were considered with greater ambivalence than most other ties."[27] The study confirmed an obvious but oft-ignored point, that closeness often creates complications, giving people good reason to avoid strong ties for given topics.[28]

More direct evidence of avoidance can be culled from the CNIA survey. Assessing this evidence is not straightforward, given several of the biases inherent in surveys that I have discussed through the book. Consider one broad measure. In the survey, for each of the people they had earlier described as important in their lives, respondents were asked the following: "How comfortable would you feel discussing a private issue regarding [*topic*] with each person?" (Recall that the average respondent had 4.2 people they considered important to their lives.) The question was asked three times per potential confidant, once for each of the following topics: "your family life," "your work," and "your health." The survey asked about each topic separately and allowed respondents to rank the comfort level on a scale of 1 to 10. Respondents reported being highly comfortable with their important alters, with averages of 8.4, 8.8, and 8.5 for family, work, and health, respectively. Yet high rates are to be expected, given that the topics are broad enough to admit many specific circumstances.[29] Furthermore, there is normative pressure to report positive relations to those important to one's lives.[30]

But their actual willingness to confide regularly in those people was telling. Since the average respondent reported 1.7 core discussion partners but 4.2 people they were close to, the average person decided not to include 2.5 of their closest friends and family as the people they regularly approach with important matters. Indeed, although they could have named up to five people as regular discussion partners, and had on average more than four close people in their lives, they opted to name fewer than two confidants. Stated differently, the average American does not approach regularly the *majority* of people he or she is close to.[31]

People Are Willing to Forgo Closeness for Empathy

But the students were not merely avoiding their close or regular confidants. We saw in Chapter 5 that many of them, motivated by the pursuit of cognitive empathy, deliberately approached people who, even if not close friends or family, were likely to understand their concern as they saw it. Still, the experience of graduate students may, again, differ from those of other populations. Many of the school-related matters that concerned graduate students had rather specialized needs, the kind for which an expert or otherwise well-informed peer might be especially appropriate. Note that a lot of the topics were related to their work, that is, highly specialized academic research. Considering that when the students were asked about their worries they were asked to focus first on the graduate experience and then on life in general, it is not difficult to imagine that the answers to the former might center on these specialized kinds of needs. The issue at hand is thus twofold: whether people in general exhibit a strong preference for potential confidants who seem especially likely to understand their concerns, and whether such a preference is a reason they are willing to forgo people they are close to when they actually confide in others.

The notion that people exhibit a preference for those relevant to their concerns assumes that people approach different individuals for different topics. That assumption has been supported in several studies focused on discussion matters.[32] Peter Bearman and Paolo Parigi found that respondents to their North Carolina survey exhibited "topic-alter dependency" when confiding in others, meaning that whom they talked to depended on the topic at hand. For example, people talked with spouses about money and finances but with relatives about their relationships.[33] Similarly, in a recent study using nationally representative data on 2,061 adults ages 18 and over, sociologist Matthew Brashears found strong associations between the topic people discussed and the particular role in respondents' lives that people played, with the roles being "parent, sibling, spouse/romantic partner, child, other family member, coworker, friend, neighbor, and other non-kin."[34]

However, what I uncovered among graduate students is more precise and more difficult to determine on a large scale—that people confided in those particularly likely to empathize with their predicament—and the existing surveys have not provided that evidence. They have not even provided evidence for the less exacting idea that people discuss important matters with those who are somehow relevant to the matter. For example, consider Bearman and Parigi's finding that people tend to talk about finances with their spouses. While it might make sense ex post facto that people will talk about money with their husband or wife, it is certainly not clear that, had we first tried to predict with whom people will talk about finances, we a priori would have hypothesized "spouses." The idea that people would talk to their spouses about their finances only makes sense after the fact, once one has learned about the discovery. But if people made their decision based primarily on who seems most likely to understand the problem, then a priori it would have made better sense to predict that they talk about finances to others with financial problems, or with bankers, or with finance experts.

The CNIA survey provides some of the needed evidence. Recall that students at times found people who could empathize directly because of their similar attributes, situations, or positions; people who could somewhat empathize, albeit less perfectly, because of their previous direct experience; and people who could generally understand the students' predicament because of their indirect experience, having talked to others about similar concerns. The CNIA survey cannot confirm the first several of these, but it can provide two forms of evidence relevant to the last.

First, it asked them. Those respondents who had been asked whom they talked to the last time they discussed something important were subsequently asked why. The answer? Twenty percent of the time they reported being motivated by the person's experience with the topic—respondents replied that the person was "an expert" or "particularly insightful on the topic." This figure, 20%, is high, but it is not the majority response. Indeed, respondents reported 45.1% of the time that they were motivated by the fact that the confidant was "good to talk to about any topic." Nevertheless, when they were motivated by the person's experience with the topic, most of the time—59%—they talked to someone they were not close to.[35] That is, when Americans reported approaching people because of their experience with the topic, they tended to approach weak ties.

A second form of evidence comes not from respondents' statements but from their behavior. Did they actually approach people experienced with the particular topics they were concerned about? Since the survey asked people to report what topic they had talked about in their last discussion of something important, it is possible to answer this question specifically. Even so, providing an answer is difficult.[36] When designing the survey, we did not know in advance what particular topics people would talk about, since respondents, as you will recall, provided the topics in their own words; for this reason, we did not know in advance what specific types of persons to indicate. For example, if someone was going to report "fitness and exercise" as the topic they talked about, we would want to have entered "physical trainer" as a kind of alter for them to talk to. Without knowing what topic all our respondents will have most recently talked about, it is impossible to list all the kinds of people who would likely understand something about what the respondents needed to discuss.

Still, the survey did include questions on whether the people respondents spoke to were one of a wide array of types of people that national surveys such as the GSS regularly ask about. With a wide enough array, we can reasonably determine whether a person is more appropriate than normal. For example, for problems involving health, we can determine whether they talk to doctors more than they typically talk to doctors. The survey asked whether the people they talked to were doctors or help professionals, advisers, and many others, making it possible to assess the question. That rationale provides great leverage into our question.

First, consider what average Americans found to be important topics. Recall that the students reported worrying primarily about work, family (including love life), social life, and finances.[37] In the CNIA survey, the average American talked to others about a wide array of large and small issues, including "drug abuse," an "argument with a relative," "financial problems," "working out and bettering my lifestyle," "religion," "changing careers," "death," "depression," "my mother passing away," "losing weight," and "how the government is ruining our life for their own greedy ass." I classified the responses into 12 topics that were then checked blindly for reliability by a separate researcher.[38] The five most common topics of discussion in the national survey were family (27% of the time), work (20%), personal finances (18%), health (14%), and happiness and life goals (13%).[39] The top four of these are largely consistent with the students' major worries, with the notable exception that students worried a lot less about health (they are clearly younger).[40] The main topics of discussion in the CNIA survey are also remarkably similar to those reported by Brashears in his national study. After conducting a separate survey, eliciting the topics through a slightly different method, and coding the topics independently, Brashears reported that the four most common topics people reported as important matters they had discussed were finances, family, "health/medical care," and work.[41] Adult Americans tend to find the same kinds of things important to talk about.

The issue is whether for the five main revealed topics in the CNIA survey—family, work, finances, health, and happiness and life goals—people talked to those who would be particularly experienced with the topic. The survey inquired about such confidants—kin members for the topic of family; coworkers for work; health professionals for health; and personal advisers for happiness and life goals. (Unfortunately, the survey did not ask whether the person they had talked to was a banker, an accountant, or someone otherwise appropriate for personal finances.) Respondents talked to some of these people more than others. The question is whether they talked to any of these people more often than they normally would when the topic was relevant to the person, which is what we would expect if they were pursuing those especially likely to understand.

With one exception, they did. When the topic was family, people talked to kin members as much as they normally do. However, when the topic was work, they were 85% more likely to talk to coworkers than they typically talk to coworkers; when it was health, 77% more likely to talk to health professionals than they typically do; when it was happiness and life goals, 72% more likely to talk to personal advisers than they typically do. Statistical models that adjusted for demographic characteristics of both respondents confirmed the significance, direction, and general magnitude of the results, and are available in Appendix B.[42] Respondents exhibited a clear and distinct bias toward topic-relevant confidants.

In sum, Americans do seem to approach confidants motivated by whether the person is especially likely to understand their predicament. They express less motivation from that factor than from others, such as whether the person is generally good to talk to. Yet, as the graduate students were, when Americans are motivated by the confidant's ability to understand their problem, they are more likely to approach weak than strong ties. Furthermore, regardless of their expressed motivations, their behavior is unambiguous. For any given topic other than family, they are far more likely to talk to those experienced in the topic than they normally talk to those people.

People Will Often Confide in Whomever Is Around

Chapter 6 uncovered that graduate students often did not deliberate much on whom to talk to, instead responding to opportunities as they emerged in the context of interacting with others. While they sometimes knew precisely whom they would confide in, they often acted incidentally, just selecting the person who happened to be before them, or even spontaneously, deciding to ask for help in the midst of an interaction. Indeed, their actions reflected that they were often "thinking fast," as Daniel Kahneman has put it, when deciding to ask for help. The question, then, is twofold—whether individuals who are not graduate students simply turn to people because the latter were easily accessible, and also, more precisely, whether they activate their networks incidentally and spontaneously, rather than just in reflective fashion.

The CNIA survey provides evidence in answer to the first of these questions.[43] First, consider respondents' reports about their motivations. The respondents who were asked to recall their last important discussion and whom they had talked to on that occasion were also asked why. Fifteen percent responded, as their primary motivation, "because [the person] was available when I needed to discuss the topic." That is, when forced to present a single reason they approached whom they approached, people reported availability almost as often (14.6% of the time) as they reported relevance (19.6%). That answer may indicate that people just turned to whomever was available, but it may also indicate that people turned to the person who was available only among those they were close to. The evidence is consistent with the former: when respondents reacted to availability, they were far more likely—59%—to talk to weak than strong ties. While neither of these facts is dispositive, both are consistent with the idea that Americans are often responsive to opportunities, speaking to those who happen to be available, and that this pattern might help explain why they confide in people they are not close to.

Still, we should not expect the average person, regardless of circumstances, to confide in others who happened to be available as frequently as graduate students did, unless they also had ample opportunities to interact with others. Instead, such practices should be common among individuals whose routine activities involve interacting with many people who are potential helpers for the kinds of problems they have. These would include not only graduate students in academic departments but also regular workers in offices, hospitals, and police precincts and institutionalized people in prisons, asylums, or care homes—contexts where repeated interactions with others in similar circumstances are unavoidable. That is, the more such opportunities individuals have, the more likely they should be to have been motivated by availability—and the more likely they should be to confide in people they are not close to.

The CNIA survey provides indirect evidence in a national population.[44] Outside of work and home, people spend most of their time in the social, voluntary, and political organizations, clubs, and associations that are characteristic of contemporary life, organizations such as churches, professional societies, sports clubs, and the like.[45] Few people spend as much time interacting with others in those organizational contexts as they do either at work or at home. Still, people vary in how much they do, and if people are responsive to how easily accessible others are, then that variation should matter. The CNIA survey asked about membership in 15 such organizations, based on a standard question asked of Americans regularly by the GSS. These included churches, professional societies, sports groups, and others.[46] Twenty percent of respondents were not members of any organization; 50.2%, of one; 29.7%, of two or more. I then examined whether such membership was related to their behavior.

The results were consistent with the idea that mere accessibility matters. The more organizations respondents were involved in, the more likely it was that, during their last discussion, they had approached whom they had approached primarily because of availability: for members of no organizations, 11.1% of the time; members of one, 16.4%; members of two or more, 17.9%. The more opportunities Americans had to interact with others regularly, the more likely they were to decide whom to confide in based primarily on availability.

While this evidence is consistent with the idea that people respond to how accessible potential confidants are, it is insufficient evidence of the prevalence of incidental or spontaneous decision making, since respondents did not indicate specifically how much they were planning on approaching their confidants before they did so. In this respect, a study of the experiences of college students is instructive. I recently commissioned an online survey on a panel of more than 2,000 college students equally divided among males and females and with equal proportions of blacks, Latinos, Asians, and whites. The Resources and Favors among College Students (RFCS) survey aimed to capture how deliberatively students had decided to seek help when they had recently received it (for details, see Appendix B).

Students were asked to recall the last time they sought someone to talk to for help on a math or economics problem, on a paper they were writing, or on a problem with a roommate; whom they asked for help; and why. Though this kind of support differs from discussing a personal matter, the results are still instructive. A similar proportion reported that their primary reason to have talked to whom they did was availability: 14.4%, 19.2%, and 23.0% for math, paper, and roommate problems, respectively.[47]

In addition, the respondents in the RFCS survey were also asked explicitly how much they had planned on asking the person they asked. Their options were "I was planning or asking this person," which indicates reflective activation; "I was planning on asking someone, not necessarily this person," incidental activation; and "I was not planning on asking anyone," spontaneous activation. Since the problems are highly specialized in nature, one would expect the majority of decisions to have been reflective. Still, notably high proportions were not: for math problems, 23.0% were incidental and 5.9% spontaneous; for paper problems, 27.9% and 8.1%, respectively; for roommate problems, 25.4% and 10.3%, respectively. In sum, the students had not planned on getting help from whom they did about a third of the time. College students often deliberated, but they also, quite often, asked for help on the spot.[48]

CONCLUSION

The existing surveys cannot perfectly test each of the book's empirical propositions precisely as stated. That task will ultimately require more detailed data on the composition of people's networks, on their decisions about support, and on their routine social interactions. It will require data collected repeatedly over time. And it will probably require more data on other national and cultural contexts, since Americans' characteristic openness may well affect their willingness to confide in people they are not especially close to.[49]

Nonetheless, the evidence suggests that the graduate students' actions with respect to confiding in others were not unique. Though they seemed to worry more about work and much less about their health than the average US adult, neither of these is surprising. The first year in graduate school, like the first year in a new job, is stressful, and the need to perform to new and not fully understood standards will often create the need to talk; and the students, who were younger than the average adult, had not yet experienced many of the health problems that people face over their lifetimes. Still, these differences in circumstances did not seem to translate into differences in responses.

Qualifiers notwithstanding, the bottom line seems clear: having examined all publicly available, large-scale US surveys that could speak to the major empirical propositions describing the students' behavior, one can reasonably conclude that, though the first year in graduate school is a unique experience, the students' responses to their circumstances were not. On the matter of confiding in others, adult Americans, like the graduate students, respond to their particular difficulties in multiple but consistent ways: they confide in family and close friends but often take pains to avoid them, they readily replace those they regularly confide in, they often pursue those likely to understand their predicament, and they willingly approach people they are not actually close to, at times doing so without giving the matter much thought.

CHAPTER 8
Theoretical Generalizability

The common-sense notion that people reserve their serious worries for close friends and family has been proposed in one way or another by thinkers as different as Adam Smith, Immanuel Kant, and contemporary network theorists.[1] Nevertheless, it is not supported by our data: Americans seem to replace confidants easily, to avoid strong ties often, and to approach weak ones readily, even without giving the matter much thought. Why?

I argue the reason is that Americans react to context, respond to expectations, seek empathy, and act on opportunities far more than they worry how close they are to potential confidants. The many elements of this argument amount to an alternative perspective on how people decide whom to talk to when they need someone to talk to. The pages that follow describe that perspective and discuss its implications. To be clear, the perspective is not a comprehensive theory of how people confide in others; it is a set of related assumptions that, by prioritizing practice over structure, introduces a new and different set of questions. In addition, the perspective does not fundamentally contradict the structural approach; instead, it brings to light important limits in structural analysis, ultimately helping to improve the latter's quality and depth.

The chapter is divided into three sections. The first examines the status quo. It probes why the otherwise powerful structural theory about what strong ties do failed to account for what the book has reported. That theory is epitomized in the pithy rule of thumb that while weak ties offer information strong ties provide support, an idea so widespread it has reached popular culture.[2] The section shows that the rule of thumb failed because the assumptions informing it are often contrary to lived experience.[3] The second section summarizes the alternative perspective. It presents three broad assumptions, each of which answers a question about how people decide whom to turn to for support: whom they consider, what they take into account, and how they make the decision. The alternative, practice-based perspective seeks to pave the way for stronger theories of how people mobilize others for support. The third section applies the perspective to specific situations beyond those of graduate students. It pinpoints three particular propositions from the book and assesses their ability to explain how doctors, soldiers, teachers, and others facing difficulties such as clinical depression, sexual victimization, and the fear of coming out, decided whom to turn to for support. It shows that shifting from structure to practice broadens our view of how networks work.

A STRUCTURAL THEORY REVISITED

Strong Ties for Support

I begin with the status quo. The rule of thumb about the separate benefits of strong and weak ties derives from Granovetter's seminal paper.[4] Granovetter believed that strong ties tend to be interconnected, such that a person's close friends will tend to be friends among themselves. (Much of what I argue will depend on how "strength" is defined, and I will follow the convention of conceiving strength as closeness.[5]) Since the strength of one tie is thereby reinforced by the others, strong ties will tend to be resilient, reliable, and supportive. But if strong ties tend to be connected, then only weak ties are likely to be bridges between networks of strongly tied groups and their separate pools of information. For this reason, weak ties will tend to be a great source of information; strong ties, of support.

The rule of thumb rests on the belief that strong ties will be interconnected. In more precise terms, it depends on the belief that in the trio of actors A, B, and C, if A and B are strongly tied and A and C are strongly tied, then B and C are likely also to be strongly tied. For B and C to be weakly tied would be uncommon, Granovetter argued, and for them to be not tied at all would be rare. In fact, he called the latter condition, with self-aware exaggeration, "the forbidden triad."

Granovetter arrived at this conclusion based on three premises. First, he reasoned that "stronger ties involve larger time commitments"[6]—they require time to maintain, and time is limited. Thus, if A spends a lot of time with B, and with C, then B and C will also likely spend a lot of time together. Second, Granovetter extrapolated from the principle of homophily, the well-known fact that people tend to resemble their close friends.[7] If

A resembles both B and C, then B and C will likely resemble each other. If so, then B and C are likely to become friends as well. Finally, Granovetter reasoned—echoing Georg Simmel and building on psychologists Fritz Heider and Theodore Newcomb—that the psychological need for balance in one's relationships would contribute to the outcome.[8] "If strong ties A-B and A-C exist," he proposed, "and if B and C are aware of one another, anything short of a positive tie would introduce 'psychological strain' into the situation, since C will want his own feelings to be congruent with those of his good friend, A, and similarly, for B and *his* friend, A."[9] Granovetter believed it would be difficult for A to maintain strong ties to B and to C with these two not being close, or even worse, disliking each other. The triad, therefore, will tend toward closure.

Four decades later, one remains struck by the elegance of Granovetter's reasoning. But the worth of a deduction depends on the soundness of its premises. And the soundness of a theoretical premise, in social science, turns on its ability to accurately capture how people think, interact with others, and make decisions in their everyday lives. The lives explored in this book were those of students entering the first year in their programs. How well did the premises fare?

Strong Ties in Practice

Consider, first, the notion that A would have difficulty spending much time with two people without the two also coming into contact. The notion appeals to common sense because time is finite. But we noted in this book that interaction always happens in some space, and spaces may affect the allocation of time. Recall Catherine, the former corporate worker with spouse and child. Catherine saw her husband at home, where they raised their child together, and her colleagues at work, where she took classes. She could therefore easily spend a lot of time with her husband and also with her closest colleague with the two of them never interacting.[10] When A spends time with B and C in different spaces, there is little reason to expect B and C to ever interact.

The second rationale was the notion that if A resembles both B and C, then the latter two should resemble each other. The notion makes sense because homophily is ubiquitous. But we saw that students could resemble different people in different ways. While Diana, the student unsure whether she fit her departmental culture, resembled her colleagues in their academic interests, she resembled her hometown friends in their "anti-academy" progressive politics. Her closest student peers and her friends in Los Angeles had little in common. This condition was not out of the ordinary, since there is no such thing as "all-purpose homophily." When A resembles B and C in different ways, there is little reason to expect B and C to resemble each other.

The third was the notion that A would feel "psychological strain" from being in a forbidden triad. The notion makes sense because balance in one's life is generally less stressful than imbalance. But we saw that what people expect of their relationships depends on formal and informal institutions, which may make such strains unlikely. Recall Oscar, who roomed with his brother Ned and would become close to his adviser Gerald. Oscar felt no "strain" that Ned and Gerald were not close, because nothing requires one's brothers and professors to be friends. In fact, for Ned and Gerald to be close might even be peculiar. Family and profession are separate institutions with different and separate expectations, few of which include the comingling of their members. When A is tied to B and C via separate institutions, there is little reason for B and C to expect to be connected.

In sum, though each of the premises is intuitive in the abstract, each is also contradicted by many lived experiences. Thus, the principle that strong ties will be interconnected depends far more than typically acknowledged on particular scope conditions. When A regularly interacts with B and C in different contexts, resembles B and C in different ways, or is tied to B and C via separate institutions, we should not expect B and C to be strongly tied. In fact, when all conditions hold, we should not expect B and C—forbidden-triad expectations notwithstanding—to be tied at all.

A Limited Rule of Thumb

An example from the General Social Survey (GSS) will illustrate the point. Suppose we consider those respondents who, like Catherine, were married, and who thought of their spouse B and of a coworker C as confidants. Assume, for the benefit of the rule of thumb, that respondents are close to B and to C.[11] If the structural theory were correct, then the B–C tie would be strong among most respondents. Nevertheless, consider a simple unweighted count: Of the 110 B–C pairs in which one is a spouse and one a coworker, only 16% are strong ties; 65% are weak ties and 18% are strangers (Figure 8.1). There are *more* supposedly forbidden triads than closed strong-tie triads, in precise contrast to the theory.[12]

But the theory is not universally wrong; it merely depends far more on context than researchers have acknowledged. Suppose we consider those

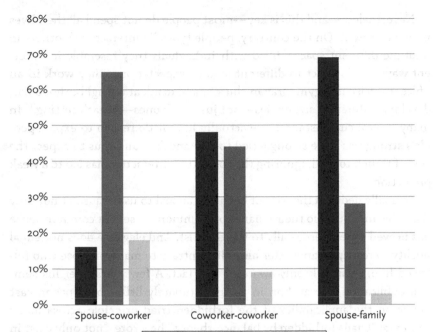

Figure 8.1. Strength of the *B–C* tie, depending on type of alter.
Source: 2004 General Social Survey, author's tabulations.

cases wherein both *B* and *C* are coworkers, and thus likely interact with *A* regularly in the same space. In the GSS, when *B* and *C* are coworkers, 48% are strong ties, 44% are weak ties, and only 9% are strangers, just as Granovetter would predict. And when *B* and *C* are a spouse and another family member, 69% are strong ties, 28% are weak ties, and 3% are strangers. Within a single space of interaction, the forbidden triad principle works largely as Granovetter theorized (see Figure 8.1).

The illustration makes clear how much the principle can depend on a shared interaction context.[13] Among a group of students in the same school, or family members in the same household, or managers in the same firm, if *A* spends time with *B* and with *C*, then the latter two are, in fact, likely to encounter each other often, to resemble each other in the ways they resemble *A*, and to feel uncomfortable with a structurally imbalanced relationship. In a single space, conditions are optimal for the forbidden triad principle to work. I would not be surprised if in the body of conflicting evidence evaluating the paper, much of the support for this specific principle derived from sociocentric studies in which networks are confined to a single context.[14]

Nevertheless—and this is key—most people do not spend all their lives in one context.[15] On the contrary, people typically interact with others in multiple different spaces, filled with individuals they resemble in different ways, and subject to different sets of expectations. They work in an office, exercise in a gym, pray in church, and drink at a neighborhood bar, developing different strong ties—not just weak ones—in each setting.[16] In many typical circumstances, we actually have little reason to expect people's strong ties to be strongly tied to one another, and thus to expect the rule of thumb to hold. Ignoring the context of interaction has led to a weak prediction.

Formally deduced theories of behavior appeal to us because of not only their elegance but also their reliance on common sense. But common sense has proved a treacherous ally to the theorist. And elegance does not equal fidelity to reality. Granovetter himself, contrary to many of those who followed him, seemed keenly aware of this fact. A few years after his seminal publication, the author, in an unfortunately little-noted paper, cast doubt on the applicability of the forbidden triad principle across many contexts: "triads forbidden by balance theory," he wrote, "not only exist in macrolevel context[s], but have . . . stabilizing roles in political conflict."[17] That is, whether this principle works depends on the context. But this qualification was lost to history, as a sensible and targeted proposition became an oft-repeated theorem and eventually, in the eyes of many, including in the popular media, a presumed social fact—that weak ties offer information and strong ties provide support.

Today we have reason to step back and theorize anew. Fully understanding how people decide whom to talk to requires a perspective not deduced from first principles but derived from lived experience. It requires openness to both inductive methods and qualitative data. And it requires asking entirely different questions.

FROM STRUCTURE TO PRACTICE

To understand how people turn to others for support, I propose a shift in perspective. The shift can be expressed in three assumptions about how the process operates that prioritize practice over structure. To be clear, I did not deduce the assumptions from first principles; I induced them from empirical observation.[18] I derived them from the students' experiences and behavior, and then confirmed with national data that their behavior was consistent with that of American adults. The assumptions help account for that behavior. Thus, the assumptions do not represent the theoretical model from which this project began; based entirely on a close engagement with the data, they represent how future projects, I believe, may move forward. The assumptions answer three questions about how people decide whom to talk to: whom people consider, what they take into account, and how they make the decision.

Whom They Consider

First, I assume that *the pool of individuals from which people decide whom to confide in is not merely the few in their network of support but also the many in their routine interactions.* As we have seen, though people are embedded in a network structure, they are also immersed in a steady stream of interactions, in a roughly consistent but constantly changing set of individuals encountered in their daily routines. Most of these ties are weak in nature. But because people are willing to turn to both weak and strong ties with the matters that concern them, everyone they encounter, in each of their contexts, becomes a potential confidant.

The two metaphors, the network of ties and the stream of interactions, provide an instructive contrast. The first invokes a net, the small group of friends and family that people believe will be there to catch them in moments of need. This net is important, because people in fact rely on it and because believing it to exist provides a sense of safety. But in the everyday flow of interaction people often find themselves relying on those who happen to be before them—the co-worker at the office, the runner at the gym, the neighbor at the social club, the clients at the barbershop, the prayer at the pew, and more—regardless of whether they thought of these as part of their social safety net. In practice, people draw sustenance from anywhere in their stream.

Few factors play a greater role in the composition of the stream itself than the formal organizations in which people participate routinely, the firms, hospitals, social clubs, schools, neighborhood restaurants, churches, barbershops, beauty salons, and other contexts where people spend most of their time.[19] Routine organizations provide two things: a space for interaction, via the hallways, dining halls, conference rooms, lobbies, waiting areas, water stations, and other physical places that make interaction possible and shape its composition; and a set of norms and rules to regulate interaction, via the expectations about hours of participation, waiting times, level of engagement, and nature of activities that affect who does what with whom.[20] Routine organizations are the most important context of social interaction, a nearly universal aspect of ordinary experience.

And when people's routine contexts change—as occurs when they start school, or get promoted, or marry, or bear children, or change churches, or divorce, or get evicted, or enter or leave prison, or emigrate, or retire—so will their regular confidants.[21] People's true pool of confidants is everyone they run into.

This shift in focus from the network of support to the social interactions is important for three reasons. First, the number of individuals people encounter over the course of their everyday activities is far larger than the number they consider their network of support. This condition requires—both ontologically and methodologically—a conception of "the network" far more expansive than is common. Whom people decide to call their confidants is probably less important than whom they actually encounter. Second, note that a stream, unlike a pool—to stretch the metaphor to its limits—changes constantly. To paraphrase Heraclitus, the particular stream a person will step into at any given time is ultimately unpredictable.[22] If so, there is no practical tool with which a scientist can reconstruct the vast number of true potential confidants by asking. There is no name generator that can reproduce, except after the fact, that an actor decided to confide in a stranger at a train station or in a distal colleague at a miscellaneous conference who also happened to be in the midst of a divorce. Third, as a result, the scientist hoping to understand these decisions will need to make room for analyses that begin not with the network but with the action, that seek to reconstruct decisions after they take place, and that try to understand the contexts in which people interact with others. To understand mobilization, network analysis must expand its scope.

What They Take Into Account

Second, I assume that *to the extent people deliberate on whom to talk to, what they consider is less the strength of the tie than its inherent expectations, and less how well the confidant is known than how well the confidant can empathize.* When people reflect on whether to confide in someone, they likely weigh the expected gain and expected harm. The common-sense view that people prefer those they are close to derives in part from the fact that confiding in others carries risk, and strong ties mitigate uncertainty; a close friend or family member is known well enough that the odds of being harmed can be assumed to be low. But the mitigation of risk and the expected gains or harms can be shaped by issues more important than the strength of the relation.

Specifically, as we have seen, people weigh issues other than closeness to assess the expected harm, they weigh especially heavily the value of the expected gain, and they include in their assessment the risk of harming the relationship. These factors reduce the relative advantages strong ties would have over weak ones, and reflect a kind of assessment in which strength is not the central issue at hand. To understand more clearly the role of these factors, consider their separate operation at the level of the tie and the level of the confidant.

At the level of the tie: People appear to consider less the strength of the tie than the expectations derived from its (a) institutional mediation and its (b) emotional reciprocity. Institutional mediation is the extent to which the norms or rules of an organization, profession, or other formal or near-formal arrangement govern the expectations underlying the tie.[23] For example, the ties between two coworkers, two spouses, a teacher and a student, a therapist and a client, and a parent and a child are subject to institutional expectations about appropriate behavior. These expectations may be explicit, as in an office's policy against sexual harassment or a teacher's requirement to listen to a student; or implicit, as in two parishioners anticipated kindness toward each other or a parent's assumed responsibility toward a child. They do not depend on whether the tie is weak or strong. Since most relationships are either formally or near-formally institutionally mediated, such expectations are inherent in most ties. And since institutional expectations shape the topics appropriate for conversation and the presumed level of support, they can weigh heavily in the decision of one party to confide in the other.

Emotional reciprocity is the extent to which the two people in the tie are mutual confidants. The tie between best friends is often, though not always, emotionally reciprocal; the tie between a therapist and a patient rarely is. When a tie is not emotionally reciprocal, the recipient of emotional support is typically expected to reciprocate in some other form, such as payment, a service, or overt appreciation. Though people typically know they must reciprocate, they may not always know how. If expectations are clear, they may weigh heavily as either benefits or drawbacks in the decision to seek help; if they are ambiguous, they alter a person's sense of the uncertainty involved in the decision. In both scenarios, the reciprocal expectations that characterize the tie also shape the decision.

At the level of the confidant: People appear to consider less how well the confidant is known than how well the confidant can empathize. People tend to believe that they are rationally self-protective, that they would avoid the unnecessary risk of confiding in someone not well known. But people need confidants when they are worried, and being worried is not an emotionally neutral state; it is a state of need or desire, where the expected gain from a potentially risky action weighs heavier than it normally would.[24] The value of empathy relative to closeness is much greater in the difficult times when people need to talk. For especially unique worries, the desire for empathetic understanding appears to surpass even other obvious priorities, such as sympathy or niceness. I suspect that the complexities of the contemporary world have created conditions in which personal experience may be increasingly unique and, thus, the yearning to be understood especially powerful.

The ideas I have sketched here do not represent a full listing of the factors that people consider when they deliberate on whom to talk to. The point is that when people reflect on whom to talk to, the strength of the relation will probably weigh less heavily than typically believed, because institutional and reciprocal expectations, and the needs associated with the pursuit of a confidant, strongly shape a person's sense of the potential harms and gains. It is not surprising that adult Americans, in their last important discussion, were as likely to have turned to weak as to strong ties. In the battery of issues that people consider, the tie's strength level does not appear especially important. In this way, too, therefore, network analysis must expand its scope.

How They Decide

Third, I assume that *although people must always decide whether to confide in others, they do not always decide through the same cognitive process.* Most theories of motivated action in the study of networks of support have proposed that people make decisions through a single process, such as the rational weighing of costs and benefits or the strategic matching of topics with potential confidants. As I have shown, people clearly sometimes deliberate on the expected gains and harm from deciding to approach or avoid a confidant. I argue, however, that the extent of deliberation in the decision-making process is heterogenous across situations. As we have seen, sometimes people deliberate; sometimes they do not.

The notion that any single process is at work in all circumstances is difficult to defend at this juncture in the development of the social sciences, where abundant evidence in psychology, sociology, and the field of judgment and decision-making suggests that people act at times deliberatively and at times intuitively.[25] In this book I found evidence of one particular form of heterogeneity, the sequence of seeking, selection, and activation decisions: at times, people decide to seek help, next select whom to talk to, and then approach that confidant; other times, they make one or more of these decisions in the midst of an interaction with the person who turns out to be the confidant. In different circumstances, people make different decisions—but also *make decisions differently.*

Psychologists have shown that this kind of heterogeneity is the natural result of the limits of the mind. Since weighing options before a decision requires mental work, the mind has good reason to take shortcuts, and it will do so, often.[26] It is simply not possible to reflect on every decision before making it; it is not always even possible to consciously decide whether to take shortcuts. Many decisions about whom to talk to will simply happen intuitively.

A key role for sociologists is to capture and unpack how the context of interaction contributes to the process. Intuitive decisions about confiding in another are always responses, in the moment, to a social interaction. As a result, they cannot be captured by reconstructing network structure; they require qualitative and quantitative methods geared at understanding what people were doing, with whom, and in what context, when they decided to talk. In this sense, too, finally, network analysis must expand its scope.

These three broad assumptions do not constitute a theory; they merely outline a perspective, developed throughout the book, which asks different kinds of questions about how people decide whom to confide in.[27] Their contrast to a structural perspective is sketched in Table 8.1. Standard network analysis calls attention to the structure of people's networks, to the strength or weakness of the ties, and to the implications of this structure for people's behavior. It has shown that people will refer only to a few individuals as their regular discussion partners. And it has demonstrated that the networks in which people are embedded ultimately affect their behavior and well-being. The alternative perspective calls attention to what people do in practice, to the contexts in which they do it, and to the expectations affecting their relationships. It has shown that whom people call their confidants does not reflect in full whom they confide in. And it has demonstrated that people's ties are themselves embedded in contexts of interaction that affect their decisions.

The implications of the practice-based perspective can be seen in its particular propositions about why people behave as they do. In what follows

Table 8.1. TWO APPROACHES

	Networks and Structure (Tradition)	Networks in Practice (This Book)
Main assumptions		
	Actors are embedded in networks whose characteristics shape their behavior	Actors are immersed in interactions whose contexts shape their decisions
	Tie and whole network characteristics are important	Expectations and context of interaction are important
		The decision-making process is heterogeneous across situations
Core elements		
Point of departure	Network, individual	Individual, decision
Key tie characteristics	Strength	Institutional mediation, emotional reciprocity
Key quality sought	Closeness	Cognitive empathy
Decisions	Not a focus	Reflective, incidental, or spontaneous
Questions asked		
About context	Characteristics of the network?	Characteristics of the interaction space?
About practice	In whom would actor confide?	In whom has actor (actually) confided?
About choice set	How many confidants?	How many people encountered regularly?
	Who is close friend or family?	Who is likely to empathize or understand?
	Who is confidant?	Who is available?
About relationship	Is it strong?	Is it institutionally mediated?
	Is it trustworthy?	Is it emotionally reciprocal?

I dig deeper into the explanatory power of three specific propositions: that people will avoid strong or otherwise potentially appropriate ties when they fear incompatible expectations; that people will approach weak ties when they have reason to expect cognitive empathy; and that even with serious or risky concerns people will at times confide in others incidentally or spontaneously. I examine directly whether each of the propositions is applicable to other contexts, and whether it helps explain how others decided whom to turn to for support.

APPLICATIONS: AVOIDING STRONG OR OTHERWISE APPROPRIATE TIES

Incompatible Expectations

The fact that people often avoid their strong ties runs counter to conventional expectations about what strong ties do. However, once reported, it also seems perfectly understandable—most people could probably list several reasons to avoid their spouse, parent, closest colleague, or adviser.[28] In fact, research has found that people often feel explicitly ambiguous about their inner circle, finding many relationships "both close and bothersome."[29] Furthermore, a structural network perspective can also explain well why people may want to avoid family members: when everyone either knows or is close to everyone else, any secret will spread quickly. Explaining why people would avoid their strong ties is not difficult.

But the students' actions suggest an important oft-neglected condition, the role of institutional expectations. Note that people will avoid a close relation less as a matter of principle than as a function of the given topic, such that A will avoid B particularly with respect to topic x.[30] Whether A will do so depends substantially on institutional expectations. Strong ties exist in many forms, but few of them are free of either formal or informal expectations, such as the rules of a graduate program, the norms of a team of coworkers, the ethical guides of a profession, or the obligations of a kin relation. People live fully aware that their roles carry expectations, which are so prevalent and dominant that, in practice, when people are deciding whom to talk to, they will often be a bigger factor than the mere strength of the relation.

Complications arise when roles in the A–B relation are multiplex—when someone is potential confidant but also provider, competitor, patron, client, evaluator, advocate, or some other behavioral role. Since not all roles are compatible with that of confidant, A will avoid B when topic x risks eliciting the wrong role, when B may react as evaluator, competitor, provider, or some role other than listener or supporter that creates the potential for conflict. This ambiguity is a powerful deterrent. A will avoid B when topic x creates fear of *incompatible expectations*.

The fear of incompatible expectations may arise among strong or weak ties. But it is common among strong ones because such ties are often multiplex. And it may be riskier among them because the consequence of conflict is emotionally greater. Consider the following two cases. The first makes clear that incompatible expectations may encourage someone to avoid a close colleague who might otherwise seem ideal to talk to. The second makes clear that in the mist of such incompatibilities, people who seem particularly appropriate for a disclosure may be avoided.

Why a Professional May Avoid Disclosing Mental Illness to Close Colleagues

People deal with mental health problems regardless of job or profession. In occupations involving professional care, as many in the fields of education, social work, and health, serious mental illness can interfere severely with the proper delivery of care or service, creating complications for those experiencing them. Some conditions such as the onset of depression, can emerge well into adulthood, and their first signs often prompt the need to talk. But when close friends are also professional colleagues, a larger set of institutional expectations enters and complicates the decision to talk, creating the possibility of incompatible expectations that makes the disclosure difficult.

Consider the case of Anne MacKenzie, a British doctor who has written about dealing with depression. Well into the course of her career, MacKenzie came to realize she was clinically depressed. "I could hardly sleep. I could not concentrate to read a book or listen to music. . . . I thought compulsively about death. I know that suicide is a terrible thing to do to other people but I endlessly worked out the scenarios of credible accidents. . . . I was very frightened that one morning I would kill myself."[31]

When she first became aware of her condition, MacKenzie felt too vulnerable to talk about it at all. She did not tell her friends or her colleagues. "I could not tell anyone when I became depressed. I could not tell my husband, my friends, or my colleagues. As a result, for two years I tried to treat myself with probably inadequate doses of whatever tricyclic drugs were lying around the surgery. I managed to suppress my symptoms enough to cope with life but not to get any pleasure from it."[32]

MacKenzie worked in "an isolated small town,"[33] which made it difficult to find someone to talk to. As any network analyst would expect, the relatively dense networks of small towns would likely mean that no news would be secret for long. Nevertheless, MacKenzie even avoided talking to her closest colleague, who should in theory be trusted to keep things to himself. In fact, the colleague was also her own doctor, a position for which he would also be expected to maintain confidentiality. But the multiplexity of the relationship—doctor, friend, colleague—which probably made it stronger also made it complicated with respect to this issue, since it engendered expectations that were not compatible in nature.

As she explained, "It would have been difficult to consult my own general practitioner. He and I shared duty [rotations]. If he knew I was ill he would be worried about the extra stress of night and weekend on call."[34] As her doctor and her friend, he might have been good to talk to, but as her colleague, he was difficult to talk to about this particular topic, because his desire to provide support might conflict with his responsibility to ensure that the clinic is operating properly and that patients are being served by fully capable doctors. Consistent with the theory, she found the two potential roles he could occupy, supportive friend and responsible professional, to be difficult to reconcile: "He could have legitimate doubts about my ability to treat his patients. To some extent the other doctors in the [isolated small] town would also be affected if I could not work."[35] MacKenzie feared forcing her friend to choose between being a supportive friend and fulfilling his professional duties. Thus, she decided to avoid him.

MacKenzie's experience makes clear why though in theory close friends may seem good to talk to, in practice particular issues may trigger multiple sets of expectations that complicate one's ability to turn to them for support.

Why a Soldier May Avoid Disclosing Victimization to Her Commander

The fear of incompatible expectations can become even more complicated between people in hierarchical positions, where the possibility of additional ambiguities may play a role. In many institutional contexts, subordinates see their superiors as not only supervisors or instructors but also mentors, supporters, advocates, and even friends. Such multiple roles come into conflict when a subordinate seeks in a superior a supporter or an advocate but the latter faces additional expectations that require enacting an alternative role. These complications are evident in the relationship between soldiers and their commanders when the soldiers have been sexually victimized.

Recent years have brought considerable attention to the high prevalence of sexual assaults in the military, and the fact that victims rarely report—indeed, they often talk to no one, even refraining from telling trusted superiors.[36] Victims often describe fearing that the expectations surrounding a person's otherwise appropriate role might make them the worst person to talk to.

For example, Army Sergeant Myla Haider had early in her career trained to join the Army's Criminal Investigation Command (CID), before her skills were discovered and her commander sent her to Iraq as an intelligence analyst.[37] Indeed, her "commander from the 101st Airborne, retired Lt. Col. Marty Herbert," a reporter explained, "describe[d] Haider as a sharp, even-keeled analyst, standing out in a battalion of hundreds. Haider went with the 101st to Kandahar in 2002, and then to Iraq in 2003."[38]

Nevertheless, Sgt. Haider did not tell any of her commanders that back while she was training for the CID, she was raped.[39] In fact, for years she refused to report the assault. As recorded in later congressional testimony, when the assault happened she confided in one peer and two friends, all of whom "promised her that they would not report the rape."[40] She refused to report the crime to her superiors because she feared the consequences for her: "I've never met one victim," she later explained, "who was able to report the crime and still retain their military career."[41]

Commanders are responsible for their units, and serious moral and criminal transgressions within their ranks reflect poorly on their own leadership. It is therefore not something they often want to hear. Retired Major General Dennis Laich put the matter bluntly to a reporter: "The last thing a company commander wants to do is make the phone call to his or her battalion commander to say: 'I have had an allegation of a rape in my unit'. . . . It will adversely affect their career."[42] The expectation to support a victim in their unit conflicts with the expectation to prevent victimization from happening in the first place, and evidence of the latter has professional consequences. Of course, many commanders report assaults immediately, refer victims to medical attention, and investigate the matter fairly. But the fear that they might not has dissuaded victims from talking. In fact, a widely disseminated 2012 report on sexual assault concluded that only 11% of victims of unwanted sexual contact reported their assault.[43]

To be clear, sexual victimization in the military is a complex and multifaceted problem requiring far deeper analysis than is possible to conduct in these pages.[44] Furthermore, many victims of sexual assault, both in and outside the military, fail to report the crime, such that factors well beyond the military as an organization are in effect as well. But there is little doubt that the institutional expectations faced by commanders and others must form part of any complete story.[45]

APPLICATIONS: APPROACHING WEAK TIES

Cognitive Empathy

Avoiding strong ties is not the sole reason people approach weak ones. Approaching others is also a three-part relation, in the sense that A will decide to approach B specifically with respect to problem, worry, or difficulty x. I have argued that A will do so when she has reason to believe that B can empathize with respect to x, in the sense of understanding the problem, worry, or difficulty as she understands it. Empathy, to be clear, is cognitive understanding, not sympathy or pity. A will expect B to either understand or come close to understanding x if B has the same characteristics (attribute similarity), faces the same problem (situational similarity), has the same relationship to the rest of a network (structural similarity), has faced x in the past (direct experience), or has often talked to others facing x (indirect experience). Finding a fully or partly empathetic ear substantially raises the expected benefits of taking the risk to share one's problem.

People can find empathy in both weak and strong ties. But when a person's difficulty is not common, one is likelier to find empathy in a weak tie than a strong one, since there are more of the former than the latter. Thus, when x is either uncommon or otherwise difficult to comprehend, A will more likely take the risk of talking to an acquaintance or even a stranger with whom they can empathize. This predicament helps explain why people facing addiction will confide intimate aspects of their lives to a room full of strangers at a Narcotics Anonymous meeting. While the norms of secrecy and the hope for recovery naturally make a difference, the possibility that, at a bare minimum, others will understand their predicament represents a major payoff. It also helps explain why renters facing eviction willingly share their difficulties with other renters, even people they have just met, in their own low-income communities.[46] There are countless difficulties, from losing one's child to violence to losing one's home to the bank, that many people experience and yet are likely to be uncommon among a person's circle of friends. There may be no greater isolation than finding no one who genuinely understands one's difficulty.

But not all uncommon problems, difficulties, or worries result from despair. Often they merely result from the uniqueness of one's position or situation. In fact, given the complexity of contemporary society and the heterogeneity of circumstances in which people may find themselves, the need to talk about uncommon problems is not itself especially uncommon. And since uncommon problems are unlikely to be shared by one's three or four closest friends and family, one is likely to seek a weak tie for cognitive empathy. Consider the following case.

Why a Doctor May Prefer Confiding Errors to a Colleague over a Spouse

A painful experience for doctors, and potentially tragic one for their patients, is making a mistake during diagnosis, treatment, or surgery. Depending on the severity of the error, medical professionals have found the experience annoying, embarrassing, unnerving, distressing, and even traumatic. Doctors' attitudes about discussing errors were the subject of a recent study of 338 faculty and resident physicians across three US medical centers by physician and ethicist Lauris Kaldjian and his colleagues. The survey confirmed the distress that doctors feel when making errors. When asked, 92% of respondents agreed that "[w]hen I make a medical mistake, I am my own worst critic."[47] It is not surprising that they often need to talk.

But what a person feels after making a medical mistake is not something that most can reasonably claim to understand. How many of us have killed someone by accident? Or hurt someone who has come to us based precisely on our ability to help them? A husband or wife, no matter how supportive, will have difficulty empathizing unless they are also medical professionals. They will certainly be sympathetic, but often not likely empathetic. If empathy matters more than sympathy or closeness, then doctors will approach other doctors more than their close friends and family.

The survey confirms the expectation. In the survey, 73% reported that they "usually discuss [their] medical mistakes with colleagues."[48] Consistent with the theory, the doctors were eight percentage points *more* likely to tell a colleague than their own "spouse/significant other, or a family member or close friend"—that is, than the presumed social safety net—about a medical mistake.[49] For the doctors, closeness mattered less than cognitive empathy. As the uniqueness of one's difficulty increases, so will the importance of empathy and the odds of relying on weak ties.

Probing Further

That colleagues might be the best people to talk to makes sense. But note that, in my discussion of Dr. MacKenzie's depression, I noted that other doctors would be the worst people to approach. The evidence amounts to the irony that, depending on the topic, a colleague can be the best or the worst person to talk to. This dual predicament runs the risk of turning any explanation based on institutional expectations into a just-so story, the kind that only makes sense after the fact.

However, that is not the case here. We can theorize, in advance, whether someone should be more or less likely to turn to a given institutionally mediated relation: If the topic is domain specific, then colleagues, who can empathize, should be especially likely to be approached—provided the disclosure would not represent a threat to the expectations of their roles. If it would, then even close colleagues are likely to be avoided.

Consider, again, the question of medical mistakes. One might think that learning of a colleague's mistake might put a doctor in the uncomfortable position of having to report the situation, rather than provide support, creating incompatible expectations. However, that is not the case, because the confidant would rarely be expected to report on the confider. Doctors see hundreds of patients every year. As a result, medical mistakes are exceedingly common, and in fact inevitable—so much so that lawsuits are par for the course, and liability insurance is ubiquitous.[50] Entirely routine bureaucratic procedures exist for reporting mistakes shortly after they take place. Disclosing a mistake to other doctors does not actually threaten the expectations of the confidant's role, since the mistake has good odds of already having been reported. However, their ubiquity does not make them less distressing to the individual who perpetrates them, which is why the doctors often need to talk.[51]

That potential threat was the difference between this case and Dr. MacKenzie's. Whereas making a medical mistake does not suggest that a doctor may be unable to perform her duties, experiencing suicidal ideation does. Thus, MacKenzie's worry that her colleagues might question her competence was well founded, and though they would understand her difficulties better than most, she had reason to avoid putting them in a difficult situation. It was a kind of catch-22.

Her solution revealed these dynamics perfectly. She confided in someone who, as a fellow doctor, could empathize with her trepidation in discussing her predicament with others but who, *no longer in practice* as a physician, did not face the complicating institutional expectations or obligations. "When finally I asked for help I could not do so face to face. I wrote a note to a friend, a doctor, not in practice, asking to be referred to a psychiatrist."[52]

Dr. MacKenzie's story ended happily. "I had anticipated a dismayed five minutes now and then, during which I was advised 'to keep on taking the tablets.' What I got [from the psychiatrist] was friendship, concern, and support. Perhaps I would have got better anyway with proper therapeutic doses of antidepressants, but it was so much easier with support." In fact, the psychiatrist became her regular confidant: "As soon as I knew that I had someone to go to if problems overwhelmed me, the problems got less. For months I got through each day to a litany of 'never mind, it'll be all right on Friday.'"[53]

APPLICATIONS: DISCLOSING SERIOUS MATTERS INADVERTENTLY

Incidental and Spontaneous Talk

I have argued that the processes of avoidance and empathy at times implied people who, like Sgt. Haider or Dr. MacKenzie, reflected on whom to talk to before approaching or not approaching a confidant. But I have also proposed that the decision process is often fluid, such that explanations focused solely on actors' careful assessments of pros and cons will miss how a lot of people actually find themselves talking to others. Sometimes, A will need to discuss x but will have yet to decide on B when an opportunity arises; at other times, A will not even have decided she needs to discuss x when a situation presents itself. People find themselves responding to circumstances as they happen, talking things through, and often finding themselves grateful. Many of those whom people ultimately confide in cannot be captured by asking them to reconstruct what they take to be their support network.

Situational contexts matter to these decisions. Research on personal disclosure in psychology has begun to address how environmental cues affect the willingness of people to divulge personal information, such as admitting that they engaged in unethical behavior. People appear to respond to micro-level aspects of the situation, such as how informal the environment appears or whether others have disclosed something personal themselves.[54] And research on decision making in psychology, behavioral economics, and choice modeling has begun to assess how conditions of the situation affect the decision process itself.[55]

But the conditions in the space of interaction itself necessarily shape any decision a person did not fully expect to make. I suggest that people will find themselves making incidental and spontaneous activation decisions when they spend much of their time in densely populated interactional spaces, when the people they regularly encounter are potentially empathetic, and when the spaces are formal organizations whose activities focus on the matters that concern them.[56] Consider a powerful case involving how people handle a personal disclosure, coming out at work. In spite of the high stakes involved, people often report having done so in ways that reveal far more about the circumstances of the social interaction than any deliberative process of selection and activation.

How a Teacher May Decide Whom To Come Out To at Work

Many who identify as LGBT report difficulties when deciding whether and how to come out at work. Some deliberate extensively on the matter, deciding on how, when, and to whom they will come out ahead of time. As Jim Bridgman, a gay Massachusetts teacher, put it, "I thought a lot about the 'why' and 'how' of coming out at school."[57] Given the risks involved, such deliberation is only rational. The potential consequences, from homophobic slurs, to moral reprobation, to violence, prompt many to give the matter careful thought. But the seriousness of the matter does not guarantee that people will not respond in unexpected ways to the interactions in which they find themselves. Nor does it guarantee that, when they disclose their sexuality, they will do so to the person they had concluded would be optimal. Consider two different scenarios.

Incidental activation. Sometimes, the decision is incidental, in the sense that a person had decided he or she needed to come out but not concluded how or when until a situation presented itself. Robert Parlin was a teacher in an affluent Massachusetts suburb considered by some to be "fairly liberal."[58] The administration had instituted a "Committee on Human Differences," a faculty-run group aimed at discussing issues of diversity and inclusion. In the few years since its inception, it "had discussed a wide range of topics, looking at anti-Semitism, racism, sexism, and class issues, and attitudes toward foreign students."[59] This particular year, homophobia might be on the agenda, and a planning meeting had been set up to discuss this and other topics.

Parlin was generally private but not particularly secretive: "I had been teaching history at the school for four years, but I was 'out' only to a few colleagues who were close friends."[60] He had decided he wanted to no longer be closeted, and saw this as a chance to come out to other colleagues. "For the first time, I began to hope that I could come out to the whole school, and that we could all work together to create a place where gay and lesbian teachers and students felt comfortable, welcome, and valued."[61]

The planning meeting, however, had not gone as he had hoped. Parlin had arrived 15 minutes late, only to find that teachers seemed to agree that homophobia was not a pressing problem in this liberal community, and the issue was best left to a future year. He was incredulous. In response, he unexpectedly came out of the closet. "I knew that it was simply not true, and my anger allowed me to overcome my fears. 'Let me tell you why we *do* have a problem,' I began. 'I am gay and I have never felt truly welcome here at this school.'"[62] He simply said it.

The depths of his disclosure surprised even him: "I told them what it was like to feel that you were sick and disgusting, and how I was taught to hate myself. I described how the pain nearly drove me to take my life the summer after my first year in college, because I could not envision a life in which I would be happy and whole. I shared the tremendous pressure of being closeted at work, afraid that one day I might let something slip, feeling that I could never be fully honest with the people around me. As I spoke, I could feel the fear slipping away, being replaced by a sense of self-confidence that I had never before known."[63] He was now out, and relieved about it.

Spontaneous activation. Many people, however, are even less open than Parlin, who, though he did not know when he would do it, had already planned to come out. Some, like Rodney Wilson, did not even want to come out. Wilson knew he was gay by age 7, had joined gay and lesbian student groups in college, and had become involved in the gay community in St. Louis when he moved there for a job. "The only place where I was still closeted," however, "was at work."[64] Wilson did not yet have tenure, and the prospects of discrimination as a result of his sexual identity were daunting, even as late as the early 1990s. "As a second-year, nontenured teacher, I felt that to reveal my true identity would have put my job in jeopardy. I had a choice: honesty or bread. At that point, I chose bread."[65]

But it was difficult. One incident in class brought matters to a head. During a discussion of civil rights, the issue arose of "whether or not a lesbian couple should be allowed to adopt children."[66] He did not expect their answers. "I was taken aback by the students' overwhelmingly negative response. Some proclaimed that they would burn down the house of any lesbian couple who moved near them."[67] The open expression of homophobic violence was both shocking and distressing. It also induced guilt. "I felt it was my duty at the time to tell my students that I was gay: they needed a human face behind the word *homosexual*. . . but [I] could not."[68] For a 24-year-old teacher making ends meet, bread superseded honesty. He remained silent in the classroom.

But the students' awful comments boiled inside him. Fortunately, shortly after class, he ran into someone who could listen sympathetically. "After the class ended, I bumped into the school's wellness counselor, Joanna Van Der Tuin, in the cafeteria."[69] So he blurted it out spontaneously. "I came out to her amidst the clamor and chaos of five hundred hungry students."[70] He was not expecting to do so. Indeed, with the rest of his colleagues, Wilson remained in the closet for three more years.[71]

To understand how Parlin and Wilson decided to come out, beginning with the standard practice of reconstructing the structure of their networks would be of little help. Someone like Joanna Van Der Tuin would likely not have appeared in Wilson's "core discussion network." In contrast, understanding the space would be essential, since incidental and spontaneous decisions always happen in the midst of some interaction. Parlin was in a faculty meeting room; Wilson, in the school cafeteria. People can sit in solitude and decide whom to call to talk, but they cannot incidentally and spontaneously talk to others on their own. The space of interaction will ultimately be part of the story.

Furthermore, the particular focus of activity and the institutional norms imposed by the formal organizations are essential.[72] Parlin, you will note, was confronting the surprise that his presumably liberal peers believed homophobia was not a local problem; Wilson had been shocked that his students opposed allowing lesbians to adopt children. Though each disclosed their status in different ways and to different people, both were shocked by the failure of people in their schools to meet the norms and expectations they had otherwise adhered to. Schools teach acceptance, and liberal ones take pride in doing so. Coming out was, in that sense, topically relevant in each situation, a fact that certainly made the decisions to come out far more likely. Topics matter; situations arise.

Topics, as one graduate student had put it, "come up," and people respond to the circumstances, in the moment, as best they can, often in ways they did not intend.

NETWORKS IN PRACTICE

The perspective I have outlined does not amount to a complete theory of how people decide whom to talk to. However, I hope to have shown that the questions introduced in this book matter, and that we cannot answer them by limiting network analysis to the study of structure. Without attending to the contexts in which people spend their lives, and to the fluid nature of their decisions in those contexts, we risk a narrow understanding of this fundamental aspect of social life.

Ultimately, the practical network of confidants—the set of individuals people actually confide in when they need someone to talk to—may be at once smaller and larger than typically suggested. It is smaller in the particular sense that, for many of the matters for which people seek confidants, they will often avoid their closest friends and family, and even decline to consider a confidant the majority of important people in their lives. Even in the midst of a strong support network, people may experience profound isolation. But it is larger in the sense that, as they seek empathy and respond to opportunities as these arrive during their social interactions, they may find themselves confiding in acquaintances, miscellaneous coworkers, and random, distal people who happened to be facing a similar problem or to have often talked to others who had, or who simply happened to be in the right place at the right time. The steady stream of social interactions is ever-changing and continuously replenished. And given people's readiness to drink from anywhere within it, the stream and its conditions deserve our full attention.

A Final Word

If there was ever a time when many of the propositions of this book should have been wrong, it is now. The reason is technology. Over the past two decades technology has dramatically changed how we communicate with our closest friends and family.[1]

The Internet and the smartphone have altered how we relate to our strong ties, not only—as the invention of the telephone did over a century ago—when they are far but also when they are near, in the same country, city, and even building.[2] As in many new technologies, the change in norms is most evident in younger cohorts, as in the 20- and 30-something graduate students we studied. For many of them, the primary modes of communication—with their close friends, spouses, and even roommates—are to text, to online-chat, and to connect via online network platforms. Platforms have evolved so quickly that many have already absorbed the text and chatting functions. Online network platforms, once a way to find friends long lost since elementary school, are now a combination news source, photo album, political mobilization tool, and communication vehicle.[3] To call by phone is increasingly uncommon. In fact, a telling indicator of the shift in norms is the decided preference among many using smartphones for unlimited text and unlimited data over unlimited minutes.[4]

As a result of these dynamics, two things should have been true. It should have been easier than ever for the students to retain their connections to close confidants in the midst of dramatic life changes. Since a lot of the communication between friends among the young happens virtually, even when they are near, the ordinary habits among close friends and confidants are as portable across space as they have ever been: if they had wanted to, the graduate students could easily have held on to their trusted and tested confidants, not only because there have never been more ways of doing so but also because there has never been a time where doing so would have required the least change in their ordinary habits for connecting with their network. G-chat, texting, Twitter, Skype, Facetime, Facebook, Snapchat—that is already how they kept in touch with many of their confidants.[5] The last conversations about difficult problems should have been Skypes or G-chats with trusted friends back home, not unexpected confessionals to miscellaneous classmates encountered down the hall.

In addition, it should have been less necessary than ever to interview people one on one and understand their interactions qualitatively, in their everyday spaces, to capture whom they talk to about their problems. The amount of communication that happens electronically with companies willing to share their data should have made more possible than ever a study that could reveal much about people's decisions by simply analyzing the "big data." Indeed, it would have been easy to imagine that, finally, today, the study of questions of this kind could become a completely structural network science. As many sociologists have reported, we exist in a networked age, where people's communities are no longer tied to a local place but spread across space.[6] And the tools of structural network analysis are optimally suited to study relationships that do not depend on space.

But those space-independent relationships, no matter how strong, long lasting, or trusted—all of which they often are—cannot override people's responsiveness to everyday contact, the fact that, day in and day out, people encounter a stream of regular and new individuals with whom they must interact, to whom they must respond, and about whom they must make decisions. In spite of what is possible online, people are deeply responsive to the social interactions they encounter routinely. They make split decisions about matters small and large in the circumstances in which they happen to find themselves. The distinctly human elements of interpersonal relations, those that lie beyond the network structure, remain indispensable to understand network behavior.[7]

To whom does a child turn when he feels bullied? To whom does a teen confide that he is considering coming out? To whom does a soldier vent upon return from another tour? To whom does a student talk when she feels guilty for her own assault? To whom does a parent confide her guilt about resenting motherhood? To whom does a renter talk about the anxiety of losing the unit? To whom does a worker vent about the shame of unemployment? To whom does a man talk on the anniversary of his widowhood? To whom does a senior turn when she fears her memory is fading? Each of these questions represents a kind of network problem—not just a network to map, but also a stream of interactions to observe, a knot of expectations to unravel, and a set of decisions to understand.

PART IV

Appendices

Appendices

This book, part of an ongoing project on personal networks, was based on a mixed-methods study. The book used qualitative data on a small number of graduate students to test a major hypothesis, to examine why it was not supported, and to generate both empirical and theoretical propositions about what should happen among other populations and in other contexts. It then assessed the empirical propositions using quantitative data from two original surveys and from secondary sources.

When designing the study, I believed that each kind of data should address the questions it can best answer, and that each collection procedure should aim to maximize that gain. Thus, the qualitative case study focused on depth, discovery, and understanding local processes; the quantitative study, on breadth, reliability, and uncovering central tendencies.[1] At each step of data collection and analysis, I paid careful attention to what I consider the core principles of social scientific inquiry: a continuous assessment of theory against evidence, an impartial examination of the data, a healthy skepticism about underlying assumptions, a studied attention to possible flaws in reasoning, and an overall orientation toward replicability and transparency.

Because the study both tested and generated theories, and thus involved both deductive and inductive analyses, it required a great deal of fluidity, such that both the questions and methods of data collection evolved over the course of the project. As a result, explaining the methodological decisions involved in the study will require some discussion of the process through which I arrived at them. This process, and the methodological decisions that resulted, are the focus of the appendices that follow.

Appendix A, "Qualitative Analysis," discusses the major decisions underlying the qualitative study, and it describes the overall process. Appendix B, "Quantitative Analysis," discusses the two surveys. It also presents that statistical analyses supporting the results reported in Chapter 7.

APPENDIX A

Qualitative Analysis

In-depth research on small groups has long been part of the network analysis tradition, as evidenced in classic studies such as Theodore Newcomb's study of the associations among 17 men entering college, or David Krackhardt's study of the perceptions of network relations among 36 workers in one firm.[1] This book follows that tradition, except the aim was not to formalize a network structure but to unravel a decision-making process. The book's qualitative data source consisted of an in-depth interview-based, four-wave longitudinal case study of 38 graduate students, who constituted nearly all enrolled first-year students across three departments in a single institution.

This design reflects the initial objective of the qualitative study, to understand how people use, perceive, and form relations to others when entering new institutional contexts. Still, the study's questions, focus, interview protocol, and relation to the quantitative data all evolved over the course of the project. This kind of evolution is common among mixed-methods and qualitative projects.[2] As Howard Becker put it recently, "successful qualitative research is an iterative process, in which the data gathered at T1 inform data gathering operations conducted at T2. Successful researchers . . . use what they learn from day to day to guide their subsequent decisions about what to observe, who to interview, what to look for, what to ask about."[3] Qualitative research is often, by necessity, iterative.[4]

Nevertheless, far too often researchers across the social sciences choose to report their methods in ways that mask this fact, representing post facto decisions as though they had been made from the start. For example, they may report results as "confirming hypotheses" even when these hypotheses had not been specified before the data collection or analysis.[5] I disagree with such practices. The core principles of scientific reportage should be clarity and transparency. In this book, many of the methodological decisions I made were only resolved well after the project had begun. For this reason, the most accurate way to discuss them is to reconstruct the process through which the book was written, explaining each methodological decision as it took place.

THE PROCESS

Background

While interviewing parents for my previous book, a study of the networks that mothers in New York made through their children's daycare centers, I discovered that the respondents, to my surprise, were willing to entrust their children to other parents who were not part of their network and whose names at times they barely even knew. (Sometimes, the two parents would later go on to become friends.) I had many questions about why and how this happened. But one of them stood out, a question prompted by what I had been reading about how networks are supposed to operate.

Everything I had read on networks of support assumed, as a matter of course, the ostensibly obvious point that for a person to turn to another for help, the latter must be part of the former's network. That is, people must *form* a tie before they can *mobilize* it. Thus, to understand how people get support from their networks, to understand how people decide whom to turn to for what, a researcher would first need to map the personal network of those they studied. The idea seemed clear and self-evident.

But that view of how networks operate, and that approach to understand them, did not seem quite right. To map the mothers' support networks, I would presumably first ask them to list their close friends and family. But some of the mothers I had interviewed were turning to people whom they did not really know and who would not have appeared on a list of friends or family. Yet clearly they were getting support from these people. I reflected on the matter, considering other social contexts and other kinds of support, and the more I did, the less the practices of the mothers seemed odd.[6] Different kinds of support would probably exhibit different dynamics—people would borrow money differently from how they vented about a personal difficulty. And yet I could find instances among many kinds of support of people going far beyond their expected "social support network" of very close friends and family. Understanding people's networks in *practice* seemed to require something other than understanding their network *structure*. I began to wonder whether reconstructing people's networks as the first step in the research process was an epistemological decision with far deeper implications, both practical and ontological, than I realized. Mobilization could actually precede formation.

After publishing that book, *Unanticipated Gains*, I decided to spend several years reading everything I could on how people use their networks. This focus led me to the question of agency.[7] Far too often in network research I saw that authors acknowledged that people were ultimately the agents of their lives, but then quickly set agency aside, adopting a kind of language that suggested that the networks, rather than individuals, were the actors. Researchers used phrases such as "the triad closed" or "the weak tie created access," which were useful as shorthand but also promoted a kind of narrative wherein individuals were somehow no longer determining their own fates.

Some of this language is inevitable: in fact, I am certain I have used it in the book. But I sensed it should probably not go unchecked. Ronald Burt, in a discussion of networks and social capital, put it well: "Everyone knows that people are the source of action. Measured networks are only the residue of how people have spent time together up to the moment a network is measured. However, agency has often been put aside to focus on describing the performance association with network structure."[8] I sought not to put it aside but to make it central. At some point, my concern narrowed from agency to decision making. To use the resources in one's network is, in the end, to make a decision and to act upon it. Thus, the core topic of the book eventually would become how people make decisions about their networks of support.

This topic placed the work line with the important research of Bernice Pescosolido, Sandra Smith, and others who sought a richer understanding of how people make decisions about turning to their networks.[9] Yet to understand these questions, I had to read far beyond what I had come to view as conventional network analysis. For several years, I studied works in psychology, anthropology, behavioral economics, and philosophy that seemed to speak to these questions. I was especially moved by the anthropological network studies of the Manchester School, the early studies on judgment and framing that would become prospect theory, the twentieth-century survey studies that pioneered large-scale ego network analysis, and the early pragmatist propositions about action and decision making—all of which I returned to repeatedly over the course of the project.[10] These works shared a preoccupation with fundamental questions, a measure of methodological innovation, and a penchant for elegant analysis.

The works helped me think about network decisions more precisely and more broadly, at some point leading to the realization that I needed to understand perception. Individuals, even when they are turning to people outside their regular network, are not approaching just anyone; they are approaching people whom they, for one reason or another, perceive as potentially helpful. It seemed important to understand where these perceptions come from and how they matter. Thus, I set as the broad theme of my project the various connections among how people use, think of, and create ties to others—the three-way relationship among network *mobilization, perception,* and *formation.*

A Commitment

While reading, I brainstormed alternative ways of collecting data to unravel this three-way relationship. I ran exploratory surveys with both descriptive and experimental components, and conducted a few small ethnographic studies. I studied how Chicago children formed friendships after changing schools unexpectedly, and how low-income mothers in Houston, Chicago, and New York avoided isolation. I explored conducting a diary study wherein participants would record their daily contacts in careful detail, and considered running an "experience sampling" study where participants would be contacted at random times throughout the day to report whom they were in contact with and why. I took copious notes—hundreds of thousands of words' worth—enough to animate well over a decade's worth of research ideas. By then I was convinced that several of my questions had not been answered, that addressing them was worthwhile, and that I should design one targeted study.

I decided to focus narrowly on how people confide in others, a most basic form of emotional support about which there had been a substantial literature in network analysis. The study would examine three "how" questions: how people form new ties (formation), think about those relationships (perception), and turn to them for support (mobilization). (The first book, this one, would end up focusing primarily on mobilization.) I would make few assumptions about how these processes worked, and I would certainly not presume that constructing a network would necessarily be the first step in the analysis. Having committed to at least one core question, I still needed to decide what type of data to collect and from which population.

THE DATA COLLECTION

Type

Early on, it became clear that a large-sample survey would be necessary. Such surveys have been essential to network analysis, particularly to the study of ego networks, at least since the pioneering work of Paul Lazarsfeld, Edward Laumann, Claude Fischer, Barry Wellman, and others. For the study of social support, the main advantage of a survey was clear: statistical representativeness and the ability to examine associations quantitatively. These advantages were important, and in the end I conducted two large-sample surveys whose details I describe in Appendix B.

However, a good survey requires the researcher to know in advance what variables one wants to capture, and much of what I found interesting were issues that the literature had not examined in depth. For example, I did not yet know exactly how to elicit good data on how people turned to those who were not in their core networks. In fact, I did not completely know what I did not know. Furthermore, because I wished to understand how people conceived of their own networks, I also needed a process where, in contrast to a structured survey, people had time to reflect on the matter, to meander as needed, to make a statement and return to it later, and even to change their minds.[11] I did not want to commit the mistake of forcing people I studied into a preconceived understanding of how they made decisions. Thus, I needed to collect data through a more inductive process, one that allowed the freedom for discoveries to emerge that I had not anticipated.[12] Qualitative work was essential.

Though I considered both ethnographic participant observation and in-depth interviews, in the end, I concluded I needed to rely on in-depth interviews.[13] There are several aspects of how people confide in others— that is, of this form of network mobilization—that cannot be captured through any means but through in-depth interviews: what people do in private, or only in the presence of one person; what people believe their motivations to be; what people thought about before making a decision; the contradictions between people's beliefs and behavior; the contradictions among their expressed beliefs themselves; their personal histories or biographies; their deepest or otherwise most serious preoccupations.[14] The centrality of these issues to my core question convinced me to conduct an interview-based study.

Nevertheless, the core limitation of interviews was clear: I could not be present when my respondents confided in others, and thus could only capture behavior indirectly. Indeed, no obtrusive social science method— including interviews, surveys, ethnographic observation, or experiments— can capture with perfect accuracy the events in people's lives as they would have taken place without the researcher's presence. Still, after both research and trial and error, I became convinced that, with the proper combination of well-known and new techniques, I could elicit both belief and behavior separately from respondents and get reasonably close to reconstructing their past behavior. Naturally, I could not get perfect representation. But in-depth interviews could get me closer than any other method to what actually took place, and they would allow me to determine some of what I was missing. (I return to these issues later in the chapter.)

Population

I knew that I was interested in adults, since they would have a fully formed personal network, a way of thinking about its members, and a set of strategies for both turning to them for help and developing new ones. I soon concluded I needed to study people who had some motivation to mobilize their networks and the opportunity to form new connections. I knew I would need to follow them over time, and that I would have to do far more than a conventional network study.

After considering many options, I concluded that graduate students beginning their professional training were ideal. They were adults, with a fully formed network. At the same time, they would have many opportunities to form new ties. Given the expected stresses and difficulties of the first year in any new context, they would have reason to seek help from others. They would be forced to confront clear choices when needing someone to talk to—rely on their trusted, pre-existing confidants or turn to their newly formed acquaintances? Moreover, if I tracked them closely over the typically demanding first year, I could understand, at the level of the individual, how people use their network to manage new and continuing difficulties. As an analytically strategic site, the graduate student context seemed perfect.

Based on what I had learned in my previous book, I believed that aspects of the institutional environments would play a role. The core idea behind the notion of the *organizational embeddedness* of networks was that what people do in light of others depends on the organizations in which they are embedded, and the institutional norms and expectations governing relations in those organizations. I had an intuition that the laboratory environment, with its team-based approach to research and the fact that students enter into a lab, might have a different environment than a humanities environment, where almost all work is sole-authored and people primarily write long-gestating books after many years of research. The social sciences, depending on their specialty, had both. For this reason, I decided on three departments, one in each of these areas. This was not a small-*n* "method of difference" comparative design, an approach that has many problems.[15] There was no "outcome variable" or "core explanatory factor." There were simply three processes—formation, perception, and mobilization—I hoped to understand in these different contexts.

THE INTERVIEWS

After deciding on an institution and three departments and completing Institutional Review Board requirements, I contacted the chairs, before the start of the semester, to inform them of the study. I then wrote every student in the entering cohort about the study asking for their participation, informing them there would be confidentiality and no consequences from nonparticipation, and offering some compensation ($60) for their time.[16] Fortunately, all but three students across all three departments agreed. To interview them all shortly after their arrival on the Hillmount campus, I needed help, and worked with two research assistants. All students were interviewed within 1 intense month. We repeated the process 6 months later and 6 months after that. After beginning to analyze a year's worth of data, I realized I needed more, so I conducted another round of interviews 12 months after the last one. At each wave, we made clear to students that they need not participate in any further waves if they did not wish to do so. Nevertheless, of those who participated in the first, all agreed to all subsequent interviews (one student, who was unreachable at the time, missed the third wave). Several of them expressed gratitude for participating in the survey. My guess is that most of those who participated did so mainly to be helpful. I am grateful for their time and generosity.

Each interview lasted between one and four hours. Of the 38 students, 50% identified as female, 50% as white or Caucasian, 29% as Asian or Asian American, and the remaining students—for which the numbers are too small to report without risking disclosure—identified as black or African American, Latino, or something else. The median age was 25.

The data reported in this book constitute only a slice of the large amount of sociometric, behavioral, attitudinal, and process data collected from the interviews. The interview contained both structured and unstructured sections.[17] A core set of questions was asked at each wave, with minor variations from wave to wave. Two research assistants and I conducted the interviews. I interviewed more than 60% of the students at least once. One research assistant conducted only three interviews in the first wave; every other interview was conducted either by the other research assistant or by me, which meant that, by the end of the project, the two of us knew the students quite well.

Structured Section

The structured section was asked first. At each of the four waves, the interview began with a word-for-word General Social Survey (GSS) name generator prompt, followed by a name interpreter (demographic questions on each alter reported) and several sociometric questions. The GSS name generator was asked first because, given its centrality to the project, I wanted to ensure it was not affected by question-order effects.[18] Claude Fischer demonstrated this matter dramatically in an evaluation of a set of conclusions from the GSS name generator. Miller McPherson and colleagues had argued that the core discussion network had declined between the 1980s and the 2000s.[19] Their argument was based on the GSS name generator, which had been elicited in 1985 and 2004. However, Fischer noted that the question was asked at different points in the survey in the two years: "In 2004, the critical question had followed a long, complicated, and nosy set of questions about respondents' organizational memberships."[20] In 1985, it was asked earlier in the interview. To determine whether this difference could account for the observed change over time, the GSS asked the question again in 2010, with some respondents receiving it in the context that those in 1985 did and others in the context that those in 2004 did. The results were extraordinary. In 2010, those who received the 1985 context questions reported rates of isolation similar to those in 1985; those who received the 2004 context questions reported rates similar to those in 2004. In sum, the presumed decline in isolation was not distinguishable from a question context effect.[21] For this reason, it was important that, in my interview study, the GSS name generator was the very first question asked.

From the structured section of the interviews, this was the only question I ultimately used in the book, given the book's eventual focus. The rest of the structured section asked a number of questions amenable to conventional sociometric analysis. Students received a roster of all others in their cohort and were asked, for each peer, whether the respondent was close to the peer and how likely the respondent was to discuss her or his academic life, love life, or the possibility of leaving academia with the peer. Respondents were given a spreadsheet with all peers listed along the columns and rows and asked how close they thought each pair of peers was. In addition, the first wave included a reconstruction of all contacts over the course of the previous day, along with follow-up questions. This question was dropped in subsequent waves, and other questions, covering smaller topics, were added at different waves. The large amount of data produced by these questions is currently being analyzed and will form part of future studies.

Unstructured Section

The unstructured section produced the heart of the material discussed in this book. This section is best described as partly semistructured, partly unstructured, in that it used a small number of guiding questions to stimulate a larger conversation about the circumstances under which people confided in others. We allowed the students to speak openly and at length, doing little more than probing, and ensuring that the interviews were experienced far more as conversations than interrogations. At the same time, this portion of the interviews sought to elicit accurate reconstructions of the students' decisions, motivations, and reactions.

In so doing, the unstructured portion was forced to deal with three important challenges involved in how people represent their experiences or themselves to others. Two of these had become clear to me after several years of reading, research, brainstorming, and reflecting on the role of in-depth interviews in the study of mobilization; the third only emerged as I began to analyze the responses from the first and second waves of the interviews. The three challenges were the tendency of people to describe what they believe typically happens, rather than what actually happened; the tendency of people to represent their motivations as rational; and the tendency of people to represent their actions as intentional, rather than unexpected. Specific techniques were required to address each of the three.

First challenge: Representation of belief as experience. As I discussed throughout the book, many of the surveys used to understand how people confide in others presume that people typically confide important matters in those whom they say they do and, thus, ask people to characterize their own typical practices. However, my prior work, and the work of others such as H. Russell Bernard and Peter Killworth, had made me question that practice.[22] There was and continues to be debate over the proper way to word survey network questions and whether people's representations of their networks could be trusted. But given my focus, it was imperative to understand, to the extent possible, what had actually happened—that is, whom they had actually turned to—regardless of whether whom they believed they typically turned to would be accurate or not.

My strategy was first to elicit their major concerns, separating graduate school from life in general. Thus, students were first asked, "What are the three things that worry you most regarding your graduate experience?" Later, they were asked three worries in their lives outside graduate school. By the end of the first wave, it was clear that graduate school was so overwhelming that few could provide three life worries; thus, future waves asked them to name only one worry outside graduate school.

Next, we focused on one of the worries they reported, and asked them to recall the last time they talked about that particular issue. We then asked whom they talked to that time.[23] We repeated the process for each of the other reported worries. In addition to capturing actual experience, the approach had two additional advantages. First, people probably remember specific events more clearly than general circumstances. Second, people certainly recall recent events far more accurately than distal ones.[24] Since rather than asking them to reconstruct the previous six months we asked them to remember the most recent instance—at times pointing to issues that had taken place within the day—we had substantially better odds of capturing actual experience, rather than belief. This difference in approach to the question turned out to be crucial, and it served as the foundation of Chapter 3.

Second challenge: Representation of self as rationally motivated. My previous work on in-depth interviews had made clear to me that, when attempting to reconstruct the students' motivations behind their actions, I would have to work around people's tendencies to represent themselves as acting based on rational motivations. The interviews quickly confirmed this concern. When explaining why they confided in whom they did, students often provided explanations that accorded with common sense. This fact did not, of course, make their account wrong. But it required me to be attentive to the fact that, as some have recently argued, rational explanations for motivated action may be appealing because they sound good—because they are consistent with common sense—rather than because they are accurate.[25]

In the interview setting, such representations can take different forms. Sometimes, they may be rationalizations, post facto justifications of a prior controversial or difficult action as founded on rational motives. In this case, a respondent is essentially trying to represent him- or herself as positively as possible. Other times, they may be explanations that accord with either common sense or a respondent's self-understanding while not actually being a motivating factor at the time the decision was made. In this case, a respondent is merely providing an explanation to him- or herself, because he or she may not remember the true motivation behind a past action. Either way, one must worry that people's depiction of the motives behind the action might be little more than a story that seems believable because it sounds reasonable.

One response to this problem might have been to disregard people's explanations of their own behavior on the view that they are unreliable. This response would be a mistake for three reasons. First, people's own explanations are a useful place from which to generate theories, and an objective of this book is to generate theories, or at least theoretical intuitions. All social theories must come from somewhere, and one derived from the population of interest is surely one step closer to reality than one derived from the researcher's imagination. Second, people's explanations might include issues a researcher has never thought of. Third, people's own explanations might in fact be correct.

An alternative response is to consider any self-reported motivation, whether it appears reasonable or not, as a proposition like any other—and to use the interview itself as a tool for probing that proposition. This was the perspective I adopted. The main tool we used to probe those statements in the interviews was to engage in what I have come to call *counterfactual questioning.*[26]

Typical in-depth interview questions seek to capture the facts as they occurred (or interviewees' opinions or attitudes about the facts as they occurred). Counterfactual interview questions seek to understand why circumstances that run counter to the facts as they occurred failed to occur. As such, I found it a powerful tool to understand motivation.

Counterfactual questioning always centers on a concrete event, not a general summary of past events. The idea is to probe the interviewee's account of motivation m as the reason to approach person P to discuss topic t by examining what would have happened if the core elements of the event they described had not occurred. Thus, we asked whether they still would have approached person P if they were not motivated by m (e.g., would they have still talked to their lab partner if they were not motivated by desperation?). We asked whether they still would have approached P if the topic were different (e.g., would they still have confided in their mother if the topic were work, rather than relationship troubles?). We asked whether m would still have motivated them to approach P if the topic were other than t (e.g., would their desperation still have mattered if the issue were a failed course instead of a failed relationship?). We asked whether topic t would still have motivated them to approach P if they were not motivated by m (e.g., would they have still talked to a professor they did not know about a given topic if they were not desperate?). And for a given motivation m or topic t, we asked why they did not approach person Q, rather than P, whenever Q would have seemed equally appropriate (e.g., why not approach a different particular graduate student to talk about their second-year paper?). For this last strategy, the fact that we had earlier elicited the core discussion network was crucial, because it gave us a list of plausible alternatives.

The purpose of these questions was a kind of triangulation aimed not at tripping up interviewees but at uncovering the pattern tying together their motivations, the topics they talked about, and the people they talked to. Most interviewees were, as they usually are, consistently honest. But for any who might not be inclined to be, it would be difficult to maintain a comprehensive story for so many different kinds of questions unless the story bore a strong relation to the underlying truth. In addition, even students most inclined to represent themselves as rational would inevitably discover inconsistencies in their understanding of their motives, inconsistencies that in interviews we then probed and sought to resolve. The result was an exceptionally rich account of what had motivated people's actions during concrete, recent events at which they had made network decisions.

Naturally, we did not ask all respondents each of the previous questions about every mentioned act in which they discussed their worries with others. Such an exercise would be not only exceptionally cumbersome but also counterproductive. Among other things, it would quickly lead to burnout. Anyone subjected to such grueling interviewing in one session would undoubtedly, at a later interview, hesitate to report many instances during which they confided in others. Furthermore, the interviews covered many different topics, and forcing the students to consistently address a narrow set of questions risked not letting the data speak for themselves, undermining the inductive aims of the investigation. The key to the strategy was balance—to exercise judgment during the interview itself and understand it as a dynamic interaction, rather than a formal survey. In the end, we engaged in counterfactual questioning more systematically in the later interviews, as their significance to our ongoing understanding of the students' decisions became clearer and clearer. Much of the data elicited through this process formed the basis of Chapters 4 and 5.

Third challenge: Representation of self as intentional. Over the course of the interviews, it became increasingly clear that a different issue was at play. The answers elicited through counterfactual questioning were exceptionally helpful, in part because they forced the interviewees to reflect carefully on their motivations. That gain, however, was also a problem. If people are asked why they have effected an action, they will often provide a motivation, regardless of whether, at the time, their actions were especially motivated. As psychologists Richard Nisbett and Timothy Wilson have shown, if people are asked to provide an account of their actions, they will do so, regardless of whether the account ultimately explains their action.[27] This tendency to explain one's own actions as motivated is especially likely to be evident among highly intelligent, thoughtful individuals who have dedicated their lives to the pursuit of knowledge. In this population, "I don't know why I did it" was an especially rare answer; "I did it for no reason at all" was all but absent.

And yet not all action, as I have discussed in the book, is motivated—at least not in the way it is most convenient to theorize, wherein an actor arrives at a conclusion mentally before proceeding to execute it. In essence, the action sometimes emerges from the interaction itself. I needed an approach that would allow me to uncover those circumstances when the action was spontaneous to some degree.

Therefore, in the later waves of the interviews, after the students had identified the last time they talked about a given topic, we began to first ask students to describe the circumstances under which the topic emerged. The core question was designed to allow them to provide an answer that did not commit them to a motivation. We asked, "How did it come up?" Sometimes, they provided an answer that made clear they had decided to talk to person P for a given motivation. In those circumstances, we proceeded with the counterfactual questioning described previously. Other times, they provided an answer that made clear the discussion was unexpected. In those circumstances, we asked them to describe where they were, why it came up, and other relevant questions as appropriate to the case, such as how often that seemed to happen. The data elicited through this process became the foundation of Chapter 6.

No single interview followed all of the procedures described here precisely as discussed. As I have argued, doing so would be counterproductive for multiple reasons. Furthermore, conducting a regimented procedure—which would be essential in a structured survey design that aims to make claims of statistical representativeness—would undermine the strengths of our in-depth interviews, the first strength of which was to uncover what we did not already know. That process requires the interviewer to guide but not control, and to react to themes as they emerge, rather than force a change toward a predetermined schedule.

Still, all of these practices would also make any claims of representativeness suspect—in the absence of additional data. For example, since not all respondents at every wave was asked, "How did it come up?" about every discussion they reported having, it would be impossible to produce reliable numbers about how frequently students reported one or another form of activation. That kind of claim requires large-sample surveys, which I conducted. I discuss these in Appendix B.

AFTER THE INTERVIEWS
The Book

By the fourth wave of interviews, it was clear I would have far more data than I could analyze in one book. I had comparative data across the three departments, data over time, data on structure, data on meaning, data on cognitive understanding of networks, data on what the students saw as their problems, and much more. It became increasingly obvious that there were many potential papers—or two or three books, not just one—to be produced from these data. At some point in the process, I decided that what was most important to the field and most immediately interesting to me was to dig deep into practice, mobilization, and decision making.

At the same time, however, many new questions had emerged. Although I originally intended to produce a study comparing institutional environments across the three departments, I quickly found that these differences were dwarfed by the similarities across them. In many of my explanatory analyses, while there were differences across the departments, any impartial observer would have to conclude that these were not the heart of the story.[28] In the matters that concerned this book, the departments looked more similar than different. Issues such as the institutional expectations surrounding a relationship and the decision-making processes involved in mobilization came to the fore. Still, I only had enough data to begin answering those questions.

Thus, it became clear that though it was time to write a book, the book could not have a complete theory, and it would need to not merely answer old questions but pose many new ones.

Confidentiality

I would also need to address the question of confidentiality. Although ensuring confidentiality is a standard element of qualitative research, the reasons for doing so are not always clear. In fact, some researchers in recent years have abandoned the practice altogether.[29] Though I do not believe that practice works under all circumstances, researchers should probably see confidentiality not necessarily as an end in itself but specifically as a means to protect people from harm that might result from the research. The fact that today confidentiality is especially difficult to maintain increases even further the need to be clear on its aims. For example, after controversy surrounded a recent book focused on criminal behavior among young men, many independent researchers quickly uncovered the identities of the men based on comments from the book and publicly available online records. Other than misrepresenting the city in which the project was conducted or distorting respondents' biographies dramatically, it is difficult to know what else the researcher might have done to ensure the anonymity of participants.[30]

In a network study, the stakes are typically even greater, because disclosure, I argue, is easier. There are two possible forms of disclosure in network studies. One is internal, wherein participants in the study identify other participants. In a sociocentric network study, all participants are directly or indirectly connected to all others, making such disclosure much easier. For this project, although I approached every single student in the three programs, three of the students declined, and all interviews were conducted in private. Thus, no student knows for sure whether any other participated unless the latter has disclosed the fact. Nevertheless, students know which department they are in and, based on the depictions in the book, might be able to identify someone in their own department's small pool (of 38/3 or ~13 persons on average).

The other form of potential disclosure is external. Even if all students did not care whether any of their peers knew of their participation, it may be more possible than normal for those in the public at large to identify a particular student. The reason is that network data makes triangulation much easier. In a regular (nonnetwork) survey, people are sampled with known probability from a population, and no information from any individual plays a role in the selection of any other. In a network survey, having any information on one means having some information on all others. For example, correctly identifying 1 student means that the enrolled university of the other 37 will be known. Indeed, this problem recently affected a major study based on Facebook data.[31] Furthermore, if one student decides to self-disclose, then some information on others—namely, their university—is immediately revealed. It is naturally not within the power of the researcher to prevent self-disclosure.

Therefore, both forms of disclosure must be considered when deciding how to manage confidentiality. I considered three approaches. One approach is to create composite characters in which the experiences of multiple people are described under one, as some researchers have done.[32] Though the sensitivity of some topics might make this an appealing option, I believe as a matter of principle that dramatic distortions of this kind are scientifically dangerous, since they shift the narrative from objective reportage into something closer to research-based fiction.

A second approach is to change all descriptive characteristics—gender, race, marital status, research topic, and so on—of each person described in the book. However, doing so would tempt even the most honest researcher into distorting issues in favor of a predetermined argument or, at a minimum, lead to inadvertent changes in favor of one or another conclusion. For example, if a student concerned about the relationships is described as single when he is not, the reader might infer a sense of isolation that the student does not necessarily experience.

A third approach is to reveal little about the respondents themselves. While this practice helps keep potentially self-serving fabrications at bay, it also unfortunately requires the researcher to leave a lot of data on the cutting room floor. Any qualitative researcher knows that doing so can be heartbreaking. More important, however, it also risks losing the most important advantage of qualitative research. In-depth interviews are indispensable to network analysis, I argue, because they represent the attitudes, felt motivations, and private interactions of respondents. Their words and actions are the heart of the data in a qualitative analysis, and the circumstances under which they undertook those actions are indispensable. Any good qualitative project is in part a repository of data, and this book represents the thoughts and actions of a set of students in a US university in the early part of the 21st century. Leaving out too much undermines its role as a source of qualitative data, and was, thus, a poor option.

My decision was a modification on the last approach. First, I changed no words and created no composite characters of any kind. Every statement reported was made as reported by the student who is said to have made it, in the wave of the study that they made it, in the context in which they made it.

Second, between the two extremes—revealing a lot but changing students' characteristics dramatically or revealing less but altering little about their traits—I opted for something closer to the latter. Because I had four waves of very rich data, even though I excluded much material, there was still sufficient data for the reader to evaluate, I hope, whether the evidence supported my conclusions. I did not reveal any student's race, sexual orientation, or place of birth, an option I find more palatable than altering any of the three. This situation of course made it impossible for me to discuss the effects of race, sexual orientation, or national origin, but I saw no way around it that would protect the confidentiality of respondents, and these are issues where confidentiality does, in fact, matter. For some ethnic or national groups, the number of students was simply too small, an all-too-common feature of today's university environments. I hope that other researchers may pursue these matters in future work. I assigned all students generic Anglo-American nicknames, only because this text is in English and the university is located in the United States. The names imply nothing about the ethnic background of respondents—e.g., "Catherine" may be Latina, Asian, black, white, Native American, or ethno-racially mixed. With respect to gender, there were sufficient numbers of women and men that changing anyone's gender was unnecessary, with the exception that

I changed the gender of one student's romantic partner because not doing so would have outed the student as same-sex partnered.

Third, I changed minor identifying details only when I was convinced they had no impact on the conclusions. I revisited these decisions several times over multiple drafts of the manuscript. If there was ever a doubt, I opted to remove the reference or detail, rather than keep a changed detail and risk introducing a self-serving statement.

These decisions all took place under a pragmatic approach to confidentiality. Given the ease of online searching and the possibility that some student might self-disclose, I proceeded with the objective that, in the event a student were unwittingly identified, the student would suffer no serious personal or professional harm. This was ultimately my most important concern. To this end, I re-read and revised the final drafts multiple times with an eye to removing anything that, in the event of inadvertent disclosure, might cause harm. The decision to remove material of this kind was both scientifically and morally difficult, since it meant dropping statements involving a few of the most important, personal, and common issues faced by students, particularly their marginalization by race or sexual orientation. These issues will have to await a later study.

The Limits

As I have argued, qualitative research should not be merely supplementary; it should be central to network analysis, particularly to any perspective in which networks, as they exist in practice, are being examined. Case studies that probe deep into micro-processes are foundational, and essential, for they serve to animate and check on the larger assumptions made in service of structural research. Nevertheless, a case study is still a case study. The experiences of 38 students in three departments in a single cohort in one university are not representative of those of American adults. To examine the applicability of my case to a national sample, I needed national data. These data are discussed in Appendix B.

Quantitative Analysis

The figures reported in Chapter 7 were based on quantitative analyses of the Core Networks and Important Alters (CNIA) survey and the Resources and Favors among College Students (RFCS) survey. The majority of the book—and the larger project behind it—devoted greater attention to generating new theories than to testing existing ones. Consequently, the two surveys contain many questions that had not been previously asked and exclude many questions to be found in existing surveys. The most important exception was the explicit replication of the General Social Survey (GSS) name generator, an essential component of the CNIA survey. Given their nature, the CNIA and RFCS surveys were preceded by a great deal of research and experimentation, which affected their size, question ordering, and format. To follow I describe each survey briefly. I then list supplementary tables for the analyses reported in Chapter 7.

LARGE-SAMPLE SURVEYS

Core Networks and Important Alters Survey

The CNIA survey was an online survey of 2,010 respondents. The survey was fielded by the research firm Qualtrics, which has a panel of thousands of respondents who are paid a small sum to complete surveys. Respondents were asked to report their core discussion networks, the people they were close to, the characteristics of the reported alters, and a set of questions regarding their decisions and motivations. For the first module of the survey, which examined whom people talked to about important matters, there were two versions, one a replica of the GSS discussion name generator and another a version designed to capture last discussions. Respondents were randomly assigned one of the two versions of the module, and roughly half of respondents received each. All other questions were identical for all respondents. Respondents were selected to match the adult, noninstitutionalized US population by gender, race, and employment status, based on the 2009 American Community Survey Public Use Micro Sample.

The CNIA survey was not designed to be a long-form survey with a large number of questions about people's networks. Instead, it was designed as a targeted survey to examine a small number of questions about the core discussion network and several unique questions not present in other studies. To help determine the survey's final form, I first conducted an exploratory online survey of 160 respondents.

The exploratory survey helped assess the feasibility of the questions, their form, and their length. This pilot study made clear that respondent fatigue would be an important consideration. Given the cognitive challenges of asking multiple questions about names elicited via several name generators in an online setting, the CNIA survey would need to be short. The exploratory survey also confirmed what other researchers had shown, that name generators in online surveys can be manipulated to produce many or few names by altering the format of the question as seen on the screen.[1] Thus, CNIA survey name generators allowed respondents to enter only one name on the screen. If they did, they were asked if there were any others, upon which, if appropriate, they proceeded to another screen where only one name could be entered. In addition, given the evidence of context effects in the GSS name generator (see Appendix A), the name generators were asked at the very start of the survey, immediately after two well-being questions and the questions required to determine eligibility.[2]

Respondents in the GSS replication sample were asked the 2004 GSS name generator. Respondents in the last-discussions sample were asked a question that began similarly but ended differently: "From time to time, most people discuss important matters with other people. Looking back over the last six months—think about the last time you discussed something that was important to you." After a pause, they were asked, "That time, what did you talk about? Two or three words are sufficient." Their options were "I talked about: _____," with space to enter the topic, and "I discussed no matters important to me." If they responded the former, they were asked for a name. The question cycle was repeated up to five times. Name interpreters followed after all names had been elicited. Additional details behind the survey may be found in Small (2013b).

The resulting sample performed well. Table B.1 presents the basic characteristics of respondents in the survey along with those of the 2000 US census.[3] With respect to gender, race, employment, and age, the sample

Table B.1. SAMPLE CHARACTERISTICS, CORE NETWORKS AND IMPORTANT ALTERS (CNIA) SURVEY

		CNIA Survey	
	US Population	Replication Sample	Last-Discussion Sample
Gender			
Female	51.6%	52.6%	50.8%
Race			
White	68.3%	69.2%	67.4%
Latino	13.7%	14.5%	16.0%
Black	11.3%	11.1%	11.0%
Other	6.8%	5.2%	5.6%
Employment			
Employed	61.4%	60.1%	61.9%
Unemployed	6.5%	6.2%	6.9%
Not in labor force	32.1%	33.6%	31.3%
Age	46	44	45
Education			
Less than high school	14.5%	3.9%	2.7%
High school graduate	28.5%	20.7%	21.4%
Some college	23.9%	30.4%	29.9%
Associate's degree	7.2%	11.5%	13.5%
Bachelor's degree	16.6%	23.1%	22.4%
Graduate or professional degree	9.2%	10.4%	10.1%
n		1,019	991

Sources: American Community Survey (ACS 2009) and CNIA survey. US figures refer to noninstitutionalized adults ages 18 and over, derived from the 2009 ACS Public Use Micro Sample (PUMS). The total number of discussion partners for the US population is derived from the 2004 General Social Survey (GSS) (McPherson et al. 2006). The GSS replication sample figures present the random half of the total sample that was asked the GSS name generator question; the last-discussion sample figures represent the other half, which was asked to report on the last important discussion respondents had.

matched the national US population, as designed. With respect to education, the online sample was slightly more educated, as expected. The proportions of respondents with some college, an associate's degree, or a bachelor's degree were each about five percentage points greater than in the US population. The proportion with an advanced degree was about the same.

Table B.2 presents the sizes of the name generators. The first column presents the sizes from the GSS. The 2004 GSS allowed people to name up to six respondents, with "six or more" as the generated category. However, it only asked name interpreter questions about the first five.

Table B.2. NUMBER OF ALTERS ELICITED BY NAME GENERATORS, GENERAL SOCIAL SURVEY (GSS) AND CORE NETWORKS AND IMPORTANT ALTERS (CNIA) SURVEY

	GSS	CNIA Survey	
Number of Alters	2004	Discussion	Important
0	24.6%	17.4%	8.0%
1	19.0%	38.8%	9.3%
2	19.2%	20.1%	15.7%
3	16.9%	11.0%	13.4%
4	8.8%	6.6%	12.4%
5	6.5%	6.2%	10.7%
6	5%	N/A	9.1%
7	N/A		7.5%
8			5.5%
9			3.2%
10			5.3%
Mean	2.08	1.69	4.2
Median	2	1	4
Mode	0	1	2

Sources: GSS (2004), CNIA survey. Note: In the GSS column, the category "6" represents "six or more" alters, per the GSS.

The next column exhibits the results of the CNIA survey, which only allowed respondents to list five alters. The CNIA survey produced a core discussion network with a slightly smaller mean and median (1.7 and 1) than the GSS (2.1 and 2), as expected given the online format and the deliberately conservative approach to the screen design. At the same time, the CNIA survey produced fewer isolates (17.4%) than the GSS (24.6%), and the mode was greater, at 1 rather than 0.

The CNIA survey also included an important alters generator asked of both the replication and the last-discussions sample, intended to capture those they were actually close to. Immediately after the first name generator cycle, respondents were given a distraction exercise to ensure they understood they were being asked a different question. They were shown three neutral images and asked to select their favorite. They were then asked, "Other than your family, who are the people you would consider important to you? These may be people you have already named, or they may be people you have not mentioned yet. Either is fine." After a pause, they were instructed, "Please list one person you consider important to you and who is not a member of your family." After they provided a name, they were offered the opportunity to list other names; the cycle was repeated to allow for five names in total. They were then asked about family: "Now, think about the family members you consider important to you. While all family [members] are significant to us, some may stand out as especially important." After a pause, they were instructed, "Please list one member of your family who is important to you." As before, they were allowed to report an additional five names.

As shown in the third column of Table B.2, the important alters list produced a large number of names (mean 4.2, median 4), even though it was asked after the GSS or modified GSS questions, and using the same conservative screen format. The results strongly suggest that the survey did not miss people who were in fact important to respondents.

The Resources and Favors among College Students Survey

The Resources and Favors among College Students (RFCS) survey was an online survey of 2,211 college students with roughly equal proportions of blacks, Latinos, Asians, and whites, and roughly equal numbers of women and men in each group. Respondents were asked to report the prevalence of problems common among college students, whom they turned to for support in addressing those problems, how, why, and under what circumstances. The survey was also administered by Qualtrics. Contrary to the CNIA survey, the RFCS survey was not designed to be representative of the US population of college students; instead, it was designed to be large enough to examine how (rather than how often) relatively uncommon processes took place.

The RFCS survey was designed to test a small number of questions that had emerged from the CNIA survey, from the fieldwork, and from a review of the literature. The survey was preceded by a pilot study of 180 students to identify issues in wording and design. The RFCS survey was concerned with broad social support, and sought not to elicit a core network but to understand experiences of support. Thus, all name generators were experience based. The survey was focused on college students because it was important to find a population that had enough problems in common, and in sufficiently large numbers, that it would be possible to identify patterns in how people addressed their problems. Contrary to the CNIA survey, it was not designed to be representative of the college student population; instead, as an analytical survey, it was designed to secure a large enough sample of students from different ethnic backgrounds that, should differences arise, could be explored in future work. Still, the core focus of the survey was not ethnic differences but how respondents made decisions about social support. The result was a number of original questions on the nature of interaction around social support networks. These questions are being analyzed in ongoing research. Additional details behind the survey design and implementation may be found in Small and Sukhu (2016).

Table B.3 exhibits the sample characteristics. The sample performed approximately as designed. There were somewhat more women (55.5%) than men. Just about 25% of the sample was of each of the four racial/ethnic categories. The mean age was just under 21. Students were only included if they were within the first four years of college; the modal student was a sophomore, and seniors, at 19.1%, constituted the smallest proportion of respondents. Eighty-eight percent of students were US born.

Table B.3. SAMPLE CHARACTERISTICS OF THE
RESOURCES AND FAVORS AMONG COLLEGE
STUDENTS (RFCS) SURVEY

Gender	
Female	55.5%
Race	
Non-Hispanic white	24.6%
Non-Hispanic black	24.7%
Non-Hispanic Asian	25.0%
Latino/a	25.7%
Age	
Mean	20.95
Year in college	
First	22.8%
Second	34.6%
Third	23.5%
Fourth	19.1%
Place of birth	
United States	87.7%
N	1,664

Source: RFCS survey.

The following tables supplement the results produced in Chapter 7, as referenced, by table title, in the chapter and its endnotes. For additional details on analytical decisions regarding Tables B.4 to B.7, see Small (2013b). For the relevant details regarding Tables B.8 to B.9b, see Small and Sukhu (2016).

Table B.4. WHY DID YOU DISCUSS (THE TOPIC YOU DISCUSSED) WITH (THE PERSON YOU TALKED TO)?

		Alter Type by Motivation		
		Important	Nonimportant	Total
S/he is good to talk to about any topic		0.45	0.58	0.42	1.00
S/he is an expert or insightful on the topic		0.20	0.41	0.59	1.00
S/he was available when I needed to discuss the topic		0.15	0.42	0.59	1.00
I am not sure		0.03	0.21	0.79	1.00
Other		0.18	0.52	0.48	1.00
	Total	1.00		
If "Other":				
Because the topic involved alter		0.44	0.56	0.44	1.00
Because alter and ego are related		0.14	0.35	0.65	1.00
Because alter had a need		0.13	0.69	0.31	1.00
Uncategorized		0.30	0.47	0.53	1.00
	"Other" total	1.00		

Source: Small 2013b. Core Networks and Important Alters (CNIA) survey, last-discussions sample (*n* = 728 last discussions; an additional 258 respondents had not discussed an important matter during the previous six months). Figures may not add to 100% due to rounding. Under "Other," "Uncategorized" reflects a wide array of understandings of motivation.

Table B.5. TOPIC OF LAST DISCUSSION OF IMPORTANT MATTER

	Main Topic	Main or Secondary Topic
Family	0.25	0.27
Career	0.16	0.20
Personal finances	0.12	0.18
Happiness and life goals	0.10	0.13
Health	0.07	0.14
Housing	0.05	0.06
Politics	0.04	0.05
Economy	0.04	0.08
Current national events	0.04	0.05
Other relationship	0.02	0.03
Current local events	0.01	0.01
Other topics	0.08	N/A
Total	1.00	N/A

Source: Small 2013b. "Other topics" includes a battery of uncategorized subjects such as "fixing license suspension," "legal matters," "zombie movies," and "a big trip."

Table B.6. RELATIONSHIP BETWEEN TOPIC AND ALTER TYPE, FIVE MOST COMMON TOPICS, LAST DISCUSSION OF IMPORTANT MATTER

	Alter Is Important	Alter Is Kin	Alter Is Coworker	Alter Is Advisor	Alter Is Health Pro.
Percentage of All Last Discussions	0.50	0.64	0.08	0.08	0.03
Percent increase in the raw probability that alter is of the listed type when the topic is					
Family	0.03	**0.07**	0.18	-0.06	-0.64
Career	0.03	-0.03	**0.85**	0.16	-0.76
Personal finances	0.02	0.07	-0.50	-0.03	0.08
Happiness and life goals	0.18	-0.02	-0.59	**0.72**	1.51
Health	-0.11	0.08	-0.31	0.34	**0.77**

Conditional increase in predicted odds that alter is of the listed type when the topic is	Alter Is Kin		Alter Is Coworker		Alter Is Advisor		Alter Is Health Pro.	
	b	e^b	b	e^b	b	e^b	b	e^b
Family	0.204	1.226						
	(0.209)							
Career			1.028***	2.796				
			(0.365)					
Happiness and life goals					0.780*	2.181		
					(0.403)			
Health							1.750**	5.752
							(0.866)	

Source: Small 2013b. Top panel presents raw figures, with bold typeset identifying theorized alter–topic matches. Bottom panel presents unstandardized conditional logit coefficients (b) and odds ratios (e^b) for regression with outcome as the alter type and predictor as the relevant topic after controlling for ego's age, gender, race, employment, education, and income and alter's age, gender, and race.
*** $p < 0.01$, ** $p < 0.05$, * $p < 0.1$.

Table B.7. MEMBERSHIP IN SOCIAL, VOLUNTARY,
AND POLITICAL ORGANIZATIONS

	Proportion of Respondents with at Least One Membership
Church or religious affiliated group	0.35
Professional or academic society	0.13
Sports group	0.13
Hobby or garden club	0.13
Labor union	0.09
Service club	0.08
Veterans' group	0.08
Literary or art discussion group	0.07
Fraternal group	0.06
Youth group	0.05
School service group	0.05
Political club	0.05
Fraternity or sorority	0.04
Nationality group	0.04
Farm organization	0.02

Source: See Small 2013b.

Table B.8. WHY DID YOU TURN TO (THE PERSON YOU TURNED TO) FOR HELP WITH (THE GIVEN PROBLEM)?

| | Primary Motivation | | | | | Mentioned Motivation | | | | |
	Accessible	Trustworthy	Skilled	Other	Total	Accessible	Trustworthy	Skilled	Other	n
Mathematics	14.4%	27.2%	46.5%	12.0%	100%	31.6%	47.5%	59.1%	20.6%	1,347
Paper	19.2%	31.1%	39.3%	10.4%	100%	36.1%	50.2%	53.1%	18.1%	1,102
Roommate	23.0%	43.0%	19.9%	14.1%	100%	38.7%	60.1%	32.1%	19.1%	801

Source: Small and Sukhu 2016. Note: The "Other" category includes "required." Respondents could indicate more than one motivation. Left panel indicates proportion of respondents who indicated the motivation was the only or primary one. Right panel indicates proportion who mentioned the motivation.

Table B.9a. LOGISTIC REGRESSION PREDICTING ODDS THAT RESPONDENT REPORTED ACCESSIBILITY AS PRIMARY OR SOLE ATTRIBUTE

	Mathematics Help					
	Model 1		Model 2		Model 3	
	b	e^b	b	e^b	b	e^b
Planning on asking someone, not necessarily this person	1.022*** (0.183)	2.779	1.532*** (0.182)	4.627	1.046*** (0.187)	2.846
Not planning on asking anyone	1.349*** (0.286)	3.857	1.908*** (0.289)	6.740	1.439*** (0.294)	4.216
Controls						
Ego characteristics	N		Y		Y	
Alter characteristics	N		N		Y	
n	1,347		1,347		1,347	

	Paper Help					
	Model 1		Model 2		Model 3	
	b	e^b	b	e^b	b	e^b
Planning on asking someone, not necessarily this person	0.770*** (0.176)	2.160	1.618*** (0.173)	5.043	0.949** (0.179)	2.583
Not planning on asking anyone	0.861*** (0.272)	2.366	1.702*** (0.272)	5.485	0.991* (0.277)	2.694
Controls						
Ego characteristics	N		Y		Y	
Alter characteristics	N		N		Y	
n	1,102		1,102		1,102	

	Roommate Help					
	Model 1		Model 2		Model 3	
	b	e^b	b	e^b	b	e^b
Planning on asking someone, not necessarily this person	1.180*** (0.207)	3.254	2.505*** (0.204)	12.244	1.382*** (0.224)	3.983
Not planning on asking anyone	0.903*** (0.307)	2.467	2.181*** (0.304)	8.855	1.140 (0.320)	3.127

Table B.9a. CONTINUED

	Roommate Help					
	Model 1		Model 2		Model 3	
	b	e^b	b	e^b	b	e^b
Controls						
Ego characteristics	N		Y		Y	
Alter characteristics	N		N		Y	
n	801		801		801	

Source: Small and Sukhu 2016. Figures are unstandardized conditional logit coefficients (b) and odds ratios (e^b) for the regression of log odds that respondent chose alter because alter was available. Ego controls are age, black, Latino, Asian, and female. Alter controls are age, black, Latino, Asian, and female. The coefficient for female ego in the math help models (0.324 in model 3) and the final paper model (0.4) were the only statistically significant controls. Controls for blacks, Latinos, Asians, and age failed to reach statistical significance in all models. Regressions include a control for question ordering (respondents were randomly assigned one of two orderings as part of an unrelated survey experiment). Based on 10 multiply imputed datasets.
*** $p < 0.01$, ** $p < 0.05$, * $p < 0.1$.

Table B.9b. LOGISTIC REGRESSION PREDICTING ODDS THAT RESPONDENT REPORTED ACCESSIBILITY AS AT LEAST ONE OF THE ATTRIBUTES

	Mathematics Help					
	Model 1		Model 2		Model 3	
	b	e^b	b	e^b	b	e^b
Planning on asking someone, not necessarily this person	0.404*** (0.137)	1.498	0.414*** (0.139)	1.513	0.412*** (0.139)	1.510
Not planning on asking anyone	0.514** (0.239)	1.672	0.599** (0.242)	1.820	0.597** (0.244)	1.817
Controls						
Ego characteristics	N		Y		Y	
Alter characteristics	N		N		Y	
n	1,347		1,347		1,347	

	Paper Help					
	Model 1		Model 2		Model 3	
	b	e^b	b	e^b	b	e^b
Planning on asking someone, not necessarily this person	0.326** (0.141)	1.385	0.337** (0.142)	1.401	0.318** (0.144)	1.374

Table B.9b. CONTINUED

Paper Help

	Model 1		Model 2		Model 3	
	b	e^b	b	e^b	b	e^b
Not planning on asking anyone	0.604***	1.829	0.618***	1.855	0.582**	1.790
	(0.227)		(0.229)		(0.232)	
Controls						
Ego characteristics	N		Y		Y	
Alter characteristics	N		N		Y	
n	1,102		1,102		1,102	

Roommate Help

	Model 1		Model 2		Model 3	
	b	e^b	b	e^b	b	e^b
Planning on asking someone, not necessarily this person	0.466***	1.594	0.526***	1.692	0.526***	1.692
	(0.175)		(0.179)		(0.184)	
Not planning on asking anyone	0.392	1.480	0.397	1.487	0.411	1.508
	(0.246)		(0.250)		(0.256)	
Controls						
Ego characteristics	N		Y		Y	
Alter characteristics	N		N		Y	
n	801		801		801	

Source: Small and Sukhu 2016. Figures are unstandardized conditional logit coefficients (b) and odds ratios (e^b) for the regression of log odds that respondent chose alter because alter was available. Ego controls are age, black, Latino, Asian, and female. Alter controls are age, black, Latino, Asian, and female. Ego controls are age, black, Latino, Asian, and female. Alter controls are age, black, Latino, Asian, and female. The coefficient for female ego in the math help models (0.344 in model 3) and the final roommate model (0.368) were the only statistically significant controls. Controls for blacks, Latinos, Asians, and age failed to reach statistical significance in all models. Regressions include a control for question ordering (respondents were randomly assigned one of two orderings as part of an unrelated survey experiment). Based on 10 multiply imputed datasets.
*** $p < 0.01$, ** $p < 0.05$, * $p < 0.1$.

NOTES

INTRODUCTION
1. Consistent with this idea, psychologists have shown that when people are anxious they are more likely to seek advice from others than they normally would (Gino, Brooks, and Schweitzer 2011).
2. Sociologists have referred to venting as a kind of "emotional support" and to thinking things through as "appraisal support" (Berkman et al. 2000). For the sake of simplicity, I will use "emotional support" as an umbrella term to capture both ideas, and to distinguish both from the kind of instrumental support people seek when they need information, a job, or other concrete goods. Throughout the text, I will clarify as needed when I am referring to one or the other form of emotional support.
3. Smith 2002/1790: 18.
4. Kant 1963/1930: 206. The original lectures from which the English text derives were not initially published by Kant in German; they were delivered by him at the University of Konigsberg around 1780. The published text reproduces his students' carefully written transcripts.
5. Cohen and Wills 1985.
6. Pennebaker and O'Heeron 1986.
7. "The groups were structured to encourage discussion of how to cope with cancer, but at no time were patients led to believe that participation would affect the course of disease. Group therapy patients were encouraged to come regularly and express their feelings about the illness and its effect on their lives. Physical problems, including side-effects of chemotherapy or radiotherapy, were discussed and a self-hypnosis strategy was taught for pain control. Social isolation was countered by developing strong relations among members. Members encouraged one another to be more assertive with doctors. Patients focused on how to extract meaning from tragedy by using their experience to help other patients and their families. One major function of the leaders was to keep the groups directed toward facing and grieving losses" (Spiegel et al. 1989: 889). And confiding in others appears to not only prevent ill health but also support well-being. A series of experimental studies recently found that disclosing personal thoughts and feelings "engage[d] neural and cognitive mechanisms associated with reward" (Tamir and Mitchell 2012: 8038).
8. The control group, asked to write about nonemotional topics, showed no effects. A parallel study of patients with rheumatoid arthritis showed smaller but still

statistically significant improvements in "overall disease activity" (Smyth, Stone, Hurewitz, and Kaell 1999).

9. Smyth 1998. An important contributor to this literature has been James Pennebaker (see Pennebaker and Beall 1986; Pennebaker, Kiecolt-Glaser, and Glaser 1988; Pennebaker, Colder, and Sharp 1990; Pennebaker 1990, 1993).

10. Cobb 1976; Berkman and Syme 1979; Berkman 1985; Kahn and Antonucci 1980; House, Landis and Umberson 1988; Kawachi and Berkman 2000, 2001.

11. There are several refined classifications of social support (see House 1981, Chapter 2, especially pp. 19–21). Fischer (1982) distinguishes emotional from instrumental support. House (1981) divides them into emotional, instrumental, informational, and appraisal (also Berkman et al. 2000). Wellman and Wortley (1990) believe there are emotional aid, small services, large services, financial aid, and companionship. For reviews of the vast work on social support, see Stack 1974; House 1981; House, Landis, and Umberson 1988; Berkman et al 2000; Antonucci et al. 2014.

12. For examples, see Stack 1974, Wellman and Wortley 1990, Pescosolido 1992, Lin 2001, Smith 2007, Small 2009b, Menon and Smith 2014.

13. Kant 1963/1930: 206. Kant's statement was ultimately about "full" disclosure. It is possible he believed people might reasonably disclose a truly personal but very narrow matter to someone other than a friend.

14. Smith 2002/1790: 28.

15. Smith et al. 2002. The question read, "Now suppose you felt just a bit down or depressed, and you wanted to talk about it. Who would you turn to first for help?" Respondents were given a long list of options.

16. McPherson, Smith-Lovin, and Brashears 2006: 354.

17. The findings will turn out to be consistent with Simmel's argument about the propensity to confide in strangers (Simmel 1950: 404).

18. Barabási and Albert 1999; Albert and Barabási 2002; Barabási and Frangos 2002; Girvan and Newman 2002; Watts 1999; Butts 2009.

CHAPTER 1

1. Marsden 1987; McPherson, Smith-Lovin, and Brashears 2006; Fischer 2009.

2. "Perfect friendship is the friendship of people who are good and alike in virtue; for they are alike in wishing each other's good, inasmuch as they are good and good in themselves" (Aristotle 1943/350 BCE: 199). "[Perfect friendships] require time and familiarity, too; for, as the adage puts it, men cannot know one another until they have eaten salt together; nor can they admit one another to friendship, or be friends at all, until each has been proved lovable and trustworthy by the other" (Aristotle 1943/350 BCE: 200).

3. "'Tis obvious, that people associate together according to their particular tempers and dispositions, and that men of gay tempers naturally love the gay; as the serious bear an affection to the serious. This not only happens, where they remark this resemblance betwixt themselves and others, but also by the natural course of the disposition, and by a certain sympathy, which always arises betwixt similar characters" (Hume 1978/1739: 354).

4. "We expect less sympathy from a common acquaintance than from a friend: we cannot open to the former all those little circumstances which we can unfold to the latter" (Smith 2002/1790: 28). The findings in this book will cast doubt on Smith's statement. It is worth noting that, in this passage, Smith is expressing his belief that the difference made it possible for people to approach an

acquaintance more calmly, since there would presumably be less to share. Being in the presence of total strangers would produce even more tranquility.

5. Simmel 1950.
6. Moreno 1934. This history, however, can be simplistic. Many researchers before Moreno were doing similar things, though perhaps less extensively. In fact, the use of sociograms to represent kinship structures has a long-standing tradition in the field of anthropology (see Lévi-Strauss 1969). See Freeman 2004 for a comprehensive history of the structural tradition of network analysis.
7. Mitchell 1969; Evens and Handelman 2006; Festinger, Schachter, and Back 1950; Homans 1950, 1958, 1961; Lorrain and White 1971; White, Boorman, and Breiger 1976. There were many others.
8. See Freeman 2004.
9. Mitchell 1969; Moreno 1934; Newcomb 1961.
10. Probably most important was Katz and Lazarsfeld (1955), wherein researchers asked respondents in Decatur, Illinois, to name whom they found trustworthy about public issues, who had influenced their opinions, and whom they talked to most often about what they heard on the radio. Lazarsfeld, Berelson, and Gaudet 1968.
11. Laumann 1973; Wellman 1979; Fischer 1982. Many important scholars, such as sociologists Peter Bearman, Claude Fischer, Charles Kadushin, Edward Laumann, Bernice Pescosolido, Lois Verbrugge, Barry Wellman, and their many students and collaborators, have contributed to this work over the past 40 years. A large sociocentric study might explain all possible relations among people in a large corporation or a major online dating site—every possible connection to everyone else. But it will miss all connections to people not in the corporation or the site. A large egocentric study might explain the connections of a nationally representative sample of 2,000 people, but by definition it does not explore the connections within the sample. The questions animating the present study are those about how individuals act, which, by definition, are egocentric in nature.
12. This idea can be traced to theoretical work by sociologists such as Coleman (1958) and anthropologists such as Mitchell (1969).
13. Laumann 1973: 264.
14. The analysis of ego networks has grown dramatically in the ensuing years. For a comprehensive and up-to-date account, see Perry, Pescosolido, and Borgatti forthcoming.
15. It was conducted annually until 1994 and biennially thereafter (see General Social Survey, http://www.norc.org/GSS+Website/, accessed July 15, 2014). See Smith et al. 2002.
16. Burt 1984: 294.
17. "I conducted the networks survey in 1977-78 that was eventually reported in several articles and in *To Dwell Among Friends,* 1982. One of the 11 name-eliciting questions we developed and used was this one: 'When you are concerned about a personal matter—for example, about someone you are close to or something you are worried about—how often do you talk about it with someone—usually, sometimes, or hardly ever? [Unless respondent volunteers "never," ask:] When you do talk with someone about personal matters, whom do you talk with?' Ron Burt, who had the office next to mine, used the data to run a reduction analysis. He concluded (in a paper published in a collection he edited, I think) that if you could ask only one question out of the 11, the one above did the best to capture the 'core' set of names. I was skeptical about using any one question. . . . And

I made the point, based on our extensive pre-testing (two pretests of about 80 cases each) in writing (p. 289 in *TDAF*, and I think in an earlier working paper), that there was too much error in any one question to conclude that *these* people and only these people provided the specified exchange. Instead, the set of people answered over a set of questions provided an accurate list of alters. (That is, a respondent might forget someone who should have been answered to a specific question, but that name will come up elsewhere.)" Fischer, personal communication, July 13, 2014.

18. In Fischer's (1982) survey, respondents were asked about "personal matters." In his GSS proposal, Burt (1984: 331) suggested that GSS respondents could be asked about "personal important matters"; in the end, they were asked about "important matters." In a qualitative study of how people interpreted the GSS question, Bailey and Marsden (1999: 298) noted that "many respondents did not find the notion of important matters to be straightforward." At the same time, however, they often seemed to infer that the question referred to important matters specifically of a personal nature (Bailey and Marsden 1999: 297).

19. Marsden 1987. Burt (1986) published what appears to be the very first scholarly paper using the GSS name generator. Burt's paper, however, was focused on whether respondents named alters in descending order of strength. (They do, with a tipping point at the third name.)

20. Marsden 1987; Ruan 1998; Völker and Flap 2002; Boessen et al. 2014; Tigges, Browne, and Green 1998; Liu, Lui, and Man 2009; Bearman and Parigi 2004. Some surveys have employed minor variations on the question wording. For a review, see Bailey and Marsden 1999.

21. Marsden 1987; Sommer et al. forthcoming; Carroll and Teo 1996; Suzman 2009.

22. Burt 1987; Hurlbert et al. 2000; Lake and Huckfeldt 1998; Mutz 20002; Glaeser, Laibson, and Sacerdote 2002; Hampton, Sessions, and Her 2011; Chen 2013; Tigges, Browne, and Green 1998; Suzman 2009.

23. Burt 1984: 317; see also Bailey and Marsden 1999; McCallister and Fischer 1978; and Straits 2000.

24. Marsden 1987: 123; see also Burt 1985. In the first report of the initial GSS survey, Marsden argued that the measure should capture overall strength: "the GSS criterion could be expected to elicit reasonably strong ties, with prominent representation of kin among those cited" (Marsden 1987: 123).

25. Moore 1990: 728.

26. Mollenhorst, Völker, and Flap 2008: 938. The authors made a similar point in a different study. "The core discussion network question was selected for this procedure, because this question delineates the inner core of one's personal network, which consists of the most intimate ties" (Mollenhorst, Völker, and Flap 2014: 68).

27. McPherson, Smith-Lovin, and Brashears 2006, 2009; Smith-Lovin, Brashears, and McPherson, 2008; Fischer 2009, 2012; Paik and Sanchagrin 2013; Brashears 2014, Small 2013b.

28. McPherson, Smith-Lovin, and Brashears 2006: 353. And later: "The closer and stronger our tie with someone, the broader the scope of their support for us . . . and the greater the likelihood that they will provide major help in a crisis. These are important people in our lives" (McPherson et al. 2006: 354). The authors based their argument in part on earlier studies of the core discussion network. "In his earlier study of California communities, Fischer (1982a)

used a similar question about discussing personal matters. He found that this relationship elicited relatively strong personal ties with a good representation of both kin and non-kin. These close relationships have theoretical importance because they are central in social influence and normative pressures (Burt 1984: 127), and have strong conceptual connections to earlier survey measures of best friends and other close socio-emotional ties. Different ways of asking about important, close interpersonal relationships (often called strong ties) tend to be convergent. Many ways of asking such questions get the same close ties. These close ties are only a small subset of a person's complete interpersonal environment, which also includes a much larger array of weak ties, which are more distant connections to people. Weak ties may occur in just one institutional context or may connect us to people who are less like us in many ways. . . . Estimates of the larger network of weak ties range between 150 (Hill and Dunbar 2003) to more than a thousand . . ." (McPherson et al. 2006: 355). The statement, however, combines arguments based on empirical evidence with arguments that had not been tested.

29. It is interesting that the field arrived at this conclusion even though the GSS was explicitly designed to elicit an exchange relation (talking to others), rather than an affective relation (closeness to others). Had the GSS designers wanted to know whom people were close to, they could have just asked them. But as use of the name generator spread, it became interpreted as more and more things than it could plausibly be said to be. See Marin and Hampton 2007 for a discussion; see also van der Poel 1993.

30. The GSS name generator has been important and widely influential, justifying its use as a starting point for our inquiry. At the same time, however, this study is not just about the GSS. As a survey question the GSS probably performed its originally intended role well. However, over the years it has been interpreted to mean much more than it should have. And part of the reason is that these interpretations are consistent with basic predictions from structural network analysis.

31. The author defines the strength of a tie as "a (probably linear) combination of the amount of time, the emotional intensity, the intimacy (mutual confiding), and the reciprocal services which characterize the tie" (Granovetter 1973: 1361). Marsden and Campbell (1984) showed that "closeness" is probably the best indicator of what researchers mean by tie strength. I will often use the words interchangeably throughout the book.

32. Granovetter 1973.

33. Wellman 1981: 185 (italics in the original).

34. Wellman 1981: 186.

35. Wellman and Wortley 1990. Wellman's ideas about emotional support coming from strong ties also owe a great deal to Homans (1950, 1961), who argued that repeated interactions between people create positive sentiments that make them reliable means of support (Homans 1961).

36. Granovetter 1983: 209

37. An interesting issue is that the 1985 GSS itself almost provided this opportunity. As part of the name interpreter, it asked how close respondents were to the alter. "Do you feel equally close to all these people?" If they answered negatively, they were then asked which of them they felt "especially close to." Unfortunately, the survey did not give them the option of indicating that they were not close at all.

38. Note that I have described two among many different kinds of survey questions in reference to this idea. In the first, GSS respondents were asked generically whom they would turn to if they were "just a bit down or depressed." In the second, the GSS name generator, people were asked to report the names of their confidants, "thinking back over the last six months." The fact that the latter introduces a specific time period means the latter question is a lot less hypothetical than the former. At the same time, however, respondents are asked to summarize six months' worth of experiences, a process in which they will inevitably generalize, rather than report concrete experiences. I should also note that the heart of my critique of the GSS name generator question lies in how it has been interpreted. The question itself is quite robust and has probably served its original purpose quite well. However, it is not a great tool to understand the everyday practice of turning to others for support or to understand why they turn to whom they turn. In a later chapter, I will also discuss why, even in a world in which respondents were accurate and truthful, the average person they confided in over the previous six months may still be someone not in the core discussion network.

39. Killworth and Bernard 1976. I discuss this and the other studies in greater detail in a later chapter.

40. Bernard and Killworth 1977.

41. Bernard and Killworth 1977: 17. Though researchers argue over aspects of these studies, the basic conclusion seems firm that people's representations of their own social networks are suspect (see Bernard, Killworth, and Sailer 1979, 1982; Bernard, Killworth, Kronenfeld, and Sailer 1984; Kashy and Kenny 1990).

42. Watts 2011.

43. A version of this pattern may be particularly true in survey-based studies. There is a probability that, when asked to recall their confidants, people tend to remember those they are closest to because of what Amos Tversky and Daniel Kahneman have called the "availability heuristic." As the authors have written, "A person is said to employ the availability heuristic whenever he estimates frequency or probability by the ease with which instances or associations could be brought to mind" (Tversky and Kahneman 1973: 208). People probably think they talk most frequently to those they are close to because they are more easily recalled.

44. As he wrote, "With the objectivity of the stranger is connected, also, . . . the fact that he often receives the most surprising openness confidences which sometimes have the character of a confessional and which would be carefully withheld from a more closely related person" (Simmel 1950: 404).

45. Stanovich and West 2000; Kahneman 2003a, 2003b, 2011; Kahneman and Tversky 2000. Similar ideas have been developed in social theory and sociology (Schutz 1964; Bourdieu 1977, 1990; Esser 1993; Kroneberg 2014).

46. Feld 1981, 1982, 1984; Small 2009b. See also Oldenburg 1989.

47. Small 2009b.

48. Personal conversations often take place in contexts (e.g., in bed between spouses) well beyond the purview of the ethnographer's eye. And for those that are not, the ethnographer's mere presence changes the dynamic of the interaction. In a deeply epistemological sense, no scientist except the lucky unnoticed eavesdropper can actually observe a naturally occurring private conversation between two people—a fatal flaw.

49. Qualitative researchers have debated the relative strengths of participant observation and in-depth interviewing for years (Becker and Geer 1957; Jessor, Colby, and Shweder 1996; DiMaggio 2014; Jerolmack and Khan 2014; Vaisey 2014). More recently, some have argued that observation is superior to in-depth interviewing when it comes to capturing actual behavior (Jerolmack and Khan 2014). While that is often true, the present case introduces a clear case where it is not, since observation is not technically possible. Here, there are two important distinctions, both of which take place strictly within the purview of interviewing: the difference between what people say they would do and what they would actually do, and the difference between what people say they have generally done and what they have actually done. A carefully constructed interview can capture the latter of each of these distinctions quite well. The problem has been that, with respect to whom people approach when they need a confidant, researchers have not seen reason to do so.

50. For more on the advantages and disadvantages of interviews versus surveys, see Richardson, Dohrenwend, and Klien 1965; Weiss 1994; Small 2009a, 2009b.

51. On social desirability bias, see King and Bruner 2000.

52. This book does not aim to examine the effects of a cause upon an outcome. It is concerned with how, not whether-or-not, questions. However, the foundations of the counterfactual model of causality provide a useful tool for the particular discussion in this paragraph. In the counterfactual model, a cause is said to have effected an outcome if, were all other conditions the same but the cause not present, the outcome would not have occurred. The difficulty lies in the fact that it is impossible for actors, groups, organizations, or any social phenomena to exist in two states, with and without the cause present. People cannot simultaneously experience and not experience a cause. Statistical techniques are therefore employed to estimate causal effects on average for statistically created groups assumed to be identical in all ways except the presence or absence of the cause (Pearl 2009; Morgan and Winship 2015; for a discussion of this and other models in the context of qualitative work, see Small 2013a). One element of the counterfactual model that is useful is its relentless pursuit of clarity about what is being compared to what. That attention helps clarify that simply examining one context statically and asserting a causal effect, especially with no careful assessment of the mechanisms at play, is an inferential mistake.

53. It is not surprising that researchers have found that the availability of confidants changes with major life transitions (e.g., Ha 2008).

54. Mechanic 1978: xv. Mechanic's *Students Under Stress* remains one of the most extensive field studies of graduate students focused specifically on stress, coping strategies, and social networks. There have been many others. See Erbe 1966; Mallinckrodt and Leon 1992; Wan et al. 1992; Hyun et al. 2006; Johnson-Bailey et al. 2008; Robotham 2008; Solem, Lee, and Schlemper 2009; Graduate Assembly 2014. For more on factors that affect graduate student success, see the Council of Graduate Schools' PhD Completion Project, http://www.phdcompletion.org/information/book4.asp. For classic studies of how individuals cope with stress, see Steiner 1945; Kadushin 1969; Lazarus and Folkman 1984.

55. See, for example, Wan et al. 1992; Johnson-Bailey et al. 2008; Smith and Moore 2000.

56. In fact, researchers have documented differences by race and by gender in the perception of graduate environment (Solem, Lee, and Schlemper 2009). See also

Johnson-Bailey at al. 2008. A classic work on the problems of being a numerical minority in organizational contexts is Kanter (1977).

CHAPTER 2

1. All students were asked the GSS name generator at the very start of every interview. In addition, following the GSS protocol, all of them were asked, "Is there anyone else?" after the student reported the last name. See appendices for details.
2. This number is higher than those resulting from national surveys, which tend to report about three members (Marsden 1987; McPherson, Smith-Lovin, and Brashears 2006; Fischer 2008, 2012; Small 2013b; see also Marin 2004). The discrepancy probably results from the fact that our students were asked for names at the start of the interview and that we were more committed than the average survey employee (see Fischer 2012; Paik and Sanchagrin 2013). In fact, respondents to the 2004 GSS, when asked by their best interviewers, also reported about six discussion partners, according to Paik and Sanchagrin 2013. "When we look at the distribution of network size across our 136 interviewers in 2004, the mean average network size is 2.02 (sd=1.28), with a min of 0 and a max of 6.5. This stat doesn't appear in any of our tables, but can be easily examined through using our public release programs" (Kenneth Sanchagrin, personal communication, October 4, 2016).
3. Granovetter 1973: 1361.
4. Marsden and Campbell 1984: 498. The authors examined closeness, duration, frequency of interaction, the breadth of topics of discussion, and confiding in others, based on three datasets. As we shall see, I will often be forced to infer closeness from other factors, such as the duration of a relationship. See also Marsden and Campbell 2012.
5. McPherson, Smith-Lovin, and Brashears 2006: 353.
6. Granovetter 1973. By contrast, see Mollenhorst, Völker, and Flap 2014, who report on changes in the core discussion network after a seven-year period.
7. Catherine's delay until early middle age before having her first child is common in a corporate environment where the childbearing decision may carry serious career consequences for women. Many sociologists and popular authors have written about this issue. See Hochschild 1989, 1997; Sandberg 2013; Slaughter 2015.
8. The relationship is also evidence of Coleman's (1988) argument that intergenerational closure cements bonds. When parents are friends of their children's friends' parents, the sense of community is stronger and informal social control is greater. Much of Coleman's discussion, however, involved a community or a school, where multiple parents could generate the social benefits of intergenerational closure. Catherine and Jenny, now living in different cities, are not part of a local group; they are a dyad.
9. In the third wave, Catherine listed her dissertation adviser and did not list Jenny. It is not uncommon for interviewees to either forget a name or add a name during one or two interviews. Even though Catherine technically did not include Jenny's name in wave three, it is still reasonable to see her case as consistent with strong tie theory, since all sociological theories must leave room for random fluctuations, and many of the better ones are probabilistic, rather than deterministic (Lieberson 1985, 1991). For this reason, I separately examined the changes in the composition of the core discussion in two separate

ways: (a) based precisely on what respondents answered and (b) assuming some random fluctuations due to chance (mistakes, memory lapses, temporary fights, etc.); the conclusions did not change (see Small, Pamphile, and McMahan 2015).

10. Social interaction is foundational to many sociological perspectives. See Simmel 1950; Homans 1950, 1961; Goffman 1967; Collins 2004.

11. See Homans 1961; Blau 2008/1964; Lawler, Thye, and Yoon 2008; Yamagishi and Cook 1993.

12. Furman 1997.

13. Small 2009b. See also Duneier 1992 and Martin and Yeung 2006.

14. Feld 1981: 1016.

15. Students were asked how close each alter pair was, with a range of 0 to 7, with 0 indicating that they did not know each other. Note that in the 1985 GSS, the average density was 0.61 (Marsden 1987). The difference could result because students are unique or because entering new contexts undermines structural strength. In Chapter 7 I show it was probably the latter. The first interviews took place within a month of their arrival, and by then several had already added people affiliated with the university, such as professors.

16. Naturally, if we had selected all people in their network, the density would have been far lower. In that particular sense, this network is more dense than average. But if we had selected all coworkers in their network, the density may well have been greater. On the whole, the network density is moderate, and certainly not the kind that represents the elegant predictions Granovetter would have made of strong ties.

17. Sometimes, students provided initials or nicknames, such as "adviser" or "mentor," instead of real names, and their approach at times changed from wave to wave. For this reason, there are two students for which we are unable to tell with complete certainty whether an alter name in the second wave was the same as a person named in the first. The figures presented earlier assume the names are different. However, only three alters in total were affected. Since there were 578 total named alters in wave 1, that possibility would not alter the conclusions.

18. See Small, Pamphile, and McMahan 2015: 100–101.

CHAPTER 3

1. Bearman and Parigi 2004.

2. Mollenhorst, Völker, and Flap 2008: 938.

3. Bernard and Killworth 1977: 17.

4. Bernard and Killworth 1977; Bernard, Killworth, and Sailer 1979, 1982; Bernard, Killworth, Kronenfeld, and Sailer 1984; Kashy and Kenny 1990.

5. Tversky and Kahneman 1973: 207. See also Brashears and Quintane 2015.

6. Unfortunately, a perspective persists across the social sciences in which uncommon events are somehow perceived as theoretically or substantively unimportant. Studying unique or rare events has repeatedly proved useful to the scientific enterprise. For example, revolutions are rare, yet their study has transformed what social scientists know about the state (Skocpol 1979). Similarly, few women or men are transsexual, yet understanding their predicament has revealed a great deal about workplace discrimination (Schilt 2010). See Small 2009a; Harding, Fox, and Mehta 2002. In fact, rare events can help identify elements of a social situation difficult to observe in ordinary activity (Ragin and Becker 1992; Small 2009a).

7. Glaser and Strauss 1967; Geertz 1973; Hammersley and Atkinson 2007; Lofland et al. 2006.
8. Simmel 1950. See also Burt 1992; Faust 2007.
9. The term appears to have been coined by French (1953; Wickstrom and Bendix 2000). In the 1920s and 1930s, a series of controlled experiments at the Hawthorne plant of the Western Electric Company were designed to improve worker productivity. Many of the studies showed that, regardless of intervention (such as changing the lighting for the experimental group), both groups improved. Further investigation suggested that all workers were merely responding to the fact of being observed. Since then, there has been a great deal of research on the effect, including a reanalysis of the plant data. See Adair 1984; Jones 1992; Wickstrom and Bendix 2000.
10. The "observer effect" is the general idea that it may be impossible to observe a phenomenon without altering the phenomenon. It is sometimes called the "Heisenberg effect," in reference to the Heisenberg uncertainty principle, though the latter refers to something somewhat different. Heisenberg argued that the more precisely one determines the position of a particle, such as an electron, the less accurately one can determine its speed, and vice versa (Heisenberg 1983/1927).
11. Different people might need a confidant to discuss different kinds of issues: acute problems, general crises, private matters, not-private but sensitive matters, neither private nor sensitive but otherwise important matters, and so on. To attain comparability across responses, we asked students what they worried about. Regardless of whether the personal issue is acute or general, if a person is worried about it, a confidant would be appropriate.
12. In the first wave of the study, we had asked them to name three worries about their life in general. However, they often did not have three.
13. That statement is true as long as there is no systematic bias induced by the time during which we held our interviews. For example, suppose our interviews were all held late in the afternoon. If most people confided in their coworkers most days while at work and in their spouses most evenings before sleep, we would wrongly infer that people mostly confide in coworkers. However, most last conversations had not happened during the day of the interview. And I can think of no related bias that would cause concern. In addition, I stress that here I refer to "statistically average" within the population of 37 students in our study, not the population of graduate students at large. To know the latter, one needs a probability survey, not a case study.
14. Interview transcripts were messy as data in a number of ways. Sometimes they reported two worries, instead of three. Other times they hesitated in describing something as a worry. They could not always recall whom they talked to the very last time they talked to someone. And so on. I addressed each of the issues as it emerged and discuss the solution throughout the text.
15. For example, see Clance and Imes 1978.
16. Hyun et al. 2006: 255.
17. Hyun et al. 2006: 247, 256.
18. Small 2009a, 2011.
19. In this wave, 35 of the 37 participants provided an alter whose core discussion network membership could be recorded. Thus, $n = 35$. The percentages will add to slightly more than 100 because (a) a few respondents' last discussions were with more than one alter simultaneously and (b) in those cases, the alters differed in

their present or past core discussion network membership. The same will be true for the "Last discussion reported" numbers.

20. In 2 of the 35 cases, neither of these names was available, so we followed the same procedure for the second issue they reported worrying about. In total, 17 of the 35 alters were of the first name reported, which may or may not have been the name of the person in the most recent conversation.

21. In 11 of 35 cases, the name is of the alter in the most recent discussion about the second worry reported; in 2 of 35, it is of the alter in the most recent discussion about the third worry reported. In 7 of 35 cases, the name of the most recent discussant is not available and the name of the first discussant mentioned is used instead.

22. Figures will add to more than 100% because several conversations took place with more than one alter.

23. Another part of the reason the numbers are so small is that in wave 3, we used this portion of the interview to examine why they did not approach others in their core discussion network, an issue we turn to in the next chapter.

24. I emphasize that especially because the portion of the interview about worries about life outside graduate school was even more open-ended than the discussion of the graduate school worries—in fact, that is the reason we only have the data for about two-thirds of the students—it would make little sense to make either strong or numerically precise claims about the distribution of graduate students' experiences. See Small 2009a.

25. One clue about why not all discussion partners were of the "strong tie" kind expected by many researchers can be gleaned from a methodological study by Stefanie Bailey and Peter Marsden of what people understood when they were asked the GSS name generator instrument. The authors conducted cognitive interviews with 50 respondents wherein the latter were asked to talk through their answers aloud, explaining how they interpreted the question. Bailey and Marsden (1999) found that 13% interpreted the question as referring to the names of close or important alters, 28% interpreted it as referring to the people with whom they discussed general topics, and 43% interpreted the question literally, as referring to the people with whom they talked most regularly about important matters. The latter group may or may not refer to people with whom respondents are close, and the students we interviewed reflected that possibility.

26. The matter may differ in a national population—I address this question in a later chapter. It is also worth recalling that the GSS instrument was designed for a different purpose, to capture the personal network of a representative population of Americans, later interpretations of the instrument notwithstanding.

27. Testing Tversky and Kahneman's full slate of expectations might require a different kind of analysis, one based on a laboratory experiment.

28. Consider Catherine, the former corporate worker concerned with the work–family balance who brought her husband and child from Dallas when she started graduate school. Catherine typically named her husband, her sister, and her friend Jenny as core discussion network members over the course of the first year. Suppose that over the course of the last six months of the year she felt the need to confide in someone—about her research, the work–family balance, health insurance, finances, or any personal or otherwise important topic—a total of 14 times, and she talked to someone each time.

Set aside for the moment that counting the number of times we need to talk to someone may be difficult for multiple reasons. That is, presume that Catherine had 14 out-of-the-ordinary conversations during which she vented to or brainstormed with someone and found catharsis, an epiphany, a sense of relief, or a deeper understanding of something that was troubling her. If she turned to her husband twice, to her sister twice, to Jenny twice, and to eight other people once, she would be accurately representing her core discussion network—the people she talked to most when she needed someone to talk to. Yet she would have still talked to those people less than half the time she needed someone to talk to. In this way, the reported list may be right about the difference between those in it and those outside it but wrong about what people do in practice most of the time. This distinction is important. In the end, the GSS name generator has probably performed well for its original intentions. Yet to infer from its results that people in reality have more conversations with people they are close to than those they are not may be mistaken.

CHAPTER 4

1. Granovetter 1973.
2. For example, there is evidence of this pattern in the broader context of social support. Carol Stack reported the phenomenon in the large kin and nonkin networks among low-income African Americans she studied. "The people living in The Flats cannot keep their resources and their needs a secret. Everyone knows who is working, when welfare checks arrive, and when additional resources are available" (Stack 1974: 37).
3. See Stinchcombe 2001 and Powell and DiMaggio 1991 on institutional relations; see also Small 2009b.
4. For an extended discussion of this question among mothers in childcare centers, see Small 2009b.
5. Love between parishioners and priests is in fact common (Nadeau 2015). In Italy, there are blogs and Facebook groups, and the number of people open about such relationships has apparently increased since the 2013 election of Pope Francis.
6. Mauss 1954; Ekeh 1974; Emerson 1976; Blau 1986/1964; Bearman 1997.
7. Blau 1986/1964: 4.
8. Stack 1974.
9. Granovetter 1973: 1361.
10. In Fischer's Northern California study they were called "just friends" or "close kin" (1982a: 41); see also Fischer 1982b. Husbands and wives may be seen as having unmediated relationships, the way siblings do. At the same time, however, when they are formally married, there is a contract with clear institutional expectations. In this respect, they may bear elements of both.
11. Lazarsfeld and Merton 1954; McPherson, Smith-Lovin, and Cook 2001.
12. See Fischer 1982; Logan and Spitze 1994, 1996. In fact, the family is a formal institution to the extent some of the expectations required of its members are encoded in the law, such as the obligation of alimony or of child support.
13. The system of expectations in kin relations has been at the heart of anthropology since at least Morgan 1871. Bott's (1957) *Family and Social Network* remains the classic treatment of class differences from a network perspective in kin-related expectations.

14. Boissevain offers a useful definition. "A social relation between two people that is based on a single role relation is described as uniplex or single-stranded, while a relation that covers many roles is termed multiplex or many stranded" (1974: 30).

15. Boissevain 1974: 28. See Biddle 1986 for a comprehensive review of how sociologists have conceived of roles in the second half of the 20th century.

16. Merton 1968/1949: 422. Merton was clear that his own conception of a role derived directly from the work of Ralph Linton.

17. Boissevain has proposed that "where multiplex relations exist, they will be more intimate (in the sense of friendly and confidential) than single-stranded relations" (1974: 32).

18. Granovetter 1974.

19. Bearman and Parigi 2004. Asking people to explain the motivations behind their own actions must be done with care. People may lie, of course; more important, they are not always aware of why they do what they do. In the methodological appendix I discuss the limits and advantages of my approach. A few researchers in recent years have pushed for qualitative and mixed-methods research in network analysis broadly (Dominguez and Hollstein 2014).

20. Both described one additional cohort member, a man in Layla's case and a woman in Andrea's, as being as close to each as the two women were to each other.

21. University professors have been documented to have, on average, more liberal political positions than the average American. However, universities are also often centuries-old institutions with long-standing norms and practices and a tendency to change only slowly. See Gross 2013.

22. The relationship bears an affinity to Roger Gould's (2003) proposition that ambiguity about rank creates conflict.

23. Bourdieu 1984.

24. On the concept of loss aversion, see Kahneman and Tversky 1984; Tversky and Kahneman 1991.

25. So many professors seem to have witnessed "the best student they've taught in decades" year after year that entire faculties in some universities must be living in multiple dimensions simultaneously, each with an allocation of once-in-a-lifetime geniuses.

26. See Nietzsche 1989/1887.

27. The student also chooses advisers in ways an employee rarely chooses bosses. Since the typical student probably has more admission offers than the average job seeker gets job offers, the student's choice set is typically larger. A strategically savvy student will place herself in an institutional context where if things do not work with one adviser she can take corrective action by simply choosing another. Employees, no matter how savvy, rarely have that choice. (How many workers would not love to fire their bosses while staying in the same company?) However, that ability, that additional power a student can deploy, is possible because the expectations of a student relationship are in a sense greater than those of an employee. A student must reciprocate more.

28. The ideas on debt, obligation, and power in this chapter owe a great deal to Nietzsche (1989/1887).

29. On conflict in interpersonal interactions, see Goffman 1967, who adopted a dramaturgical metaphor as an underlying analytical tool. Goffman's work on interaction centered primarily on the presentation of self before others and the importance of saving face. Saving face probably sometimes played a role here, as

in students' avoidance of others in competitive contexts. But many of the other dynamics, such as avoiding one's own mother, were less about saving face than about avoiding getting upset or becoming uncomfortable. A broader notion, centering on expectations, is therefore more appropriate.

30. Boissevain 1974: 32.

CHAPTER 5

1. The term "loss" is more common in the literature. "Harm" is probably more appropriate for our purposes. I will use both throughout the chapter.

2. The qualifier, "all other factors being equal," is especially important here. Clearly, losing some weak ties—such as one's relationship to a boss—is quite costly.

3. More precisely, they would need the potential benefit to be high and the potential harm to be minimal, and reason to believe that the probability of receiving that benefit is high and of suffering that harm is low. The discussion in this chapter is consistent with aspects of rational actor theory. There is an enormous literature in economics, psychology, and marketing on choice under uncertainty dating back at least to Blaise Pascal. I seek to make no contributions to that theory. As I argue throughout the book, rational actor models are useful tools that work in some circumstances and fail in others (see also Pescosolido 1992). The model is a useful starting point here because it helps frame the stakes in one particular set of issues: how people sometimes decide to confide in others when they reflect on the matter before making the decision. The discussion owes something to Coleman's formulation of trust, in which the three issues that matter are the risk, the potential gain from being right, and the potential loss from being wrong. Coleman posited a risk as worth taking if the odds of success are greater than the potential loss relative to the potential gain—that is, when $(p/(1-p)) > L/G$, where p is the probability of success (Coleman 1990: 98ff). Coleman's model is a useful staring point, but it has some problems. One can be seen in practice. If the potential loss is greater than the potential gain, then L/G is > 1, which means that according to the model, no odds of success in such circumstances would be enough for the decision to trust to be worth the risk. Yet there is evidence of people trusting others when the potential losses greatly surpass the potential gains. For example, in Small (2009b), I showed that mothers were willing to trust their kids with other mothers in their children's centers whom they barely knew even though the potential loss (something terrible could happen to their child) greatly surpassed the potential gain (they could receive great babysitting for a few hours). The second problem is conceptual. The model posits p or the "chance of winning" as relative to the "chance of losing," or $1-p$ (Coleman 1990: 99). But gains and losses are separate things, and a person can both gain and lose something at the same time—for example, feel relieved at having vented a preoccupation but also feel a little embarrassment. Thus, a better way of specifying the model would be to state that the potential gain times the probability of the gain is greater than the potential loss times the probability of the loss (or $p_g * G > p_l * L$). The chapter's discussion adopts this framework. For one of many sophisticated critiques models that view gains and losses differently, see Kahneman and Tversky 1979.

4. Asking people to explain their motivation is a risky proposition—people may lie, of course, but, more important, they do not always know why they do what they do. They may also have a natural bias toward rationality, toward accounting for their behavior in ways that make their decisions comprehensible (Nisbett and

Wilson 1977; Shafir, Simonson, and Tversky 1993; Tilly 2006). Indeed, people's representations of their decisions are so potentially suspect that in some disciplines they are explicitly ignored, based on the notion that preferences must be revealed in behavior and only behavior can be believed (Samuelson 1938). I believe ignoring people's representations altogether is scientifically incurious and analytically problematic. If truthful rational actors are engaging in a thought process orthogonal to that predicted by rational actor theory, then theory is suspect. Even if the predictions of the theory were to hold, the mechanisms theorized to give rise to those predictions would have to be incomplete or either partly or fully incorrect. The purpose of our analysis, therefore, will be to assess whether the students' accounts of their own behavior are consistent with one or the other set of theoretical predictions regarding their behavior.

5. Hardin 2002; Baier 1986.
6. Baier 1986: 236.
7. Wellman and Wortley 1990; see also Wellman and Wortley 1989.
8. However, the authors analyzed rather broad categories of behavior, and they were only able to report that, with respect to their category closest to our present concerns, the pursuit of "emotional aid," people tended to go to "strong ties." As we have seen, this is often, quite often, not the case. Yet the broad notion that individuals go to different people for different needs is appropriate to our discussion, especially when we add that an important motivator is substantive relevance. Bearman and Parigi (2004), Small (2013b), and Brashears (2014) address this issue more explicitly in the context of confidants. I discuss these studies in detail in a later chapter.
9. Bearman and Parigi 2004: 544. See also Agneesens et al. 2006.
10. Perry and Pescosolido 2010: 346. See also Perry and Pescosolido 2012, 2015.
11. Later, they argue that "individuals seek out conversations with network members believed to be sympathetic, helpful, or knowledgeable about a given *topic*" (Perry and Pescosolido 2010: 346). This statement is more specific but, as the interviews show, not quite a match to the students' accounts.
12. The psychological literature on empathy is enormous, and the term has been used to capture many different ideas. As C. Daniel Batson (2009: 3) has put it, "The term *empathy* is currently applied to more than a half-dozen phenomena. These phenomena are related to one another, but they are not elements, aspects, facets, or components of a single thing that is empathy, as one might say that an attitude has cognitive, affective, and behavioral components. Rather, each is a conceptually distinct, stand-alone psychological state." In fact, Batson identifies eight distinct uses. (Cuff et al. [2014] manage to identify 43 discrete definitions.) My use of the term relies on a distinction some psychologists have made between cognitive and emotional empathy (Smith 2006; Shamay-Tsoory, Aharon-Peretz, and Perry 2009). The former, sometimes also referred to as "perspective taking," is the general ability to understand what someone else is experiencing; the latter, sometimes understood as emotional contagion, is the sensation of feeling someone else's emotion. The interviews with the students suggest that they often acted in anticipation of cognitive empathy, that their interlocutor would understand the student's situation from the student's perspective. "Cognitive empathy" is also the sixth of Batson's eight concepts, the one he associated with prior work by Adam Smith and George Mead. Note also that empathy here does not refer to sympathy, the sense of pity or positive consideration for the difficulties of others. Though both sympathy

and emotional empathy were at times likely a part of students' experiences with confidants, their interviews, as we shall see, suggested primarily a pursuit for a cognitive understanding of their own situation.

13. My view bears some parallels to Adam Smith's view that what he calls "sympathy" matters to the development of moral sentiments. Smith's view of morality is rooted in what he calls "fellow-feeling," or the act of "conceiving what ourselves should feel in [another person's] situation" (Smith 2002/1790: 11). Unfortunately, and somewhat confusingly, Smith uses the term "sympathy" quite broadly, to include not only pity or sorrow but also any other sensation that derives from one's attempt to feel what another is feeling: "Pity and compassion are words appropriated to signify our fellow-feeling with the sorrow of others. Sympathy, though its meaning was, perhaps, originally the same, may now, however, without much impropriety, be made of use to denote our fellow-feeling with any passion whatever" (Smith 2002/1790: 13).

14. Psychologists in recent years have found evidence in support of a similar idea, that empathy is greater among members of the same groups, and may even require same-group membership under some circumstances. For example, see Cikara, Bruneau, and Saxe 2011; Cikara et al. 2014.

15. See Lazarsfeld and Merton 1954; McPherson, Smith-Lovin, and Cook 2001.

16. Economists refer to the tendency of people to pick similar spouses as "assortative mating." Kanter (1977) referred to the tendency of hiring similar people as "homosocial reproduction."

17. Lazarsfeld and Merton (1954) referred to something similar as "status homophily." They distinguished this kind from "value homophily," or similarity in values and beliefs. The latter is probably important for friendship formation, the purpose of their study. We did not find much evidence that, when seeking confidants, students thought much about the values of those they might speak to, though it is easy to imagine values being important in some circumstances. For example, a woman considering an abortion is unlikely to confide in someone pro-life (see, on abortion and secrets, Cowan 2014).

18. Burt 1976; White, Boorman, and Breiger 1976, Lorrain and White 1971; DiMaggio and Powell 1983.

19. Burt 2010: 336.

20. Notice that in this example, we are forced to discuss equivalence in reference to a very specific network, the faculty and graduate students in a program. In reality, the students will be part of a network that includes a large enough group of people that they are not actually equivalent. This is less likely to be the case if the network is bounded to, say, the university campus. Even then strict equivalence is unlikely.

21. Burt has distinguished "felt equivalence from actual equivalence" (2010: 272) in a network, the former referring to the extent to which two actors feel themselves to be in similar positions vis-à-vis others in the network. People can be in structurally equivalent positions and not feel it—and not even know one another. However, my focus in this chapter, and book, is on subjective experience.

22. Burt 1992, 2005, 2010.

23. The condition is stable only to the extent the network itself is.

24. The assumption that action is preceded by deliberation is a foundation of classical rational choice theory (see Coleman 1990; Becker 1993; Elster 2007). Economist Gary Becker put it well: "In human capital theory, people rationally

evaluate the benefits and costs of activities" (Becker 1993: 402). An example is the family: "The economic approach to the family assumes that even intimate decisions such as marriage, divorce, and family size are reached through weighing the advantages and disadvantages of alternative actions" (Becker 1993: 402). The idea is that people will choose the action that maximizes subjective utility and will reflect on that matter before acting. However, there are many models of purposive action that assume deliberative actors but do not subscribe to other aspects of rational choice theory (Merton 1936; Weber 1978; Kadushin 2002). The present discussion is consistent with a rational model of action in the very narrow sense that it presumes the act is (a) decided upon before being undertaken and (b) purposive, both traits that rational actor models tend to have. However, the act may be both reflective and purposive yet still not consistent with rational choice theory in many ways—if it is not driven primarily by self-interest, if it is not made autonomously, and so on. The next chapter will discuss why a rational actor approach alone does not work.

CHAPTER 6

1. Coleman 1990; Becker 1993; Elster 2007.
2. Becker 1993: 402.
3. Becker 1993: 402.
4. Coleman 1990: 14. His ambivalence is reflected in the early part of his *Foundations of Social Theory*, where he acknowledges some limits but makes a case for the importance of assuming both a purposive actor and a utility-maximizing one (1990: 16–19).
5. Perry and Pescosolido 2010: 346.
6. Perry and Pescosolido 2015: 116
7. Merton 1936; Weber 1978; see also Kadushin 2002.
8. In *Human Nature and Conduct*, Dewey sought to integrate a better understanding of human nature with the study of moral action. He expressly disagreed with the notion that "deliberation consists in calculation of courses of action on the basis of the profit and loss to which they did," in part because deliberation, in his mind, is simply a means to resolve the "entanglements" that arise when habit is confronted with a new and difficult circumstance (1922: part III, section 4). He believed the utilitarian view misunderstood how deliberation works in practice and exaggerated the role of deliberation in ordinary action.
9. Dewey 2004/1916: 10. Hans Joas (1996) followed this and other insights to build a powerful pragmatist theory of action in which creativity was central. Dewey's larger point about the relationship between means and ends is more subtle than can be discussed here in depth. He argued that ends or objectives are best conceived as the ends not of action but of deliberation. Dewey believed that "ends arise and function within action. They are not, as current theories too often imply, things lying beyond activity at which the latter is directed. They are not strictly speaking ends or termini of action at all. They are terminals of deliberation, and so turning points *in* activity" (1922: part III, section 6).
10. Schutz 1964: 78.
11. Schutz 1964: 78. There are parallels between this work and that of Bourdieu, who posited that people have dispositions toward action that manifest themselves unconsciously in behavior (1977, 1990). See also Emirbayer and Goodwin 1994.
12. Bourdieu 1977, 1990; Esser 1993a, 1993b; Kroneberg 2014. In fact, Schutz believed that rational calculation should be rare. Hartmut Esser hoped to build

on this idea by arguing when such calculation should take place. "Something like a rational calculation starts only if the usual rules of thumb (and relevance structures) no longer yield results that fit the expectations" (Esser 1993a: 17). The work of Bourdieu and others has been especially influential in the sociology of culture, where related ideas about the role of culture-as-cognition in action have been proposed (for example, see Vaisey 2008, 2009; Vaisey and Lizardo 2009; Moore 2017).

13. Kahneman 2003: 698; see Kahneman and Tversky 2000; Kahneman 2011. In an earlier review, Stanovich and West (2000: 658) tied the two systems more explicitly to computational capacity: "System 1 is characterized as automatic, largely unconscious, and relatively undemanding of computational capacity. . . . System 2 encompasses the processes of analytic intelligence that have traditionally been studied by information processing theorists trying to uncover the computational components underlying intelligence." See also Strack and Deutsch 2004.

14. Kahneman 2011.

15. Tversky and Kahneman 1974.

16. Kroneberg (2014; Kroneberg, Yaish, and Stocké 2010), building on Esser (1993a, 1993b), has done a lot to bring this work into sociology. In the field of social support, there appear to be few (but see Pescosolido 1992). One interesting study is Pescosolido, Gardner, and Lubell (1998), who examine how people enter mental health services and find that they sometimes do not exactly choose (or are coerced); they just "muddle through."

17. See Nisbett and Wilson 1977; Tilly 2006. A conversation with Betsy Paluck was instrumental in helping clarify some of my thoughts on these questions.

18. Shafir, Simonson, and Tversky 1993:13. Psychologists have proposed that people often do not have access to the factors that caused their own behavior. As Nisbett and Wilson have argued in an important paper: "When reporting on the effects of stimuli, people may not interrogate a memory of the cognitive processes that operated on the stimuli; instead, they may base their reports on implicit, a priori theories about the causal connection between stimulus and response" (1977: 233).

19. See Watkins-Hayes 2013; Steiner 1945. Sociologists have documented such scenarios. Sociologist Sandra Smith (2007) studied black low-income job seekers wondering whether their difficulty in the job search was affected by what theorists such as William J. Wilson (1987) had proposed, their lack of social connections to people with information about jobs. Instead, she found that many of the seekers did not get help for their networks because they did not ask for it. They refused as a result of "defensive individualism," a sense that people should succeed based on their own efforts and should not incur social debts. See also Pescosolido 1992; Bearman and Parigi 2004; Addis and Mahalik 2003.

20. Sociologists Barry Wellman and Scot Wortley (1990) used the term "different strokes from different folks" to explain a phenomenon similar to what we have discussed, wherein residents of a Toronto suburb were shown to turn to different network helpers for different problems. Although the authors do not distinguish the selection from the seeking decision explicitly, they certainly seem to be pointing to the consequences of that specific decision. Sociologists Peter Bearman and Paolo Parigi (2004) interviewed people in North Carolina and found a similar process, which they referred to as "topic-alter dependency."

21. For example, sociologist Nan Lin (2001) has proposed that having access to social capital and mobilizing social capital are different phenomena, and has called attention to the process of mobilization as important in its own right.
22. Decision models of this kind have been traditional in the help-seeking literature (Gross and McMullen 1983; Perry and Pescosolido 2010, 2015). For a version regarding how people decide to go to psychiatrists, see Kadushin 1969.
23. Granovetter 1974.
24. Simmel 1950.
25. Oldenburg 1989.
26. Many of Granovetter's respondents were not explicitly looking for job. As he explained, "A frequent answer went something like: 'Sure. You always *think* about different jobs. If you didn't, you'd be a vegetable.' Nearly one in five of my sample, then, are definitely *not* searching for a new job, but are keeping their ears open for possibilities" (Granovetter 1974: 37).
27. Dewey (2004/1916) made this point eloquently.
28. There is a parallel issue in Granovetter's study of job seekers. Granovetter found that "only 57.4% of [respondents who found job through contacts] report having actively searched" (1974: 33). Rather than searching actively, they merely had the idea in mind.
29. Simmel 1950: 404. Simmel notes, further, that strangers often hear revelations that people would not tell their closer counterparts. As I discussed in a previous chapter, close friends and family are often the worst people to approach with personal confidences.
30. Rubin 1975; see also John, Acquisti, and Loewenstein 2011; Huang et al. in press.
31. Becker 1993: 402.
32. Indeed, this would be a straightforward way of interpreting the heuristics literature in behavioral economics. People always calculate—they just use shortcuts that often lead to cognitive errors or nonrational decisions.
33. As Selten (2001: 16) put it: "Much of human behavior is automatized in the sense that it is not connected to any conscious deliberation. In the process of walking, one does not decide after each step which leg to move next and by how much."
34. There is also the larger debate over whether rationality requires calculation at all—some economists just posit that, regardless of how people make decisions, they arrive at rational actions over the long run. Simon's (1997/1945) concept of bounded rationality, which ultimately is an attempt to deal with different aspects of this question, does not ultimately resolve the issue either, since it merely indicates that people calculate within the limits of cognitive capacity at that particular time. Still, as I discuss previously, one's position on these limitations is not an obstacle to the arguments presented.
35. It is possible that in some future time the tools for such analysis might exist. Kahneman (2011: 32–36) discusses laboratory research showing that pupils dilate as people perform increasingly complex calculations. If so, in some not-too-distant future, it might be possible to assess people's dilation levels over the course of their ordinary lives. Furthermore, there might be justification for a philosophical position that admits different possibilities in different circumstances. There are at least two rather different ways of thinking about intuitive decisions. One is that they involve fast calculations that depend on heuristics; the other, that they result from habit, and thus no reflection of any kind. It seems clear that both occur. As Kahneman has written, in reference to

his work of the 1970s: "We did not ask ourselves whether all intuitive judgments under uncertainty are produced by the heuristics we studied; it is now clear that they are not. In particular, the accurate intuitions of experts are better explained by the effects of prolonged practice than by heuristics" (2011: 11).

36. See Kroneberg and Kalter 2012 for an excellent recent review. See also McCarthy 2002 for a useful discussion.

37. For a discussion of the importance of organizational embeddedness for network action, see Small 2009b.

38. In recent years, experts on judgment and decision making may have been increasingly paying attention to the environments in which people operate. See the recent review by Bruch, Hammond, and Todd 2015.

39. Frank, Muller, and Mueller 2013.

40. Festinger, Schachter, and Back 1950. See also Doreian and Conti 2012; Sailer and McCulloh 2012. Volume 34, Issue 1 of the journal *Social Networks* is devoted to spatial network analysis.

41. Simmel 1955; Blau and Schwartz 1977; Verbrugge 1977.

42. Feld 1981. This chapter purports not to present a comprehensive discussion of the role of context in personal networks, but merely to introduce one set of issues deserving greater attention. For a sampling of additional work on networks and contexts relevant to our discussion, see Huckfeldt 1983; Mollenhorst, Völker, and Flap 2008, 2011, 2014; Hsun, Lin, and Breiger 2009; Völker, Flap, and Mollenhorst 2009.

CHAPTER 7

1. The core question motivating the book may be divided into two—what do people do and why? The former is descriptive; the latter, explanatory. This chapter assesses the descriptive questions, for which statistical generalizability is the core issue. For the explanatory questions, the matter is conceptual generalizability, sometimes referred to as portability, which is the extent to which the theories about why people do what they do depend strictly on the population being graduate students. In the following chapter, I address conceptual generalizability more broadly.

2. Bidart and Lavenou 2005; Fischer and Beresford 2015; Smith et al. 2015. See Suitor, Wellman, and Morgan 1997.

3. Cornwell, Laumann, and Schumm 2008.

4. Cornwell 2015: 36.

5. Mollenhorst, Völker, and Flap 2014. The researchers used a slightly modified version of the GSS name generator. It asked, "With whom did you discuss important personal matters during the last six months?" (2014: 67).

6. Mollenhorst, Völker, and Flap 2014: 70.

7. Cornwell and Laumann 2015: 100.

8. Mollenhorst, Völker, and Flap 2014: 72.

9. Marsden 1987: 123.

10. Mollenhorst, Völker, and Flap 2008.

11. McPherson, Smith-Lovin, and Brashears 2006: 354.

12. Burt 1984: Table 2.

13. Small 2013b: 474. For question wording, see Appendix B.

14. The following discussion is important: "Notice that the question asks about important alters, rather than close ones. Throughout the discussion, we have used the terms more or less interchangeably, as has much of the literature,

with some justification. If an alter is truly close, then she or he is very likely also important to ego. However, an important alter need not be a close one; e.g., many who are not close to their mother still consider her important to their lives. The umbrella category 'people we consider important' includes the sub-categories 'people to whom we are close' and 'people to whom we are not.' Ideally, the CNIA survey might have separately asked whether discussion partners were important and whether they were close. However, asking both questions risked generating attrition (and noise), given that respondents might feel themselves to be answering the same questions repeatedly about multiple alters. Asking about the umbrella category provides a conservative test of the mobilization prediction that the core discussion network will include many weak ties. If, say, 40% of alters are not important, we know that *at least* that many are not close" (Small 2013b: 474).

15. Small 2013b.
16. Coromina and Coenders 2006.
17. It is important to note that people explicitly defined some kin members as not important to them. This finding was also reported in Fischer (1982: 80): "Many people in our sample were estranged from their relatives. For example, one woman claimed that none of her relatives was 'important' to her because of a family feud over committing her grandmother to a sanitarium and disposing of the grandmother's tiny estate."
18. Bailey and Marsden 1999.
19. Part of the reason researchers have thought of it as a network of intimates is how they have interpreted previous studies. Those studies have shown that, when one compares people in the core discussion network and people not in it, alters in the former are on average closer to respondents than those in the latter. That does not imply, however, that everyone on the former list is a close friend and family member. After all, the second list is much larger than the first, which means that if people are only close to a small number in their network, the average person in the former will likely be closer than that in the latter. When survey respondents name (a) all the people they regularly discuss important matters with and (b) all their friends, family, coworkers, neighbors, advisers, colleagues, and acquaintances, the proportion of people in the former list who are close will surely be greater than that in the latter list, since the overwhelming majority of most people's relationships are weak ties. For example, if the average married person has about three confidants and one of them is a spouse, then at least 33% of their core discussion network is composed of strong ties (if they are close to their spouse), and it would be extremely unlikely for 33% of all other ties in the personal network to also be strong. But this finding does not imply that people do not regularly confide in coworkers, neighbors, or acquaintances.
20. About 26% of respondents had not talked about anything important over the previous six months. This finding is similar to that of the Bearman and Parigi (2004) study, which found, among 600 adult North Carolinians, that about "20% of the respondents reported not talking about anything important with anyone" (2004: 547). Some nonnegligible portion of the population rarely discusses important matters regularly—they are not talkers, are slow to trust, or simply have little to talk about. In fact, in the Bearman and Parigi study, about half of those who had not talked to anyone had not done so because they had nothing important to talk about.

21. Fischer 1982; Burt 1984; Marsden 1987; McPherson, Smith-Lovin, and Brashears 2006.
22. For one set of scholars whose work is relevant to our discussions, see Fingerman 2001; Fingerman, Hay, and Birditt 2004; Birditt and Fingerman 2003, 2005; Birditt, Fingerman, and Almeida 2005.
23. Fingerman, Hay, and Birditt 2004: 796.
24. Fingerman, Hay, and Birditt 2004: 796.
25. Fingerman, Hay, and Birditt 2004: 796.
26. Fingerman, Hay, and Birditt 2004: 800 (italics added).
27. Fingerman, Hay, and Birditt 2004: 800.
28. In an interesting set of studies, Norton, Frost, and Ariely (2007) have shown that familiarity may breed contempt, in the sense that people find themselves liking an individual less the more they know about the latter, because greater information reveals new forms of dissimilarity between them, which in turn affects how they interpret each new piece of information. One implication would be complicated feelings toward close relations.
29. The question was worded as such for a separate study, currently in progress, of compartmentalization, the extent to which people discuss different kinds of issues with different individuals.
30. Still, I categorized the responses as not comfortable (1–3), somewhat comfortable (4–7), and very comfortable (8–10). Respondents were either uncomfortable or only somewhat comfortable discussing private issues regarding family, work, and health matters with 27.5%, 19.5%, and 23.4%, respectively, of their closest friends and family. That is, between roughly a fifth and a quarter of the time, Americans felt something other than very comfortable discussing major life topics with those closest to them.
31. This finding is related to that in a quota-based study of 140 first- and second-generation Italian Americans conducted in the 1960s. Respondents were asked to name their "intimate friends," in addition to several questions about what they were willing to do with friends. Respondents indicated a willingness to "confide in about personal matters" to only 64% of their "intimate friends" (Palisi 1966).
32. Wellman and Wortley 1989; Bearman and Parigi 2004; Brashears 2014; Perry and Pescosolido 2010.
33. Bearman and Parigi 2004.
34. Brashears 2014: 498.
35. See Appendix B, Table B.4. See also Small 2013b: 475.
36. The following discussion is based on Small 2013b: 477.
37. Note that the figures are not strictly comparable to those in the national survey because (a) graduate students were first asked specifically to discuss work-related issues, and (b) they were asked to discuss the topics that worried them, not the topics they had talked about when they had recently talked about something important. See relevant discussions in Chapters 3 and 5.
38. See Small 2013b for details.
39. See Appendix B, Table B.5. The "work" category includes education and career issues. Often, topics overlapped, as when an illness caused financial difficulties. For additional details regarding coding and classifications, see Small 2013b.
40. The high degree of overlap is especially remarkable given that the topics were elicited through very different questions (about "worries" rather than about "important matters" discussed), and that the coding scheme in each study was

conducted independently and entirely inductively. If I were to apply the coding scheme from the national survey to the student data, there would likely be much greater overlap. For example, many of the students' responses about social isolation could be classified as "happiness and life goals." However, given that an objective is to develop a more grounded approach to theorizing, the inductive coding approach was more appropriate.

41. Brashears 2014: 500.
42. See Appendix B, Table B.6 for full results. See also Small 2013b: 478–80.
43. The results discussed in the next several paragraphs are presented in Small 2013b.
44. This discussion is based on Small 2013b.
45. Fischer 1982; Putnam 2000.
46. For the full list of organizations, see Appendix B, Table B.7.
47. See Appendix B, Table B.8 for full results.
48. For results showing the association between incidental or spontaneous activation and responding to accessibility, see Appendix B, Tables B9a and B9b and Small and Sukhu 2016.
49. For example, a recent survey, still being analyzed, of Netherlands respondents suggests the Dutch may be more reticent to confide in weak ties (Beate Völker, personal communication, November 2016). That survey, however, also uses a wording narrower than that of the GSS instrument: "personal important matters," which probably elicits closer ties.

CHAPTER 8

1. I must emphasize that Kant's (1963/1930) point was primarily about what he called full disclosure, and he did not say much about closeness and confiding one particular but worrisome issue. Smith (2002/1790) had more complex notions about sympathy than I can discuss in this book; he believed, among other things, that we reveal less to acquaintances than to friends but that this fact gives us tranquility before acquaintances.
2. See, for example, Darling 2010; Lehrer 2010; Smith 2015.
3. Krackhardt 1992 provides one of the few examination of these assumptions.
4. Granovetter 1973, 1983. See also Granovetter 1985 for the broader defense of the idea that actors are embedded in networks of relations.
5. Marsden and Campbell 1984, 2012. See Krackhardt 1992 for a discussion of the strength of strong ties. My focus on the affective characteristics of strong ties is different from that on the structural characteristics of weak ones, as many have chosen to read the paper. When weak ties are bridges—and they need not always be bridges, as Granovetter (1983: 208) later clarified—they may well be especially important for the diffusion of information, social integration, and other phenomena, regardless of whether the arguments about why strong ties tend to close are suspect.
6. Granovetter 1973: 1362.
7. Lazarsfeld and Merton 1954.
8. Simmel 1950: 135–36, 145–46; Heider 1946; Newcomb 1961. Heider believed that "the state of imbalance will produce tension" (1946: 108). Cartwright and Harary generalized Heider's theory and drew out broader implications for network analysts. Newcomb applied it specifically to the context of network formation. See also Cartwright and Harary 1956.
9. Granovetter 1973: 1362.

10. Interacting with different people in different spaces is typical in contemporary society (Simmel 1955; Blau and Schwartz 1997; Small 2009b). On the importance of context of interaction, see Feld 1981; Small 2009b; Mollenhorst, Völker, and Flap 2011, 2014.

11. If we assume they are not, we are granting that the rule of thumb is wrong, regardless, since *A* would be getting support from weak, not strong, ties.

12. Based on 2004 GSS. Mollenhorst, Völker, and Flap (2011) recently found that a substantial number of the triads in the core discussion networks of the Dutch were not closed triads.

13. To be clear, my argument applies specifically to the strong-tie principle when strength is viewed as closeness. Note that though aspects of my argument probably apply to the related principles of balance in signed relations or transitivity in directed ones, a more detailed examination would be required.

14. For some reviews of the conflicting evidence, see, for example, Granovetter 1983; Faust 2007; Tutic and Wiese 2015. In fact, in the 1973 paper, Granovetter's egocentric study evidence centers mostly on his own work on job seekers, which shows that people got more information from weak than from strong ties but not that strong ties were particularly inbred. Of course, a person's strong ties are more likely to be inbred than the weak ones, since there are far, far more of the latter than the former. But forbidden ties may still be quite prevalent, rather than rare, among strong ties, which calls attention to the need for different kinds of analyses.

15. The boundary problem, a long-standing difficulty in network research, has often been ignored for the sake of the practical progress of research but is too consequential in this case to ignore (Laumann, Marsden, and Prensky 1989). But with the notable exception of people in forced confinement, ordinary life is rarely limited to such boundaries, no matter the inconvenience to the researcher. If scientists repeatedly test an idea in the context best suited to find support for it, they will come to believe the idea represents a truth about the social world, even if that context fails to represent how people actually carry out their existence.

16. A feature of contemporary society, as Simmel has argued, is existing in a web of multiple affiliations (Simmel 1955; Blau and Schwartz 1997). My argument is that people form not just weak but also strong ties in those separate interactional spaces, leaving little reason for the strong ties to be connected.

17. Granovetter 1979: 513. I thank Henk Flap for pointing me to this paper.

18. My own prior work also played a role. For a full discussion of the process, see Appendix A.

19. Small 2009b. See also Feld 1981, 1982, 1984. For a few among countless case studies, see Harris-Lacewell 2004 on the black church, barbershop and beauty salon; Pattillo-McCoy 1998 on the black church; Oldenburg 1989 on the English pub, German American beer garden, French café, and American tavern; Duneier 1992 on the neighborhood restaurant.

20. On spaces, see among many others Festinger, Schachter, and Back 1950; Goffman 1961. On institutional norms and rules, see among many others Berger and Luckman 1966; Meyer and Rowan 1977; Powell and DiMaggio 1991; Scott 1995; Nee and Ingram 1998; Small 2009b.

21. See Feld, Suitor, and Hoegh 2007; Mollenhorst, Völker, and Flap 2014; Small and Sukhu 2016.

22. "Socrates: Heracleitus says, you know, that all things move and nothing remains still, and he likens the universe to the current of a river, saying that you cannot step twice into the same stream" (Plato 1926: 67).
23. Note that this conception of institutions is largely normative, rather than cognitive or regulatory (Meyer and Rowan 1977; Scott 1995). The normative view of institutions can be traced to the work of Durkheim (1951/1897); the cognitive work, to Berger and Luckman (1966).
24. Gino, Brooks, and Schweitzer 2012.
25. For examples across sociology and psychology, see Esser 1993; Pescosolido, Gardner, and Lubell 1998; Stanovich and West 2000; Kroneberg, Yaish, and Stocké 2010; Kahneman 2011; Small 2013b; Kroneberg 2014; Small and Sukhu 2016; Larrick 2016; Bruch and Feinberg 2017.
26. Tversky and Kahneman 1973, 1974; Gilovich, Griffin, and Kahneman 2002; Mullainathan and Shafir 2013.
27. Among the issues I have not discussed are the many additional reasons people avoid strong ties and approach weak ones; the positive and negative consequences of the decision to confide in others for overall wellbeing, network formation, or network structure; and the several possible ways that, informed by the enormous literature on decision-making, the propositions throughout the book could be represented formally, and thereby assessed more clearly.
28. These include the fear that they might disapprove, as when people do not tell others about an abortion (Cowan 2014); the fear that sharing something intimate with one member of a close-knit network will quickly spread it to all others, as we saw with Carver and his mother; and many others.
29. Fingerman, Hay, and Birditt 2004.
30. This proposition directly parallels, and is informed by, Annette Baier's (1986) notion of trust as a three-part predicate and Russell Hardin's (2002) notion of trust as a three-part relation.
31. MacKenzie 1985: 1044.
32. MacKenzie 1985: 1044.
33. MacKenzie 1985: 1044.
34. MacKenzie 1985: 1044.
35. MacKenzie 1985: 1044.
36. See Department of Defense 2013: 25.
37. Lawrence and Peñaloza 2013.
38. Lawrence and Peñaloza 2013.
39. Parker 2011.
40. Law Offices of Susan L. Burke 2011. See also Murphy and Haider 2006.
41. Lawrence and Peñaloza 2013. As another reporter who covered male victims of rape in the military put it, "Fear of a ruined career is a major factor preventing victims from coming forward" (Ellison 2011). For a review of research on this question, see Lucero 2015; see also Turchik and Wilson 2010.
42. Aguilar 2012.
43. Department of Defense 2013: 25. After widespread attention to the issue in the national media, the number of assaults reported rose by more than 60% in three years (Department of Defense 2016: 11).
44. See, for example, the narratives in Erdely 2013.
45. Indeed, every formal investigation of the matter has pointed to institutional factors such as these. For a comprehensive review of research on sexual assault in the military, see Turchik and Wilson 2010. One notable study is Sadler et al.

2003, which found that female rape victims in the military typically did not report their assaults officially as a result of not one but multiple joint factors, the most prevalent being (in descending order) embarrassment, worries about negative impact on career, belief that nothing would be done, belief it would make things worse, and belief she would be blamed by coworkers. A Human Rights Watch (2015) report based on interviews with hundreds of service men and women discusses these questions at length (https://www.hrw.org/report/2015/05/18/embattled/retaliation-against-sexual-assault-survivors-us-military, accessed July 2, 2016). See also Response Systems to Adult Sexual Assault Crimes Panel 2014.

46. See Desmond 2012, 2016.
47. Kaldjian et al. 2008: 719.
48. Kaldjian et al. 2008: 719.
49. Kaldjian et al. 2008: 719.
50. In fact, 22% of respondents had "been named as a defendant in a malpractice case" (Kaldjian et al. 2008: 719).
51. It is notable that even respondents who did not find it hard to disclose their mistakes often thought about "loss of reputation from colleagues" when disclosing their errors. The need to talk was overwhelming (Kaldjian et al. 2008: 719).
52. MacKenzie 1985: 1044.
53. MacKenzie 1985: 1044. By the end, this medical doctor became convinced of the importance of talking to others. "If nothing else I have learnt that the worst thing I could do—to my family, my friends, my doctor—is come to grief because I did not ask for help" (1985: 1044).
54. In one study people admitted to more unethical behavior when asked through a website that appeared unprofessional and casual rather than one that appeared professional, even though respondents reported that the latter was more likely to protect privacy and security. As the authors wrote, "These three experiments show that people seem naturally more comfortable disclosing personal information on unprofessional sites—which are arguably more likely to misuse it. This occurs even though participants in a pilot study judged the unprofessional site to be higher in disclosure danger. Experiment 3 shows that participants in the unprofessional condition, whose privacy concern has been suppressed, perceive the questions to be less intrusive than do those in the professional condition. Experiment 4 replicates and extends these findings by showing that the effect of the survey interface on disclosure is eliminated when privacy concerns are evoked from the outset of the study" (John, Acquisti, and Loewenstein 2011: 868).
55. Bruch and Feinberg forthcoming.
56. This discussion owes a lot to Feld 1981, 1982, 1984 and especially Small 2009b.
57. Jennings 1994: 124.
58. Jennings 1994: 219.
59. Jennings 1994: 219.
60. Jennings 1994: 220.
61. Jennings 1994: 220.
62. Jennings 1994: 221.
63. Jennings 1994: 221.
64. Jennings 1994: 200.
65. Jennings 1994: 201.

66. Jennings 1994: 200.
67. Jennings 1994: 200.
68. Jennings 1994: 200–01.
69. Jennings 1994: 201.
70. Jennings 1994: 201.
71. Still, Van Der Tuin's "support was a key element in keeping me going in the years to come" (Jennings 1994: 201).
72. See Feld 1981.

A FINAL WORD
1. Rainie and Wellman (2012) refer to it as a "triple revolution"—the rise of social networks that transcend space, the growth of the Internet as a means of communication, and the spread of smartphones.
2. On the impact of the telephone, see Fischer 1994.
3. Pew reports a 10-fold increase in the proportion of adults using social media from 2005 to 2015, to 65% (Perrin 2015).
4. I learned a telling lesson when my undergraduates informed me that many of them consider phoning even their best friends out of the blue to be rude—text is primary. And if they wish to call, they first text asking if they may call.
5. There are countless books, ranging from the serious to the alarmist, on the consequences of these changes (Baym 2010; Carr 2010; Fischer 2011; Marche 2012; Rainie and Wellman 2012).
6. Wellman 1979, 1999.
7. Several researchers are bucking that trend. See Pescosolido 1992; Wellman 2007; Doreian and Conti 2012.

APPENDICES
1. In the literature on mixed-methods research, this book would be classified as a nonnested, complementary study (Small 2011).

APPENDIX A
1. Newcomb 1961; Krackhardt 1990.
2. See Glaser and Straus 1967 for a systematic approach to inductive empirical research.
3. Becker 2009.
4. See Small 2009a, 2009b.
5. There are many versions of this practice. One of the most unfortunate is what Kerr (1998) called "HARKing," or "hypothesizing after the results are known."
6. That is, the problem shifted from a substantive one (about mothers and childcare) to a formal one (about people and support). This approach to understanding ethnographic cases can be traced to Glaser and Strauss (1967) and Simmel (1950).
7. Emirbayer and Goodwin 1994; Emirbayer and Mische 1998.
8. As he wrote, "This is the question of agency: How much do individuals matter relative to the structure around them? . . . With some exceptions, much of the social capital research on performance and network structure reads as though performance springs directly from structure" (Burt 2010: 221).
9. Pescosolido 1992; Smith 2007.
10. Barnes 1954, Gluckman 1961, Mitchell 1969; Tversky and Kahneman 1973; Kahneman 2011; Laumann 1973; Fischer 1982; Dewey 1922; Schutz 1964.

11. An advantage of an in-depth interview is time. As Sudman, Bradburn, and Schwarz have written, "Searching memory to retrieve specific information asked for in a survey question takes time. . . . The more difficult the task, the longer it takes. Thus, survey accuracy may decline if too many questions are asked within the allotted survey time" (1996:178). For at least some kinds of difficult questions, time increases accuracy substantially. An open-ended interview made this possible. Our longest interview was over four hours long.

12. In a sense, I was animated by the same concerns that have given rise to the grounded theory perspective (Glaser and Strauss 1967).

13. Participant observation methods have the advantage that social interactions can be observed as they take place. They eliminate completely the need to believe people about their actions, a point that ethnographers have always made about their work (Lofland et al. 2005; Becker and Geer 1957; Jerolmack and Khan 2014). And since I wanted to know what people did, I naturally found ethnographic observation appealing. Nevertheless, I ultimately concluded that participant observation would not work. All participant observation changes the nature of social interaction. In some circumstances, the change is trivial, because the interaction would have transpired in roughly the same way in the absence of the observer. But in circumstances with very few people or where the presence of the observer is out of the ordinary, the change to the nature of the interaction is dramatic. In the case of people confiding their personal problems to another, direct observation would change the dynamics dramatically. I considered ways of getting around this problem at length, including shifting the topic to how people talk to others in groups, planning a long-term observation period, or experimenting with recording devices. But none of these solutions proved compelling. To confide in another person is a quintessentially personal act between two. The presence of a third, as Simmel (1950) presciently observed, changes everything, including not only what people are willing to discuss but also how they do so. Unless I changed the question from personal to group confidences, there would be no way for me to avoid the well-documented observer effect, even with the passage of time (see French 1953; Heisenberg 1927).

14. See also Hollstein 2011.

15. The methods of agreement and of difference, articulated by Mill, have often been used to approach comparative analysis in the social and political sciences. However, Mill himself was clear that these methods were poor choices for social scientific research (Mill 1970/1843).

16. I have almost never paid participants for interviews. In this case, however, the cohorts were small, and I risked getting no one to agree.

17. On interview-based methods, see Weiss 1994; Hammersley and Atkinson 2007.

18. For an extensive discussion of question-order effects, as part of a large discussion of context effects in survey design, see Schwartz and Sudman 1992.

19. McPherson, Smith-Lovin, and Brashears 2006.

20. Fischer 2012. See also Fischer 2011; Paik and Sanchagrin 2013.

21. The debate over the controversial findings by McPherson, Smith-Lovin, and Brashears (2006) involved far more issues than I can discuss here. See Fischer 2009; McPherson, Smith-Lovin, and Brashears 2009; Brashears 2011; Paik and Sanchagrin 2013; Small 2013b.

22. Killworth and Bernard 1976; Bernard and Killworth 1977; Bernard, Killworth, and Sailer 1979. See Schwartz 1999, 2007; Scwhartz and Sudman 1992, 1994 for extensive, thoughtful, and empirically supported discussions of these issues.
23. While for any given topic for any single person the last experience might have been out of the ordinary, if I asked the same question of all students, then for enough people and enough topics, the answer should approximate the actual typical experience.
24. See Sudman, Bradburn, and Schwarz 1996: 163ff.
25. Many have made different versions of this point. For examples in psychology, see Nisbett and Wilson 1977; Shafir, Simonson, and Tversky 1993. For examples in sociology, see Tilly 2006; Watts 2014. Watts (2014) makes a case that this temptation affects all of sociology, wherein causal explanations are too often found to be convincing because they are, essentially, understandable stories.
26. Please note that this notion only bears a general relation to the counterfactual model of causal inference (Pearl 2009; Morgan and Winship 2015). As I have written, the counterfactual model of causality "conceives of causes as treatments; it seeks to compare what happens to an individual (or organization, group, or other entity) experiencing the treatment to what would have happened had the person not experienced the treatment. Since no one can both experience and not experience a treatment at the same time, the purpose of analysis is to estimate treatment effects on average for populations" (Small 2013a:597). The notion of counterfactual questioning in an interview context simply seeks to probe people's *accounts* of an outcome by probing what they believe would have happened in the absence of the conditions said to produce the outcome.
27. Nisbett and Wilson 1977.
28. For example, laboratory students tended to publish much earlier in their careers, and saw all of their work as a collaborative effort. But on how to confide in others, the differences between departments turned out to be trivial.
29. Duneier 1999. See Jerolmack and Murphy in press for a thoughtful discussion.
30. Goffman 2014.
31. Lewis et al. 2008. See Parry 2011.
32. Anderson 1999.

APPENDIX B

1. Vehovar et al. 2008. See also Coromina and Coenders 2006; Manfreda et al. 2008.
2. For a longer discussion, see Small 2013b. On context effects in the GSS, see Fischer 2012.
3. Reproduced from Small 2013b: Table A1.

REFERENCES

Adair, John G. 1984. "The Hawthorne Effect: A Reconsideration of the Methodological Artifact." *Journal of Applied Psychology* 69(2):334–45.

Addis, Michael E., and James R. Mahalik. 2003. "Men, Masculinity, and the Contexts of Help Seeking." *American Psychologist* 58(1):5–14.

Agneessens, Filip, Hans Waege, and John Lievens. 2006. "Diversity in Social Support by Role Relations: A Typology." *Social Networks* 28(4):427–41.

Aguilar, Rose. 2012. "Military Rape: The Invisible War." *Al Jazeera*, July 3. Retrieved August 15, 2016 (http://readersupportednews.org/opinion2/282-98/ 12244-military-rape-the-invisible-war).

Albert, Réka, and Albert-László Barabási. 2002. "Statistical Mechanics of Complex Networks." *Reviews of Modern Physics* 74(1):47–97.

Anderson, Elijah. 1999. *Code of the Street: Decency, Violence, and the Moral Life of the Inner City*. New York: Norton.

Antonucci, Toni C., Kristine J. Ajrouch, and Kira S. Birditt. 2014. "The Convoy Model: Explaining Social Relations from a Multidisciplinary Perspective." *The Gerontologist* 54(1):82–92.

Aristotle. 1943. *On Man in the Universe*, edited by L. R. Loomis. Roslyn, NY: Walter J. Black.

Baier, Annette. 1986. "Trust and Antitrust." *Ethics* 96(2):231–60.

Bailey, Stefanie, and Peter V. Marsden. 1999. "Interpretation and Interview Context: Examining the General Social Survey Name Generator Using Cognitive Methods." *Social Networks* 21(3):287–309.

Barabási, Albert-László, and Réka Albert. 1999. "Emergence of Scaling in Random Networks." *Science* 286(5439):509–12.

Barabási, Albert-László, and Jennifer Frangos. 2002. *Linked: The New Science of Networks*. New York: Perseus Books Group.

Barnes, John. 1954. *Class and Committees in a Norwegian Island Parish*. New York: Plenum.

Batson, C. Daniel. 2009. "These Things Called Empathy: Eight Related but Distinct Phenomena." In *The Social Neuroscience of Empathy, Social Neuroscience*, edited by J. Decety and W. Ickes, 3–15. Cambridge, MA: MIT Press.

Baym, Geoffrey. 2010. *From Cronkite to Colbert: The Evolution of Broadcast News*. Boulder, CO: Paradigm.

Bearman, Peter. 1997. "Generalized Exchange." *American Journal of Sociology* 102(5):1383–1415.

Bearman, Peter, and Paolo Parigi. 2004. "Cloning Headless Frogs and Other Important Matters: Conversation Topics and Network Structure." *Social Forces* 83(2):535–57.

Becker, Gary S. 1993. "Nobel Lecture: The Economic Way of Looking at Behavior." *Journal of Political Economy* 101(3):385–409.

Becker, Howard. 2009. "How to Find Out How to Do Qualitative Research." Online document. Retrieved April 29, 2017 (http://home.earthlink.net/~hsbecker/articles/NSF.html).

Becker, Howard, and Blanche Geer. 1957. "Participant Observation and Interviewing: A Comparison." *Human Organization* 16(3):28–32.

Berger, Peter L., and Thomas Luckmann. 1966. *The Social Construction of Reality: A Treatise in the Sociology of Knowledge.* New York: Doubleday.

Berkman, Lisa F. 1985. "The Relationship of Social Networks and Social Support to Morbidity and Mortality." In *Social Support and Health*, edited by S. Cohen and S. L. Syme, 241–62. San Diego, CA: Academic Press.

Berkman, Lisa F., Thomas Glass, Ian Brissette, and Teresa E. Seeman. 2000. "From Social Integration to Health: Durkheim in the New Millennium." *Social Science & Medicine* 51(6):843–57.

Berkman, Lisa F., and S. Leonard Syme. 1979. "Social Networks, Host Resistance, and Mortality: A Nine-Year Follow-up Study of Alameda County Residents." *American Journal of Epidemiology* 109(2):186–204.

Bernard, H. Russell, and Peter D. Killworth. 1977. "Informant Accuracy in Social Network Data II." *Human Communication Research* 4(1):3–18.

Bernard, H. Russell, Peter D. Killworth, David Kronenfeld, and Lee Sailer. 1984. "The Problem of Informant Accuracy: The Validity of Retrospective Data." *Annual Review of Anthropology* 13:495–517.

Bernard, H. Russell, Peter D. Killworth, and Lee Sailer. 1979. "Informant Accuracy in Social Network Data IV: A Comparison of Clique-Level Structure in Behavioral and Cognitive Network Data." *Social Networks* 2(3):191–218.

Bernard, H. Russell, Peter D. Killworth, and Lee Sailer. 1982. "Informant Accuracy in Social Network Data V. An Experimental Attempt to Predict Actual Communication from Recall Data." *Social Science Research* 11(1):30–66.

Bidart, Claire, and Daniel Lavenu. 2005. "Evolutions of Personal Networks and Life Events." *Social Networks* 27(4):359–76.

Biddle, B. J. 1986. "Recent Development in Role Theory." *Annual Review of Sociology* 12:67–92.

Birditt, Kira S., and Karen L. Fingerman. 2003. "Age and Gender Differences in Adults' Descriptions of Emotional Reactions to Interpersonal Problems." *Journals of Gerontology Series B: Psychological Sciences and Social Sciences* 58(4):P237–45.

Birditt, Kira S., and Karen L. Fingerman. 2005. "Do We Get Better at Picking Our Battles? Age Group Differences in Descriptions of Behavioral Reactions to Interpersonal Tensions." *Journals of Gerontology Series B: Psychological Sciences and Social Sciences* 60(3):P121–28.

Birditt, Kira S., Karen L. Fingerman, and David M. Almeida. 2005. "Age Differences in Exposure and Reactions to Interpersonal Tensions: A Daily Diary Study." *Psychology and Aging* 20(2):330–40.

Blau, Peter Michael. 1986 [1964]. *Exchange and Power in Social Life.* New York: John Wiley & Sons.

Blau, Peter Michael, and Joseph E. Schwartz. 1997. *Crosscutting Social Circles: Testing a Macrostructural Theory of Intergroup Relations*, 2nd edition. New York: Academic Press.

Boessen, Adam, et al. 2014. "Networks, Space, and Residents' Perception of Cohesion." *American Journal of Community Psychology* 53(3–4):447–61.

Boissevain, Jeremy. 1974. *Friends of Friends: Networks, Manipulators and Coalitions*. New York: St. Martin's Press.

Bott, Elizabeth. 1957. *Family and Social Network: Roles, Norms, and External Relationships in Ordinary Urban Families*. London: Tavistock.

Bourdieu, Pierre. 1977. *Outline of a Theory of Practice*. New York: Cambridge University Press.

Bourdieu, Pierre. 1984. *Distinction: A Social Critique of the Judgement of Taste*. Cambridge, MA: Harvard University Press.

Bourdieu, Pierre. 1990. *The Logic of Practice*. Stanford, CA: Stanford University Press.

Brashears, Matthew E. 2011. "Small Networks and High Isolation? A Reexamination of American Discussion Networks." *Social Networks* 33(4):331–41.

Brashears, Matthew E. 2014. "'Trivial' Topics and Rich Ties: The Relationship Between Discussion Topic, Alter Role, and Resource Availability Using the 'Important Matters' Name Generator." *Sociological Science* 1:493–511.

Brashears, Matthew E., and Eric Quintane. 2015. "The Microstructures of Network Recall: How Social Networks Are Encoded and Represented in Human Memory." *Social Networks* 41:113–26.

Bruch, Elizabeth, Ross A. Hammond, and Peter M. Todd. 2015. "Coevolution of Decision-Making and Social Environments." In *Emerging Trends in the Social and Behavioral Sciences*, 1–16. Hoboken, NJ: John Wiley & Sons.

Bruch, Elizabeth, and Fred Feinberg. 2017. "Decision Making Processes in Social Contexts." *Annual Review of Sociology* 43.

Burt, Ronald S. 1976. "Positions in Networks." *Social Forces* 55(1):93–122.

Burt, Ronald S. 1984. "Network Items and the General Social Survey." *Social Networks* 6(4):293–339.

Burt, Ronald S. 1985. "General Social Survey Network Items." *Connections* 8(1):19–23.

Burt, Ronald S. 1986. "A Note on Sociometric Order in the General Social Survey Network Data." *Social Networks* 8(2):149–89.

Burt, Ronald S. 1987. "Social Contagion and Innovation: Cohesion Versus Structural Equivalence." *American Journal of Sociology* 92(6):1287–335.

Burt, Ronald S. 1992. *Structural Holes: The Social Structure of Competition*. Cambridge, MA: Harvard University Press.

Burt, Ronald S. 2005. *Brokerage and Closure: An Introduction to Social Capital*. New York: Oxford University Press.

Burt, Ronald S. 2010. *Neighbor Networks: Competitive Advantage Local and Personal*. New York: Oxford University Press.

Butts, Carter T. 2009. "Revisiting the Foundations of Network Analysis." *Science* 325(5939):414–16.

Carr, Nicholas. 2010. The Shallows: What the Internet is Doing to Our Brains. New York: Norton.

Carroll, Glenn R., and Albert C. Teo. 1996. "On The Social Networks of Managers." *Academy of Management Journal* 39(2):421–40.

Cartwright, Dorwin, and Frank Harary. 1956. "Structural Balance: A Generalization of Heider's Theory." *Psychological Review* 63(5):277–93.

Chen, Wenhong. 2013. "Internet Use, Online Communication, and Ties in Americans' Networks." *Social Science Computer Review* 31(4):404–23.

Cikara, Mina, Emile G. Bruneau, and Rebecca R. Saxe. 2011. "Us and Them: Intergroup Failures of Empathy." *Current Directions in Psychological Science* 20(3):149–53.

Cikara, Mina, Emile G. Bruneau, Jay J. Van Bavel, and Rebecca R. Saxe. 2014. "Their Pain Gives Us Pleasure: How Intergroup Dynamics Shape Empathic Failures and Counter-Empathic Responses." *Journal of Experimental Social Psychology* 55:110–25.

Clance, Pauline R., and Suzanne A. Imes. 1978. "The Imposter Phenomenon in High Achieving Women: Dynamics and Therapeutic Intervention." *Psychotherapy: Theory, Research & Practice* 15(3):241–47.

Cobb, Sidney. 1976. "Social Support as a Moderator of Life Stress." *Psychosomatic medicine* 38(5):300–314.

Cohen, Sheldon, and Thomas A. Wills. 1985. "Stress, Social Support, and the Buffering Hypothesis." *Psychological Bulletin* 98(2):310–57.

Coleman, James. 1958. "Relational Analysis: The Study of Social Organizations with Survey Methods." *Human Organization* 17(4):28–36.

Coleman, James S. 1988. "Social Capital in the Creation of Human Capital." *American Journal of Sociology* 94:S95–120.

Coleman, James S. 1990. *Foundations of Social Theory*. Cambridge, MA: Belknap Press of Harvard University Press.

Collins, Randall. 2004. *Interaction Ritual Chains*. Princeton, NJ: Princeton University Press.

Cornwell, Benjamin. 2015. "Social Disadvantage and Network Turnover." *Journals of Gerontology Series B: Psychological Sciences and Social Sciences* 70(1):132–42.

Cornwell, Benjamin, and Edward O. Laumann. 2015. "The Health Benefits of Network Growth: New Evidence from a National Survey of Older Adults." *Social Science & Medicine* 125:94–106.

Cornwell, Benjamin, Edward O. Laumann, and L. Philip Schumm. 2008. "The Social Connectedness of Older Adults: A National Profile." *American Sociological Review* 73(2):185–203.

Coromina, Lluís, and Germà Coenders. 2006. "Reliability and Validity of Egocentered Network Data Collected via Web: A Meta-Analysis of Multilevel Multitrait Multimethod Studies." *Social Networks* 28(3):209–31.

Cowan, Sarah K. 2014. "Secrets and Misperceptions: The Creation of Self-Fulfilling Illusions." *Sociological Science* 1:466–92.

Cuff, Benjamin M. P., Sarah J. Brown, Laura Taylor, and Douglas J. Howat. 2014. "Empathy: A Review of the Concept." *Emotion Review* 7:1–10.

Darling, Nancy. 2010. "Facebook and the Strength of Weak Ties." *Psychology Today*, May 14.

Department of Defense. 2013. *Annual Report on Sexual Assault in the Military Fiscal Year 2012*. Washington, DC: Department of Defense. Retrieved June 30, 2016 (http://www.sapr.mil/public/docs/reports/FY12_DoD_SAPRO_Annual_Report_on_Sexual_Assault-volume_one.pdf).

Department of Defense. 2016. *Annual Report on Sexual Assault in the Military Fiscal Year 2015*. Washington, DC: Department of Defense. Retrieved June 30, 2016 (http://sapr.mil/public/docs/reports/FY15_Annual/FY15_Annual_Report_on_Sexual_Assault_in_the_Military.pdf).

Desmond, Matthew. 2012. "Disposable Ties and the Urban Poor." *American Journal of Sociology* 117(5):1295–1335.

Desmond, Matthew. 2016. *Evicted: Poverty and Profit in the American City*. New York: Crown.

Dewey, John. 1922. *Human Nature and Conduct: An Introduction to Social Psychology*. New York: Henry Holt & Co.

Dewey, John. 2004 [1916]. *Democracy and Education*. Mineola, NY: Courier Corporation.

DiMaggio, Paul. 2014. "Comment on Jerolmack and Khan, 'Talk Is Cheap': Ethnography and the Attitudinal Fallacy." *Sociological Methods & Research* 43(2):232–35.

DiMaggio, Paul J., and Walter W. Powell. 1983. "The Iron Cage Revisited: Institutional Isomorphism and Collective Rationality in Organizational Fields." *American Sociological Review* 48(2):147–60.

Domínguez, Silvia, and Betina Hollstein. 2014. *Mixed Methods Social Networks Research: Design and Applications*. New York: Cambridge University Press.

Doreian, Patrick, and Norman Conti. 2012. "Social Context, Spatial Structure and Social Network Structure." *Social Networks* 34(1):32–46.

Duneier, Mitchell. 1992. *Slim's Table: Race, Respectability, and Masculinity*. Chicago: University of Chicago Press.

Duneier, Mitchell. 1999. *Sidewalk*. New York: Farrar, Straus, and Giroux.

Durkheim, Emile. 1951 [1897]. *Suicide: A Study in Sociology*, translated by John A. Spaulding and George Simpson. New York: Free Press.

Ekeh, Peter P. 1974. *Social Exchange Theory: The Two Traditions*. Cambridge, MA: Harvard University Press.

Ellison, Jesse. 2011. "The Military's Secret Shame." *Newsweek*, April 3. Retrieved June 30, 2016 (http://www.newsweek.com/militarys-secret-shame-66459).

Elster, Jon. 2007. *Explaining Social Behavior: More Nuts and Bolts for the Social Sciences*. Cambridge: Cambridge University Press.

Emerson, Richard M. 1976. "Social Exchange Theory." *Annual Review of Sociology* 2:335–62.

Emirbayer, Mustafa, and Jeff Goodwin. 1994. "Network Analysis, Culture, and the Problem of Agency." *American Journal of Sociology* 99(6):1411–54.

Emirbayer, Mustafa, and Ann Mische. 1998. "What Is Agency?" *American Journal of Sociology* 103(4):962–1023.

Erbe, William. 1966. "Accessibility and Informal Social Relationships Among American Graduate Students." *Sociometry* 29(3):251–64.

Erdely, Sabrina Rubin. 2013. "The Rape of Petty Officer Blumer." *Rolling Stone*, February 14. Retrieved August 15, 2016 (http://www.rollingstone.com/politics/news/the-rape-of-petty-officer-blumer-20130214).

Esser, Hartmut. 1993a. "How 'Rational' Is the Choice of 'Rational Choice'? A Response to Randall Collins, Christopher Prendergast, and Ilja Srubar." *Rationality and Society* 5(3):408–14.

Esser, Hartmut. 1993b. "The Rationality of Everyday Behavior: A Rational Choice Reconstruction of the Theory of Action by Alfred Schütz." *Rationality and Society* 5(1):7–31.

Evens, T. M. S., and Don Handelman, eds. 2006. *The Manchester School: Practice and Ethnographic Praxis in Anthropology*. New York: Berghahn Books.

Faust, Katherine. 2007. "Very Local Structure in Social Networks." *Sociological Methodology* 37(1):209–56.

Feld, Scott L. 1981. "The Focused Organization of Social Ties." *American Journal of Sociology* 86(5):1015–35.

Feld, Scott L. 1982. "Social Structural Determinants of Similarity Among Associates." *American Sociological Review* 47(6):797–801.

Feld, Scott L. 1984. "The Structured Use of Personal Associates." *Social Forces* 62(3):640–52.

Feld, Scott L., J. Jill Suitor, and Jordana Gartner Hoegh. 2007. "Describing Changes in Personal Networks over Time." *Field Methods* 19(2):218–36.

Festinger, Leon, Stanley Schachter, and Kurt W. Back. 1950. *Social Pressures in Informal Groups: A Study of Human Factors in Housing.* Stanford, CA: Stanford University Press.

Fingerman, Karen L. 2001. "A Distant Closeness: Intimacy Between Parents and Their Children in Later Life." *Generations,* Summer:26–32.

Fingerman, Karen L., Elizabeth L. Hay, and Kira S. Birditt. 2004. "The Best of Ties, the Worst of Ties: Close, Problematic, and Ambivalent Social Relationships." *Journal of Marriage and Family* 66(3):792–808.

Fischer, Claude S. 1982a. *To Dwell Among Friends: Personal Networks in Town and City.* Chicago: University of Chicago Press.

Fischer, Claude S. 1982b. "What Do We Mean by 'Friend'? An Inductive Study." *Social Networks* 3(4):287–306.

Fischer, Claude S. 1994. *America Calling: A Social History of the Telephone to 1940.* Berkeley: University of California Press.

Fischer, Claude S. 2009. "The 2004 GSS Finding of Shrunken Social Networks: An Artifact?" *American Sociological Review* 74(4):657–69.

Fischer, Claude S. 2011. *Still Connected: Family and Friends in America Since 1970.* New York: Russell Sage Foundation.

Fischer, Claude S. 2012. "The Loneliness Scare Is Back." Retrieved December 14, 2016 (https://madeinamericathebook.wordpress.com/2012/04/24/the-loneliness-scare-is-back/).

Fischer, Claude S., and Lauren Beresford. 2015. "Changes in Support Networks in Late Middle Age: The Extension of Gender and Educational Differences." *Journals of Gerontology Series B: Psychological Sciences and Social Sciences* 70:S123–31.

Frank, Kenneth A., Chandra Muller, and Anna S. Mueller. 2013. "The Embeddedness of Adolescent Friendship Nominations: The Formation of Social Capital in Emergent Network Structures." *American Journal of Sociology* 119(1):216–53.

Freeman, Linton. 2004. *The Development of Social Network Analysis: A Study in the Sociology of Science.* Vancouver, BC, Canada: Empirical Press.

French, J. R. P. 1953. "Experiments in Field Settings." In *Research Methods in the Behavioral Sciences,* edited by L. Festinger and D. Katz, 98–153. New York: Holt, Rinehart and Winston.

Furman, Frida Kerner. 1997. *Facing the Mirror: Older Women and Beauty Shop Culture.* New York: Routledge.

Geertz, Clifford. 1973. *The Interpretation of Cultures: Selected Essays.* New York: Basic Books.

Gilovich, Thomas, Dale Griffin, and Daniel Kahneman. 2002. *Heuristics and Biases: The Psychology of Intuitive Judgment.* New York: Cambridge University Press.

Gino, Francesca, Alison Wood Brooks, and Maurice E. Schweitzer. 2012. "Anxiety, Advice, and the Ability to Discern: Feeling Anxious Motivates Individuals to Seek and Use Advice." *Journal of Personality and Social Psychology* 102(3):497–512.

Girvan, Michelle, and M. E. J. Newman. 2002. "Community Structure in Social and Biological Networks." *Proceedings of the National Academy of Sciences* 99(12):7821–26.

Glaeser, Edward L., David Laibson, and Bruce Sacerdote. 2002. "An Economic Approach to Social Capital." *Economic Journal* 112:F437–58.

Glaser, Barney G., and Anselm L. Strauss. 1967. *The Discovery of Grounded Theory: Strategies for Qualitative Research*. Chicago: Aldine.

Gluckman, Max. 1961. "Ethnographic Data in British Social Anthropology." *Sociological Review* 9(1):5–17.

Goffman, Alice. 2014. *On the Run: Fugitive Life in an American City*. Chicago: University Of Chicago Press.

Goffman, Erving. 1959. *The Presentation of Self in Everyday Life*. Oxford, UK: Doubleday.

Goffman, Erving. 1961. *Asylums: Essays on the Social Situation of Mental Patients and Other Inmates*. New York: Anchor Books.

Goffman, Erving. 1967. *Interaction Ritual: Essays on Face-to-Face Interaction*. Oxford, UK: Aldine.

Gould, Roger V. 2003. *Collision of Wills: How Ambiguity About Social Rank Breeds Conflict*. Chicago: University of Chicago Press.

Granovetter, Mark. 1973. "The Strength of Weak Ties." *American Journal of Sociology* 78(6):1360–80.

Granovetter, Mark. 1974. *Getting a Job: A Study of Contacts and Careers*. Cambridge, MA: Harvard University Press.

Granovetter, Mark. 1979. "The Theory-Gap in Social Network Analysis." In *Perspectives on Social Network Research*, edited by P. Holland and S. Leinhardt, 501–18. New York: Academic Press.

Granovetter, Mark. 1983. "The Strength of Weak Ties: A Network Theory Revisited." *Sociological Theory* 1:201–33.

Granovetter, Mark. 1985. "Economic Action and Social Structure: The Problem of Embeddedness." *American Journal of Sociology* 91(3):481–510.

Gross, Alan, and Peg McMullen. 1983. "Models of Help-Seeking Process." In *New Directions in Helping*, vol. 2, edited by J. D. Fisher, A. Nadler, and B. M. DePaulo, 45–61. New York: Academic Press.

Gross, Neil. 2013. *Why Are Professors Liberal and Why Do Conservatives Care?* Cambridge, MA: Harvard University Press.

Ha, Jung-Hwa. 2008. "Changes in Support from Confidants, Children, and Friends Following Widowhood." *Journal of Marriage and Family* 70(2):306–18.

Hammersley, Martyn, and Paul Atkinson. 2007. *Ethnography: Principles in Practice*. Third Edition. London and New York: Routledge.

Hampton, Keith N., Lauren F. Sessions, and Eun Ja Her. 2011. "Core Networks, Social Isolation, and New Media." *Information, Communication & Society* 14(1):130–55.

Hardin, Russell. 2002. *Trust and Trustworthiness*. New York: Russell Sage Foundation.

Harding, David J., Cybelle Fox, and Jal D. Mehta. 2002. "Studying Rare Events Through Qualitative Case Studies Lessons from a Study of Rampage School Shootings." *Sociological Methods & Research* 31(2):174–217.

Harris-Lacewell, Melissa. 2004. *Barbershops, Bibles, and BET: Everyday Talk and Black Political Thought*. Princeton: Princeton University Press.

Heider, Fritz. 1946. "Attitudes and Cognitive Organization." *Journal of Psychology* 21(1):107–12.

Heisenberg, Werner. 1927. "Über den anschaulichen Inhalt der quantentheoretischen Kinematik und Mechanik." *Zeitschrift für Physik* 43(3–4):172–98.

Heisenberg, Werner. 1983 [1927]. "The Actual Content of Quantum Theoretical Kinematics and Mechanics." NASA Technical Memorandum.

Hill, R. A., and R. I. M. Dunbar. 2003. "Social Network Size in Humans." *Human Nature* 14(1):53–72.

Hochschild, Arlie Russell. 1989. *The Second Shift*. New York: Avon Books.

Hochschild, Arlie Russell. 1997. *The Time Bind: When Work Becomes Home and Home Becomes Work*. New York: Metropolitan Books.

Hollstein, Betina. 2011. "Qualitative Approaches." In *The SAGE Handbook of Social Network Analysis*, edited by John Scott and Peter J. Harrington, 404–16. London: SAGE Publications.

Homans, George C. 1950. *The Human Group*. New York: Harcourt, Brace & Company.

Homans, George C. 1958. "Social Behavior as Exchange." *American Journal of Sociology* 63(6):597–606.

Homans, George C. 1961. *Social Behavior: Its Elementary Forms*. New York: Harcourt, Brace and World.

House, James S. 1981. *Work Stress and Social Support*. Reading, MA: Addison-Wesley Educational Publishers.

House, James S., Karl R. Landis, and Debra Umberson. 1988. "Social Relationships and Health." *Science* 241(4865):540–45.

House, James S., Debra Umberson, and Karl R. Landis. 1988. "Structures and Processes of Social Support." *Annual Review of Sociology* 14:293–318.

Huang, Karen, Mike Yeomans, Alison Wood Brooks, Julia Minson, and Francesca Gino. In Press. "It Doesn't Hurt to Ask: Question-Asking Increases Liking." *Journal of Personality and Social Psychology*.

Hsung, Ray-May, Nan Lin, and Ronald L. Breiger. 2009. *Contexts of Social Capital: Social Networks in Markets, Communities and Families*. New York: Routledge.

Huckfeldt, R. Robert. 1983. "Social Contexts, Social Networks, and Urban Neighborhoods: Environmental Constraints on Friendship Choice." *American Journal of Sociology* 89(3):651–69.

Human Rights Watch. 2015. *Embattled: Retaliation Against Sexual Assault Survivors in the US Military*. Human Rights Watch. Retrieved August 15, 2016 (https://www.hrw.org/report/2015/05/18/embattled/retaliation-against-sexual-assault-survivors-us-military).

Hume, David. 1978 [1739]. *A Treatise of Human Nature*, 2nd edition, edited by L. A. Selby-Bigge and P. H. Nidditch. Oxford: Oxford University Press.

Hurlbert, Jeanne S., Valerie A. Haines, and John J. Beggs. 2000. "Core Networks and Tie Activation: What Kinds of Routine Networks Allocate Resources in Nonroutine Situations?" *American Sociological Review* 65(4):598–618.

Hyun, Jenny K., Brian C. Quinn, Temina Madon, and Steve Lustig. 2006. "Graduate Student Mental Health: Needs Assessment and Utilization of Counseling Services." *Journal of College Student Development* 47(3):247–66.

Jennings, Kevin. 1994. *One Teacher in 10: Gay and Lesbian Educators Tell Their Stories*. Los Angeles: Alyson Books.

Jerolmack, Colin, and Shamus Khan. 2014. "Talk Is Cheap Ethnography and the Attitudinal Fallacy." *Sociological Methods & Research* 43(2):178–209.

Jerolmack, Colin and Alex Murphy. In Press. "The Ethical Dilemmas and Social Scientific Trade-offs of Masking in Ethnography." *Sociological Methods and Research*.

Jessor, Richard, Anne Colby, and Richard A. Shweder. 1996. *Ethnography and Human Development: Context and Meaning in Social Inquiry*. Chicago: University of Chicago Press.

Joas, Hans. 1996. *The Creativity of Action*. Chicago: University of Chicago Press.

John, Leslie K., Alessandro Acquisti, and George Loewenstein. 2011. "Strangers on a Plane: Context-Dependent Willingness to Divulge Sensitive Information." *Journal of Consumer Research* 37(5):858–73.

Johnson-Bailey, Juanita, Thomas S. Valentine, Ronald M. Cervero, and Tuere A. Bowles. 2008. "Lean on Me: The Support Experiences of Black Graduate Students." *Journal of Negro Education* 77(4):365–81.

Jones, Stephen R. G. 1992. "Was There a Hawthorne Effect?" *American Journal of Sociology* 98(3):451–68.

Kadushin, Charles. 1969. *Why People Go to Psychiatrists*. New York: Atherton Press.

Kadushin, Charles. 2002. "The Motivational Foundation of Social Networks." *Social Networks* 24(1):77–91.

Kahn, Robert L., and Toni C. Antonucci. 1980. "Convoys over the Life Course: Attachment, Roles, and Social Support." *Life-Span Development and Behavior* 3:253–86.

Kahneman, Daniel. 2003a. "A Perspective on Judgment and Choice: Mapping Bounded Rationality." *American Psychologist* 58(9):697–720.

Kahneman, Daniel. 2003b. "Maps of Bounded Rationality: Psychology for Behavioral Economics." *American Economic Review* 93(5):1449–75.

Kahneman, Daniel. 2011. *Thinking, Fast and Slow*. New York: Macmillan.

Kahneman, Daniel and Amos Tversky. 1979. "Prospect Theory: An Analysis of Decision under Risk." *Econometrica* 47(2):263–92.

Kahneman, Daniel, and Amos Tversky. 1984. "Choices, Values, and Frames." *American Psychologist* 39(4): 341.

Kahneman, Daniel, and Amos Tversky, eds. 2000. *Choices, Values, and Frames*. New York: Cambridge University Press.

Kaldjian, Lauris C., Valerie L. Forman-Hoffman, Elizabeth W. Jones, Barry J. Wu, Benjamin H. Levi, and Gary E. Rosenthal. 2008. "Do Faculty and Resident Physicians Discuss Their Medical Errors?" *Journal of Medical Ethics* 34(10):717–22.

Kant, Immanuel. 1963 [1930]. *Lectures on Ethics*, edited by L. W. Beck, translated by Louis Infield. Indianapolis: Hackett.

Kanter, Rosabeth Moss. 1977. *Men and Women of the Corporation*. New York: Basic Books.

Kashy, Deborah A., and David A. Kenny. 1990. "Analysis of Family Research Designs: A Model of Interdependence." *Communication Research* 17(4):462–82.

Katz, Elihu, and Paul F. Lazarsfeld. *Personal Influence, The Part Played by People in the Flow of Mass Communications*. New York: Free Press.

Kawachi, Ichiro, and Lisa Berkman. 2000. "Social Cohesion, Social Capital, and Health." In *Social Epidemiology*, edited by L. F. Berkman and I. Kawachi, 174–90. Oxford: Oxford University Press.

Kawachi, Ichiro, and Lisa F. Berkman. 2001. "Social Ties and Mental Health." *Journal of Urban Health* 78(3):458–467.

Kerr, Norbert L. 1998. "HARKing: Hypothesizing After the Results Are Known." *Personality and Social Psychology Review* 2(3):196–217.

Killworth, Peter, and H. Russell Bernard. 1976. "Informant Accuracy in Social Network Data." *Human Organization* 35(3):269–86.

Killworth, Peter D., and H. Russell Bernard. 1976. "A Model of Human Group Dynamics." *Social Science Research* 5(2):173–224.

King, Maryon F., and Gordon C. Bruner. 2000. "Social Desirability Bias: A Neglected Aspect of Validity Testing." *Psychology and Marketing* 17(2):79–103.

Krackhardt, David. 1990. "Assessing the Political Landscape: Structure, Cognition, and Power in Organizations." *Administrative Science Quarterly* 35(2):342–69.

Krackhardt, David. 1992. "The Strength of Strong Ties." In *Networks and Organizations; Structure, Form and Action*, edited by N. Nohria and B. Eccles, 216–39. Boston: Harvard Business School Press.

Kroneberg, Clemens. 2014. "Frames, Scripts, and Variable Rationality: An Integrative Theory of Action." In *Analytical Sociology*, edited by G. Manzo, 95–123. West Sussex, UK: John Wiley & Sons.

Kroneberg, Clemens, and Frank Kalter. 2012. "Rational Choice Theory and Empirical Research: Methodological and Theoretical Contributions in Europe." *Annual Review of Sociology* 38(1):73–92.

Kroneberg, Clemens, Meir Yaish, and Volker Stocké. 2010. "Norms and Rationality in Electoral Participation and in the Rescue of Jews in WWII: An Application of the Model of Frame Selection." *Rationality and Society* 22(1):3–36.

La Due Lake, Ronald, and Robert Huckfeldt. 1998. "Social Capital, Social Networks, and Political Participation." *Political Psychology* 19(3):567–84.

Larrick, Richard P. 2016. "The Social Context of Decisions." *Annual Review of Organizational Psychology and Organizational Behavior* 3:441–67.

Laumann, Edward O. 1973. *Bonds of Pluralism: Form and Substance of Urban Social Networks*. New York: John Wiley & Sons.

Laumann, Edward O., Peter V. Marsden, and David Prensky. 1989. "The Boundary Specification Problem in Network Analysis." In *Applied Network Analysis: A Methodological Introduction*, edited by R. S. Burt and M. J. Minor, 18–34. Beverly Hills, CA: Sage.

Law Offices of Susan L. Burke. 2011. "First Amended Complaint." Retrieved July 16, 2016 (http://burkepllc.com/files/2011/11/FIRST-AMENDED-COMPLAINT.pdf).

Lawler, Edward J., Shane R. Thye, and Jeongkoo Yoon. 2008. "Social Exchange and Micro Social Order." *American Sociological Review* 73(4):519–42.

Lawrence, Quil, and Maria Penaloza. 2013. "Sexual Violence Victims Say Military Justice System Is 'Broken.'" *WBUR News*, March 21. Retrieved June 30, 2016 (http://www.npr.org/2013/03/21/174840895/sexual-violence-victims-say-military-justice-system-is-broken).

Lazarsfeld, Paul F., and Robert K. Merton. 1954. "Friendship as a Social Process: A Substantive and Methodological Analysis." In *Freedom and Control in Modern Society*, edited by M. Berger, T. Abel, and C. H. Page, 18–66. New York: Van Nostrand.

Lazarsfeld, Paul Felix, Bernard Berelson, and Hazel Gaudet. 1968. *The People's Choice: How the Voter Makes Up His Mind in a Presidential Campaign*. New York: Columbia University Press.

Lazarus, Richard S., and Susan Folkman. 1984. *Stress, Appraisal, and Coping*. New York: Springer.

Lehrer, Johah. 2010. "Weak Ties, Twitter and Revolution." *Wired*, September 29. Retrieved December 13, 2016 (https://www.wired.com/2010/09/weak-ties-twitter-and-revolutions/).

Lévi-Strauss, Claude. 1969. *The Elementary Structures of Kinship*. Boston: Beacon Press.

Lewis, Kevin, Jason Kaufman, Marco Gonzalez, Andreas Wimmer, and Nicholas Christakis. 2008. "Tastes, Ties, and Time: A New Social Network Dataset Using Facebook.com." *Social Networks* 30(4):330–42.

Lieberson, Stanley. 1985. *Making It Count: The Improvement of Social Research and Theory*. Berkeley: University of California Press.

Lieberson, Stanley. 1991. "Small N's and Big Conclusions: An Examination of the Reasoning in Comparative Studies Based on a Small Number of Cases." *Social Forces* 70(2):307–20.

Lin, Nan. 2001. *Social Capital: A Theory of Social Structure and Action*. New York: Cambridge University Press.

Liu, Wei-ping, Steven S. Lui, and Derek C. Man. 2009. "Individual Change Schemas, Core Discussion Network, and Participation in Change: An Exploratory Study of Macau Casino Employees." *Journal of Hospitality & Tourism Research* 33(1):74–92.

Lofland, John, David A. Snow, Leon Anderson, and Lyn H. Lofland. 2005. *Analyzing Social Settings: A Guide to Qualitative Observation and Analysis*, 4th edition. Belmont, CA: Wadsworth.

Logan, John R., and Glenna D. Spitze. 1994. "Family Neighbors." *American Journal of Sociology* 100(2):453–76.

Logan, John R., and Glenna D. Spitze. 1996. *Family Ties*. Philadelphia: Temple University Press.

Lorrain, François, and Harrison C. White. 1971. "Structural Equivalence of Individuals in Social Networks." *Journal of Mathematical Sociology* 1(1):49–80.

Lucero, Gabrielle. 2015. "Military Sexual Assault: Reporting and Rape Culture." *Sanford Journal of Public Policy* 6(1):1–32.

Mackenzie, Anne. 1985. "Personal View." *British Medical Journal* 291(6501):1044.

Mallinckrodt, Brent, and Frederick T. Leong 1992. "International Graduate Students, Stress, and Social Support." *Journal of College Study Development* 33(1):71–78.

Manfreda, Katja Lozar, Michael Bosnjak, Jernej Berzelak, Iris Haas, Vasja Vehovar, and N. Berzelak. 2008. "Web Surveys Versus Other Survey Modes: A Meta-Analysis Comparing Response Rates." *Journal of the Market Research Society* 50(1):79.

Marche, Stephen. 2012. "Is Facebook Making Us Lonely?" *The Atlantic*, May. Retrieved August 15, 2016 (http://www.theatlantic.com/magazine/archive/2012/05/is-facebook-making-us-lonely/308930/).

Marin, Alexandra. 2004. "Are Respondents More Likely to List Alters with Certain Characteristics?: Implications for Name Generator Data." *Social Networks* 26(4):289–307.

Marin, Alexandra, and Keith N. Hampton. 2007. "Simplifying the Personal Network Name Generator Alternatives to Traditional Multiple and Single Name Generators." *Field Methods* 19(2):163–93.

Marsden, Peter V. 1987. "Core Discussion Networks of Americans." *American Sociological Review* 52(1):122–31.

Marsden, Peter V., and Karen E. Campbell. 1984. "Measuring Tie Strength." *Social Forces* 63(2):482–501.

Marsden, Peter V., and Karen E. Campbell. 2012. "Reflections on Conceptualizing and Measuring Tie Strength." *Social Forces* 91(1):17–23.

Martin, John Levi, and King-To Yeung. 2006. "Persistence of Close Personal Ties over a 12-Year Period." *Social Networks* 28(4):331–62.

Mauss, Marcel. 1954. *The Gift: Forms and Functions of Exchange in Archaic Societies.* New York: Routledge.

McCallister, Lynne, and Claude S. Fischer. 1978. "A Procedure for Surveying Personal Networks." *Sociological Methods & Research* 7(2):131–48.

McCarthy, Bill. 2002. "New Economics of Sociological Criminology." *Annual Review of Sociology* 28:417–42.

McPherson, Miller, Lynn Smith-Lovin, and Matthew E. Brashears. 2006. "Social Isolation in America: Changes in Core Discussion Networks over Two Decades." *American Sociological Review* 71(3):353–75.

McPherson, Miller, Lynn Smith-Lovin, and Matthew E. Brashears. 2009. "Models and Marginals: Using Survey Evidence to Study Social Networks." *American Sociological Review* 74(4):670–81.

McPherson, Miller, Lynn Smith-Lovin, and James M. Cook. 2001. "Birds of a Feather: Homophily in Social Networks." *Annual Review of Sociology* 27:415–44.

Mechanic, David. 1978. *Students Under Stress: A Study in the Social Psychology of Adaptation.* Wisconsin: University of Wisconsin Press.

Menon, Tanya, and Edward B. Smith. 2014. "Identities in Flux: Cognitive Network Activation in Times of Change." *Social Science Research* 45:117–30.

Merton, Robert K. 1936. "The Unanticipated Consequences of Purposive Social Action." *American Sociological Review* 1(6):894–904.

Merton, Robert K. 1968. *Social Theory and Social Structure.* New York: Free Press.

Meyer, John W., and Brian Rowan. 1977. "Institutionalized Organizations: Formal Structure as Myth and Ceremony." *American Journal of Sociology* 83(2):340–63.

Mill, John Stuart. 1970 [1843]. *System of Logic.* London: Prentice Hall Press.

Mitchell, James Clyde. 1969. *Social Networks in Urban Situations: Analyses of Personal Relationships in Central African Towns.* Manchester: Manchester University Press.

Mollenhorst, Gerald, Beate Völker, and Henk Flap. 2008. "Social Contexts and Core Discussion Networks: Using a Choice-Constraint Approach to Study Similarity in Intimate Relationships." *Social Forces* 86(3):937–65.

Mollenhorst, Gerald, Beate Völker, and Henk Flap. 2011. "Shared Contexts and Triadic Closure in Core Discussion Networks." *Social Networks* 33(4):292–302.

Mollenhorst, Gerald, Beate Völker, and Henk Flap. 2014. "Changes in Personal Relationships: How Social Contexts Affect the Emergence and Discontinuation of Relationships." *Social Networks* 37:65–80.

Moore, Gwen. 1990. "Structural Determinants of Men's and Women's Personal Networks." *American Sociological Review* 55(5):726–35.

Moore, Rick. 2017. "Fast or Slow: Sociological Implications of Measuring Dual-Process Cognition." *Sociological Science* 4:196–223.

Moreno, J. L. 1934. *Who Shall Survive: A New Approach to the Problem of Human Interrelations.* Washington, DC: Nervous and Mental Disease Publishing Co.

Morgan, Lewis Henry. 1871. *Systems of Consanguinity and Affinity of the Human Family.* Washington, DC: Smithsonian Institution.

Morgan, Stephen L., and Christopher Winship. 2015. *Counterfactuals and Causal Inference,* 2nd edition. New York: Cambridge University Press.

Mullainathan, Sendhil and Eldar Shafir. 2013. *Scarcity: Why Having So Little Means So Much*. New York: Henry Holt.

Murphy, Wendy, and Myla Haider. 2006. "Congressional Testimony of the Military's Response to Rape Victims." *Sexual Assault Report*, August. Retrieved July 16, 2016 (http://www.mncasa.org/assets/PDFs/CongressionalTestimonyonSAinArmedForces_06.pdf).

Mutz, Diana C. 2002. "The Consequences of Cross-Cutting Networks for Political Participation." *American Journal of Political Science* 46(4):838–55.

Nadeau, Barbie Latza. 2015. "Woman's Forbidden Love with Priest Has Her Living in Sin—And, Often, Loneliness." *Women in the World in Association with The New York Times*, April 6. Retrieved December 13, 2016 (http://nytlive.nytimes.com/womenintheworld/2015/04/06/womans-forbidden-love-with-priest-has-her-living-in-sin-and-often-loneliness/).

Nee, Victor, and Paul Ingram. 1998. "Embeddedness and Beyond: Institutions, Exchange, and Social Structure." In *The New Institutionalism in Sociology*, edited by Mary C. Brinton and Victor Nee, 19–45. New York: Russell Sage Foundation.

Newcomb, Theodore Mead. 1961. *The Acquaintance Process*. New York: Holt, Rinehart and Winston.

Nietzsche, Friedrich. 1989 [1887]. *On the Genealogy of Morals and Ecce Homo*, edited by Walter Kaufmann, translated by Walter Kaufmann and R. J. Hollingdale. New York: Vintage.

Nietzsche, Friedrich. 1998 [1887]. *On the Genealogy of Morality*. Indianapolis: Hackett Publishing.

Nisbett, Richard E., and Timothy D. Wilson. 1977. "Telling More Than We Can Know: Verbal Reports on Mental Processes." *Psychological Review* 84(3):231–59.

Norton, Michael I., Jeana H. Frost, and Dan Ariely. 2007. "Less Is More: The Lure of Ambiguity, or Why Familiarity Breeds Contempt." *Journal of Personality and Social Psychology* 92(1):97–105.

Oldenburg, Ray. 1989. *The Great Good Place: Cafes, Coffee Shops, Bookstores, Bars, Hair Salons, and Other Hangouts at the Heart of a Community*. Boston: Da Capo Press.

Paik, Anthony, and Kenneth Sanchagrin. 2013. "Social Isolation in America an Artifact." *American Sociological Review* 78(3):339–60.

Palisi, Bartolomeo J. 1966. "Ethnic Patterns of Friendship." *Phylon* 27(3):217–25.

Parker, Ashley. 2011. "Lawsuit Says Military Is Rife with Sexual Abuse." *New York Times*, February 15. Retrieved August 15, 2016 (http://www.nytimes.com/2011/02/16/us/16military.html).

Parry, Marc. 2011. "Harvard's Privacy Meltdown." *The Chronicle of Higher Education*, July 10. Retrieved December 13, 2016 (http://www.chronicle.com/article/Harvards-Privacy-Meltdown/128166/).

Pattillo-McCoy, Mary. 1998. "Church Culture as a Strategy of Action in the Black Community." *American Sociological Review* 63(6):767–84.

Pearl, Judea. 2009. *Causality*. Cambridge: Cambridge University Press.

Pennebaker, James W. 1990. *Opening Up: The Healing Power of Confiding in Others*. New York: William Morrow & Company.

Pennebaker, James W. 1993. "Putting Stress into Words: Health, Linguistic, and Therapeutic Implications." *Behaviour Research and Therapy* 31(6):539–48.

Pennebaker, James W., and Sandra K. Beall. 1986. "Confronting a Traumatic Event: Toward an Understanding of Inhibition and Disease." *Journal of Abnormal Psychology* 95(3):274–81.

Pennebaker, James W., Michelle Colder, and Lisa K. Sharp. 1990. "Accelerating the Coping Process." *Journal of Personality and Social Psychology* 58(3):528–37.

Pennebaker, James W., Janice K. Kiecolt-Glaser, and Ronald Glaser. 1988. "Disclosure of Traumas and Immune Function: Health Implications for Psychotherapy." *Journal of Consulting and Clinical Psychology* 56(2):239–45.

Pennebaker, James W., and Robin C. O'Heeron. 1984. "Confiding in Others and Illness Rate Among Spouses of Suicide and Accidental-Death Victims." *Journal of Abnormal Psychology* 93(4):473–76.

Perrin, Andrew. 2015. *Social Networking Usage: 2005-2015*. Pew Research Center. Retrieved August 15, 2016 (http://www.pewinternet.org/2015/10/08/social-networking-usage-2005-2015/).

Perry, Brea L., and Bernice A. Pescosolido. 2010. "Functional Specificity in Discussion Networks: The Influence of General and Problem-Specific Networks on Health Outcomes." *Social Networks* 32(4):345–57.

Perry, Brea L., and Bernice A. Pescosolido. 2012. "Social Network Dynamics and Biographical Disruption: The Case of 'First-Timers' with Mental Illness." *American Journal of Sociology* 118(1):134–75.

Perry, Brea L., and Bernice A. Pescosolido. 2015. "Social Network Activation: The Role of Health Discussion Partners in Recovery from Mental Illness." *Social Science & Medicine* 125:116–28.

Perry, Brea L., Bernice A. Pescosolido, and Stephen Borgatti. Forthcoming. *Ego Network Analysis: Foundations, Methods, and Models*. Cambridge: Cambridge University Press.

Pescosolido, Bernice A. 1992. "Beyond Rational Choice: The Social Dynamics of How People Seek Help." *American Journal of Sociology* 97(4):1096–138.

Pescosolido, Bernice A., Carol Brooks Gardner, and Keri M. Lubell. 1998. "How People Get into Mental Health Services: Stories of Choice, Coercion and 'Muddling Through' from 'First-Timers.'" *Social Science & Medicine* 46(2):275–86.

Plato. 1926. *Cratylus*, translated by Harold North Fowler. Cambridge, MA: Harvard University Press.

Powell, Walter W., and Paul DiMaggio, eds. 1991. *The New Institutionalism in Organizational Analysis*. Chicago: University of Chicago Press.

Putnam, Robert D. 2000. *Bowling Alone: The Collapse and Revival of American Community*. New York: Simon & Schuster.

Ragin, Charles C., and Howard S. Becker. 1992. *What Is a Case?: Exploring the Foundations of Social Inquiry*. Cambridge: Cambridge University Press.

Rainie, Lee, and Barry Wellman. 2012. *Networked: The New Social Operating System*. Cambridge, MA: MIT Press.

Response Systems to Adult Sexual Assault Crimes Panel. 2014. *Report of the Response Systems to Adult Sexual Assault Crimes Panel*. Arlington, VA. Retrieved July 2, 2016 (http://www.ncdsv.org/images/DOD_Report-of-the-response-systems-to-adult-SA-crimes-panel_6-2014.pdf).

Richardson, Stephen A., Barbara S. Dohrenwend, and David Klein. 1965. *Interviewing: Its Forms and Functions*. New York: Basic Books.

Robotham, David. 2008. "Stress Among Higher Education Students: Towards a Research Agenda." *Higher Education* 56(6):735–46.

Ruan, Danching. 1998. "The Content of the General Social Survey Discussion Networks: An Exploration of General Social Survey Discussion Name Generator in a Chinese Context." *Social Networks* 20(3):247–64.

Rubin, Zick. 1975. "Disclosing Oneself to a Stranger: Reciprocity and Its Limits." *Journal of Experimental Social Psychology* 11(3):233–60.

Sadler, Anne G., Brenda M. Booth, Brian L. Cook, and Bradley N. Doebbeling. 2003. "Factors Associated with Women's Risk of Rape in the Military Environment." *American Journal of Industrial Medicine* 43(3):262–73.

Sailer, Kerstin and Ian McCulloh. 2012. "Social Networks and Spatial Configuration— How Office Layouts Drive Social Interaction." *Social Networks* 34(1):47–58.

Samuelson, Paul A. 1938. "A Note on the Pure Theory of Consumer's Behaviour." *Economica* 5(17):61–71.

Sandberg, Sheryl. 2013. *Lean In: Women, Work, and the Will to Lead*. New York: Alfred A. Knopf.

Schilt, Kristen. 2010. *Just One of the Guys?: Transgender Men and the Persistence of Gender Inequality*. Chicago: University of Chicago Press.

Schutz, Alfred. 1964. *Collected Papers, Vol. II: Studies in Social Theory*, edited by Arvid Brodersen. The Hague: Martinus Nijhoff.

Schwarz, Norbert. 1999. "Self-Reports: How the Questions Shape the Answers." *American Psychologist* 54(2):93–105.

Schwarz, Norbert. 2007. "Cognitive Aspects of Survey Methodology." *Applied Cognitive Psychology* 21(1):277–87.

Schwarz, Norbert, and Seymour Sudman, eds. 1992. *Context Effects in Social and Psychological Research*. New York: Springer-Verlag.

Schwarz, Norbert, and Seymour Sudman, eds. 1994. *Autobiographical Memory and the Validity of Retrospective Reports*. New York: Springer-Verlag.

Scott, W. Richard. 1995. *Institutions and Organizations. Foundations for Organizational Science*. London: SAGE Publications.

Selten, Reinhard. 2001. "What Is Bounded Rationality?" In *Bounded Rationality: The Adaptive Toolbox*, edited by G. Gigerenzer and R. Selten, 13–36. Cambridge, MA: MIT Press.

Shafir, Eldar, Itamar Simonson, and Amos Tversky. 1993. "Reason-Based Choice." *Cognition* 49(1–2):11–36.

Shamay-Tsoory, Simone G., Judith Aharon-Peretz, and Daniella Perry. 2009. "Two Systems for Empathy: A Double Dissociation between Emotional and Cognitive Empathy in Inferior Frontal Gyrus versus Ventromedial Prefrontal Lesions." *Brain* 132(3):617–27.

Simmel, Georg. 1950. *The Sociology of Georg Simmel*, edited by K. H. Wolff. New York: Simon & Schuster.

Simmel, Georg. 1955. *Conflict and the Web of Group Affiliations*, translated by Kurt H. Wolff and Reinhard Bendix. New York: Free Press.

Simon, Herbert A. 1997 [1947]. *Administrative Behavior: A Study of Decision-Making Processes in Administrative Organizations*. New York: Free Press.

Skocpol, Theda. 1979. *States and Social Revolutions: A Comparative Analysis of France, Russia and China*. Cambridge: Cambridge University Press.

Slaughter, Anne-Marie. 2015. *Unfinished Business: Women Men Work Family*. New York: Random House.

Small, Mario L., and Christopher Sukhu. 2016. "Because They Were There: Access, Deliberation, and the Mobilization of Networks for Support." *Social Networks* 47:73–84.

Small, Mario Luis. 2009a. "'How Many Cases Do I Need?' On Science and the Logic of Case Selection in Field-Based Research." *Ethnography* 10(1):5–38.

Small, Mario Luis. 2009b. *Unanticipated Gains: Origins of Network Inequality in Everyday Life*. Oxford: Oxford University Press.

Small, Mario Luis. 2011. "How to Conduct a Mixed Methods Study: Recent Trends in a Rapidly Growing Literature." *Annual Review of Sociology* 37(1):57–86.

Small, Mario Luis. 2013a. "Causal Thinking and Ethnographic Research." *American Journal of Sociology* 119(3):597–601.

Small, Mario Luis. 2013b. "Weak Ties and the Core Discussion Network: Why People Regularly Discuss Important Matters with Unimportant Alters." *Social Networks* 35(3):470–83.

Small, Mario Luis, Vontrese D. Pamphile, and Peter McMahan. 2015. "How Stable Is the Core Discussion Network?" *Social Networks* 40:90–102.

Smith, Adam. 2006. "Cognitive Empathy and Emotional Empathy in Human Behavior and Evolution." *Psychological Record* 56(1):3–21.

Smith, Adam. 2002 [1790]. *The Theory of Moral Sentiments*. New York: Cambridge University Press.

Smith, Emily J., Christopher S. Marcum, Adam Boessen, Zack W. Almquist, John R. Hipp, Nicholas N. Nagle, and Carter T. Butts. 2015. "The Relationship of Age to Personal Network Size, Relational Multiplexity, and Proximity to Alters in the Western United States." *Journals of Gerontology Series B: Psychological Sciences and Social Sciences* 70(1):91–99.

Smith, Ned. 2015. "How Social Networks Can Keep the Poor Down and the Rich Up." *Forbes*, January 21. Retrieved December 8, 2016 (http://www.forbes.com/sites/datafreaks/2015/01/21/how-social-networks-can-keep-the-poor-down-and-the-rich-up/).

Smith, Sandra S. 2007. *Lone Pursuit: Distrust and Defensive Individualism Among the Black Poor*. New York: Russell Sage Foundation.

Smith, Sandra S., and Mignon R. Moore. 2000. "Intraracial Diversity and Relations Among African-Americans: Closeness Among Black Students at a Predominantly White University." *American Journal of Sociology* 106(1):1–39.

Smith, Tom W., Peter V. Marsden, Michael Hout, and Jibum Kim. 2002. *General Social Surveys, 1972-2014*. Chicago: NORC at the University of Chicago.

Smith-Lovin, Lynn, Matthew Brashears and Miller McPherson. 2008. "The Ties That Bind Are Fraying." *Contexts* 7(3):32–36.

Smyth, Joshua M. 1998. "Written Emotional Expression: Effect Sizes, Outcome Types, and Moderating Variables." *Journal of Consulting and Clinical Psychology* 66(1):174.

Smyth, Joshua M., Arthur A. Stone, Adam Hurewitz, and Alan Kaell. 1999. "Effects of Writing About Stressful Experiences on Symptom Reduction in Patients with Asthma or Rheumatoid Arthritis: A Randomized Trial." *Jama* 281(14):1304–9.

Solem, Michael, Jenny Lee, and Beth Schlemper. 2009. "Departmental Climate and Student Experiences in Graduate Geography Programs." *Research in Higher Education* 50(3):268–92.

Sommer, Teresa Eckrich, et al. Forthcoming. "Promoting Parents Social Capital to Increase Children's Attendance in Head Start: Evidence from an Experimental Intervention." *Journal of Research on Educational Effectiveness*.

Spiegel, David, Helena C. Kraemer, Joan R. Bloom, and Ellen Gottheil. 1989. "Effect of Psychosocial Treatment on Survival of Patients with Metastatic Breast Cancer." *The Lancet* 334(8668):888–91.

Stack, Carol B. 1974. *All Our Kin: Strategies for Survival in a Black Community*. New York: Basic Books.

Stanovich, Keith E., and Richard F. West. 2000. "Advancing the Rationality Debate." *Behavioral and Brain Sciences* 23(5):701–17.

Steiner, Lee R. 1945. *Where Do People Take Their Troubles?* Boston: Houghton Mifflin.

Stinchcombe, Arthur L. 2001. *When Formality Works: Authority and Abstraction in Law and Organizations*. Chicago: University of Chicago Press.

Strack, Fritz, and Roland Deutsch. 2004. "Reflective and Impulsive Determinants of Social Behavior." *Personality and Social Psychology Review* 8(3):220–47.

Straits, Bruce C. 2000. "Ego's Important Discussants or Significant People: An Experiment in Varying the Wording of Personal Network Name Generators." *Social Networks* 22(2):123–40.

Sudman, Seymour, Norman M. Bradburn, and Norbert Schwarz. 1996. *Thinking About Answers: The Application of Cognitive Processes to Survey Methodology*. San Francisco: Jossey-Bass.

Suitor, J. Jill, Barry Wellman, and David L. Morgan. 1997. "It's About Time: How, Why, and When Networks Change." *Social Networks* 19(1):1–7.

Suzman, Richard. 2009. "The National Social Life, Health, and Aging Project: An Introduction." *Journals of Gerontology Series B: Psychological Sciences and Social Sciences* 64B(S1):i5–11.

Tamir, Diana I., and Jason P. Mitchell. 2012. "Disclosing Information About the Self Is Intrinsically Rewarding." *Proceedings of the National Academy of Sciences* 109(21):8038–43.

Tigges, Leann M., Irene Browne, and Gary P. Green. 1998. "Social Isolation of the Urban Poor." *Sociological Quarterly* 39(1):53–77.

Tilly, Charles. 2006. *Why? What Happens When People Give Reasons . . . and Why*. Princeton, NJ: Princeton University Press.

Tilly, Charles. 2008. *Credit and Blame*. Princeton, NJ: Princeton University Press.

Turchik, Jessica A., and Susan M. Wilson. 2010. "Sexual Assault in the US Military: A Review of the Literature and Recommendations for the Future." *Aggression and Violent Behavior* 15(4):267–77.

Tutić, Andreas, and Harald Wiese. 2015. "Reconstructing Granovetter's Network Theory." *Social Networks* 43:136–48.

Tversky, Amos, and Daniel Kahneman. 1973. "Availability: A Heuristic for Judging Frequency and Probability." *Cognitive Psychology* 5(2):207–32.

Tversky, Amos, and Daniel Kahneman. 1974. "Judgment Under Uncertainty: Heuristics and Biases." *Science* 185:1124–31.

Tversky, Amos, and Daniel Kahneman. 1991. "Loss Aversion in Riskless Choice: A Reference-Dependent Model." *Quarterly Journal of Economics* 106(4):1039–61.

University of California, Berkeley Graduate Assembly. 2014. *Graduate Student Happiness & Well-Being Report*. University of California, Berkeley. Retrieved December 14, 2016 (http://ga.berkeley.edu/wellbeingreport/).

Vaisey, Stephen. 2008. "Socrates, Skinner, and Aristotle: Three Ways of Thinking About Culture in Action." *Sociological Forum* 23(3):603–13.

Vaisey, Stephen. 2009. "Motivation and Justification: A Dual-Process Model of Culture in Action." *American Journal of Sociology* 114(6):1675–715.

Vaisey, Stephen, and Omar Lizardo. 2010. "Can Cultural Worldviews Influence Network Composition?" *Social Forces* 88(4):1595–618.

Vaisey, Stephen. 2014. "The 'Attitudinal Fallacy' Is a Fallacy Why We Need Many Methods to Study Culture." *Sociological Methods & Research* 43(2):227–31.

Van der Poel, Mart G. M. 1993. "Delineating Personal Support Networks." *Social Networks* 15(1):49–70.

Verbrugge, Lois M. 1977. "The Structure of Adult Friendship Choices." *Social Forces* 56(2):576–97.

Völker, Beate, and Henk Flap. 2002. *The Survey on the Social Networks of the Dutch (SSND1): Data and Codebook*. Utrecht: Utrecht University.

Völker, Beate, Henk Flap, and Gerald Mollenhorst. 2009. "Changing Places: The Influence of Meeting Places on Recruiting Friends." In *Contexts of Social Capital: Social Networks in Markets, Communities and Families*, edited by R. M. Hsung, N. Lin, and R. L. Breiger, 28–48. New York: Routledge.

Wan, Teh-yuan, David W. Chapman, and Donald A. Biggs. 1992. "Academic Stress of International Students Attending U.S. Universities." *Research in Higher Education* 33(5):607–23.

Watkins-Hayes, Celeste. 2013. "The Micro Dynamics of Support Seeking: The Social and Economic Utility of Institutional Ties for HIV-Positive Women." *Annals of the American Academy of Political and Social Science* 647(1):83–101.

Watts, Duncan J. 1999. *Small Worlds: The Dynamics of Networks Between Order and Randomness*. Princeton, NJ: Princeton University Press.

Watts, Duncan J. 2011. *Everything Is Obvious: Once You Know the Answer*. New York: Crown Publishing Group.

Watts, Duncan J. 2014. "Common Sense and Sociological Explanations." *American Journal of Sociology* 120(2):313–51.

Weber, Max. 1978 [1922]. *Economy and Society: An Outline of Interpretive Sociology*. Berkeley: University of California Press.

Weiss, Robert S. 1994. *Learning from Strangers: The Art and Method of Qualitative Interview Studies*. New York: Free Press.

Wellman, Barry. 1979. "The Community Question: The Intimate Networks of East Yorkers." *American Journal of Sociology* 84(5):1201–31.

Wellman, Barry. 1981. "Applying Network Analysis to the Study of Support." In *Social Networks and Social Support*, edited by Benjamin H. Gottlieb, 171–200. Beverly Hills, CA: SAGE Publications.

Wellman, Barry, ed. 1999. *Networks in the Global Village*. Boulder, CO: Westview Press.

Wellman, Barry. 2007. "The Network Is Personal: Introduction to a Special Issue of Social Networks." *Social Networks* 29(3):349–56.

Wellman, Barry, and Scot Wortley. 1989. "Brothers' Keepers: Situating Kinship Relations in Broader Networks of Social Support." *Sociological Perspectives* 32(3):273–306.

Wellman, Barry, and Scot Wortley. 1990. "Different Strokes from Different Folks: Community Ties and Social Support." *American Journal of Sociology* 96(3):558–88.

White, Harrison C., Scott A. Boorman, and Ronald L. Breiger. 1976. "Social Structure from Multiple Networks. I. Blockmodels of Roles and Positions." *American Journal of Sociology* 81(4):730–80.

Wickström, Gustav, and Tom Bendix. 2000. "The 'Hawthorne Effect'—What Did the Original Hawthorne Studies Actually Show?" *Scandinavian Journal of Work, Environment & Health* 26(4):363–67.

Wilson, William Julius. 1987. *The Truly Disadvantaged: The Inner City, the Underclass, and Public Policy*. Chicago: University of Chicago Press.

Yamagishi, Toshio, and Karen S. Cook. 1993. "Generalized Exchange and Social Dilemmas." *Social Psychology Quarterly* 56(4):235–48.

INDEX

Page numbers followed by *f* indicate figures; *t* indicate tables

strong ties as reflecting, 236n13
tie strength and, 29, 220n4
CNIA. *See* Core Networks and
  Important Alters
coding, of worries, 54, 56
cognitive empathy, 93–100, 106
  from similarity, three types, 92–101
  from direct experience in past,
    101–2, 145
  from indirect experience, 102–4, 145
  weak-tie confidants example
    of, 167–68
Coleman, James, 220n8, 229n4
colleagues, as confidants
  best or worst predicament, 169–70
  as preferred over spouse, 168
college students, RFCS survey on, 149
"Committee on Human Differences," 171
common sense, 5–6, 17, 151, 156
competition, 69
  funding, 77
  grant application, 77–79
  institutional mediation and, 77
  listener *vs.* competitor case, 74–76
  supporters *vs.* applicants case, 76–79
conceptual generalizability, 232n1
confidants. *See also* decision making;
    disclosure; strong ties; weak-tie
    confidants
  accessibility factor, 210t–12t
  availability heuristic in
    recalling, 218n43
  average number of graduate student,
    28, 220n2
  closeness not required for, 36, 38, 40–43
  common-sense answer on nature of,
    5–6, 17
  common-sense notion about
    discussing worries with, 151
  core discussion network *vs.*
    actual, 141–42
  dropped and replaced, 39–40
  empathy required from, 159–60
  first-year graduate student
    actual, 59–62
  GSS expectations for, 45–52, 138
  institutionally mediated, 66–69,
    68t, 106
  length of time in ties to, named, 41f
  modeling behavior of, 123

mothers as, 86–87
mutual, 159
network-related thinking on, 11,
  214nn2–3
practical network of, 173–74
in private issues, 18–19
reciprocity factor in, 67–68
repeated social interaction and,
  35–36, 221n10
role of, 88
serious worries discussed with old or
  new, 45–52
in social interaction absence, 40
social interaction spaces and,
  127–28, 156
sorting by topic, 91–92
steady set of, 101
strangers as, 6–8, 19, 123, 214n17,
  218n44, 231n29
survey respondents on, 11
types of potential, 68–70, 68t
unplanned conversations with, 122–24
whom people consider for selection
  as, 157–58
confidants, of average adults
  context-based replacement of named,
    136–38, 232n5, 232n14
  critical factors in choice of, 158–60
  depression example, 164–65,
    168–69, 238n53
  as forgoing closeness for empathy,
    143–47, 234n37, 234n40
  frequent use of non-close,
    140–42, 233n20
  strong ties avoided by, 142–43,
    234nn28–31
  topic-relevant, 146–47
  two approaches to
    understanding, 162t
confidentiality, 22–23, 194–97
confiding. *See also* social and emotional
    support
  improved health from, 4, 213n7
  psychologists on, 213n1
  recent survey on, 5, 214n15
  risk of, 4–5
  scientific studies on, 3–4
  stress motive for increased, 3
  written expression and, 4
confirming hypotheses process, 181–82

approach to understanding students', 113–14
assumption of action preceded by, 110–11
critical factors in, 158–60
critiques on theories of, 112–13, 229nn8–9, 229nn11–12
data available from interviews on, 115
inability to prove existence of, 231n35
intuition and, 160–61
LGBT and, 171
memory and, 124–25
mobilization in standard model of, 115
in practice-based perspective, 160–62
rational choice theory and, 110–11, 113, 124, 228n24
sociology critiques on, 112, 229nn11–12, 230n16
weak-tie confidants in student, 108, 228n24
demographics, participant, 187, 201t
density, of social networks
first-year graduate patterns and, 38–39, 221nn15–16
stability and, 39
depression, 164–65, 168–69, 238n53
Dewey, John, 112, 229n8
direct experience, empathy based on, 101–2, 145
disclosure
full, 235n1
inadvertent, 170–73, 238n54
participant anonymity and, 194–97
personal, 123
sexual assault, 165–66, 237n41, 237n43, 237n45
of unethical behavior, 170–71, 238n54
dual-process model, 112–13, 125
Dutch studies, 15, 137, 232n5, 233n49, 235n49

economics
behavioral, 112, 230n13, 231n32
rationality debate in, 231n34
on similarity, 228n16
ego-centric perspective, 12–13, 215n12, 215n14
emotional reciprocity, 68, 71. See also social and emotional support
expectations of, 159

empathy, 9
cognitive, 93–101, 101–2, 106, 167–68
context and plausibility for, 129
direct experience as basis of, 101–2
forgoing closeness for, 143–47, 234n37, 234n40
indirect experience as basis of, 102–4
as more important than strength of ties, 159–60
psychology literature on, 227n12
required from confidants, 159–60
result of not finding, 108
similarity as basis of, 92–3, 99–101
sympathy distinguished from, 93
weak-tie confidants chosen for, 92–93, 101–4, 227n12, 228n14
empirical generalizability, 10. See also adults, empirical propositions for
conceptual and statistical generalizability, 232n1
conclusion and overview of, 150
core questions and, 232n1
graduate student uniqueness and, 135–36
propositions and, 136–49, 232n5, 232n14
empirical observation, 156–57
environmental factors, in decision making, 232n38
equivalence
felt, 228n21
structural, 228n20
Esser, Hartmut, 112, 229n12, 230n16
ethnography, 20, 184
Hawthorne effect and, 52, 222n9
problem of participant observation and, 240n13
expectations
anthropology understanding of kin relation, 224n13
confidant types and, 70
as deliberation factor, 158–60
emotional reciprocity, 159
incompatible, 74–87, 163–66
institutional mediation and, 159, 165–66, 237n23
strong-tie theory and GSS, 45–52, 138
types and sources of, 159
uncertainty and, 107–8
unstated, 83

sociable interaction, 119
social and emotional support
  classifications of, 214n11
  documentation on, 4
  information *vs.*, 104–5
  physical *vs.* emotional, 227n8
  reciprocity in, 67
  shift necessary for
    understanding, 156–57
  from strong ties, 17, 217n35
  structural theory on strong ties for,
    152–53, 235n5, 235n8
  structured opportunities for, 128–29
  survey choice for studying, 185
  use of term, 213n2
  venting as, 3, 213n2
social interaction. *See also* contexts,
    social interaction
  absence of, 40
  contemporary society and,
    157–58 236n16
  focus theory of, 36, 129, 232n42
  four elements of, 130
  Goffman's work on, 225n29
  metaphors for, 157
  network structure *vs.*, 38
  routine, 157
  space for, 127–28, 156, 176
  stream metaphor, 157, 237n22
  structured opportunities for, 128–29
  trust created by repeated,
    35–36, 221n10
social networks. *See also* activation, of
    social network; core discussion
    network; Core Networks and
    Important Alters (CNIA) survey;
    network analysis; organizational
    embeddedness
  deciding to mobilize, 5–10
  density of, 38–39, 221nn15–16
  of mothers, 182, 239n6
  network of ties metaphor, 157
  in practice, 173–74
  respondents representations of
    own, 218n41
  social interaction *vs.*, 38
  spaces impact on, 127, 156
  three-way relationship in, 184
Social Networks, 139
social science

confirming hypotheses process
  in, 181–82
context understanding in, 21
core discussion network
  according to, 11
deliberation assumption in, 110–11
experiments, 20
name generators use by, 14
skills required in, 46
uncommon events viewed by, 221n6
sociograms, 7, 8, 215n6
sociology
  deliberation critiques in, 112,
    229nn11–12, 230n16
  network analysis in, 12, 215nn10–11
  rational actor perspective in, 111
  repeated social interaction perspective
    in, 221n10
  on activation decision process, 230n21
  on seeking decision process, 230n19
  on selection decision process, 230n20
Socrates, Heraclitus speech to,
  157, 237n22
soldiers, sexual assault disclosure of,
  165–66, 237n41, 237n43, 237n45
spaces
  relationships independent of, 176
  social interaction, 127–28, 156
spontaneous activation, 118–22, 172–73,
  231n26, 231n28, 232n38
spontaneous decision making, context
  importance in, 126–30
spouse, colleague preferred over, 168
stability
  density and, 39
  strong ties and, 29–30
Stack, Carol, 67, 224n2
statistical averages, 53, 222n13
statistical generalizability, 232n1
status homophily, 228n17
steady stream of interactions metaphor,
  157, 237n22
strangers, as confidants, 6–8, 19, 123,
  214n17, 218n44, 231n29
stress, 219n54
  confiding during times of, 3
  financial, 64–66
  first-year graduate student, 22
  among graduate students, 22, 59
  psychologists on confiding and, 213n1

ties, to confidants. *See also* strong ties; weak-tie confidants
  length of, 41*f*
To Dwell Among Friends (Fischer), 215n17
topic-alter dependency, 92, 144
topic-relevant confidants, of average adults, 146–47
topics
  RCFS on discussed, 206*t*
  RCFS table on alter type and, 205*t*
  relationship between alter type and, 207*t*
  RFCS on five most common, 207*t*
  sorting confidants by, 91–92
train stations, study on behavior modeling, 123
triads, 152–6
  forbidden triad principle, 152–6
triangulation, 191–92
Tversky, Amos, 113, 218n43, 230n18

uncommon worries, 167–68

Verbrugge, Lois, 128
Völker, Beate, 15, 137, 232n5, 233n49, 235n49

weak-tie confidants, 9, 27–28, 33–34
  in applications of theoretical generalizability, 167–68
  availability factor in, 147–49, 210*t*–12*t*
  basic patterns, 38–40, 221nn15–17
  CNIA survey findings on, 139, 233n17
  cognitive empathy in, 167–68
  context as reason for, 151
  counting and interpretation issue, 223n28
  deeper patterns, 40–42, 41*f*, 221n17
  distribution, 38–42
  GSS and, 44
  importance of, 16
  most confidants kept prediction for, 29–32, 220n8
  in practice, 62–63, 223n25
  strong tie theory and, 220n9
  structural theory and, 235n5
  students replacing confidants prediction for, 35–38
  three-part relation with, 167
  Wellman on strong and, 17, 217n35

why students approached
  cognitive empathy and, 106
  conclusion overview, 105–8
  as deliberate decision, 108, 228n24
  emotional support and physical services distinction, 227n8
  emotional support *vs.* information basis of, 104–5
  empathy motivation, 92–93, 101–4, 227n12, 228n14
  expectation and uncertainty in, 107–8
  homophily concept and, 97–99
  motivation question, 91, 226n4
  risk of loss or harm, 90–91, 226nn1–3
  similarity reason, 93, 94–96, 228n16
  similarity types in, 99–101
  sorting by topic, 91–92
  understanding from direct experience, 101–2
Weber, Max, 111
websites, unethical behavior disclosure on, 238n54
Wellman, Barry, 12, 16–17, 98, 215n11, 217n35
Wilson, Rodney, 172–73
Wilson, Timothy, 192
Wilson, William J., 230n19
work-life balance, 31–32
worries
  categories of, 106
  coding of, 54, 56
  common-sense notion about confiding, 151
  confiding serious, 45–52
  first-wave question on, 53, 222n12
  of first-year graduate students, 54–59, 222n14
  about graduate experience, 55*t*, 56–58, 61
  important topics and, 146
  inadvertent disclosure of serious, 170–73, 238n54
  about life in general, 56*t*, 58
  open-ended interviews on, 223n24
  at start of second year, 61
  uncommon, 167–68
Wortley, Scot, 98
written expression, 4

Printed in the USA/Agawam, MA
September 12, 2022

798393.014